DIVINE SCIENCE AND THE SCIENCE OF GOD

DIVINE SCIENCE

AND THE SCIENCE OF GOD

A REFORMULATION OF

THOMAS AQUINAS

BY VICTOR PRELLER

PRINCETON, NEW JERSEY

PRINCETON UNIVERSITY PRESS

1967

Publication of this book has been aided by the
Whitney Darrow Publication Reserve Fund of
Princeton University Press
Printed in the United States of America
by Princeton University Press

TO MY PARENTS

THE question of the meaningfulness of religious language has enjoyed something of a vogue in British-American philosophy over the past ten years. The following is an attempt to rethink that question in the context of an explicit rejection of the epistemological presuppositions of traditional empiricism. The writings of Aquinas are used as a model of religious language, not because I feel that Thomistic theology either is or ought to be a model for contemporary theologizing, much less philosophizing, but simply because Aquinas holds a place of extraordinary authority both within the official circles of contemporary Roman Catholicism and within the less official discussions of contemporary philosophers, both religious and antireligious. That Aquinas failed to make some of the mistakes attributed to him by friend and foe alike is one of the theses of this book—it is in no way implied, however, that Aquinas failed to make mistakes.

It is important to note that the following study is not an instance of theological discourse. Nor is it, in any traditional sense, an essay in "The Philosophy of Religion." I do not pretend, for example, to give a theologically adequate account of the doctrine of the Trinity, but merely to discuss some of the minimal implications of that doctrine for an epistemological analysis of the claims of faith. On the other hand, it is certainly not my intention to mount a philosophical defense of theological language or a philosophical proof of religious propositions. At most I have stated some of the things that must be true of human thought and language if theological claims are not to be rejected out of hand.

It will be noted that, just as I have felt free to modify Aquinas' positions on some important points, I have also felt free to put the insights and vocabulary of contemporary philosophers to somewhat new and—from their viewpoints—possibly unjustified uses. For example, I have extended Sellars' phrase, "material moves," to cover not only S-R-learned moves from one material position in the observation language to another ("There is smoke, so there is fire."), but also S-R-learned instances of coming to occupy a position in the observation language ("Red!"). Clearly, Sellars' term, "language

· vii ·

entry," is more appropriate for the latter. In the context of the final chapter of this study, however, it seemed an unnecessary complication, and I have simply used *one* of Sellars' terms for any instance of coming to occupy a linguistic position on the basis of S-R learning alone. Similar examples of willful misuse can easily be found.

The original version of this study was submitted as a doctoral dissertation to the Department of Religion at Princeton University. I should like to thank my adviser, Professor George F. Thomas, for his assistance, and especially for his patient understanding of positions with which he is not in agreement. My particular gratitude is owed to Professor Malcolm Diamond, who, as friend and colleague, spent long hours discussing with me positions taken in this study; to him I owe a great deal of such clarity as may from time to time be present in the final version. Professor Richard Rorty, of the Philosophy Department at Princeton, was kind enough to read the manuscript and to make crucial suggestions. I am also grateful to Professor Dennis O'Brien for his encouragement. Day-to-day conversations at that time with my colleagues in the Department of Religion, and especially with Professor Arthur McGill, have undoubtedly contributed ideas and insights which I unknowingly claim as my own. I owe a debt to Myron McClellan for reading much of the manuscript with a sensitive theological eye. Any teacher must finally thank those long-suffering students who are inevitably the original sounding boards of any academic analysis, and who contribute more to the published research of those who do not perish than is often recognized.

VICTOR PRELLER

Munich 1966

CONTENTS

DIVINE SCIENCE AND THE SCIENCE OF GOD

ABBREVIATIONS USED

Ad Heb.	Expositio in Epistola ad Hebreos
Ad Rom.	Expositio in Epistola ad Romanos
C. G.	De Veritate Catholicae Fidei Contra Gentiles
Comm. in Sent.	Commentum in Quatuor Libros Sententiarum
De Trin.	In De Trinitate Boethii Commentarium
De Pot.	De Potentia
De Ver.	De Veritate
In Meta.	In XII Libros Metaphysicorum Aristoteles
In Phys.	In VIII Libros Physicorum Aristoteles
Peri Herm.	In Peri Hermeneias Expositio
Post. Anal.	In Posteriorum Analyticorum Expositio
S. T.	Summa Theologiae

NOTE: Unless otherwise noted, all translations are mine. I have, of course, consulted the standard English versions.

CHAPTER ONE

A CAUTIONARY NOTE AND ASSORTED

PROMISSORY NOTES

INTRODUCTION ACCORDING to Saint Thomas Aquinas there are two distinct "sciences" to which the name "Theology" may be given. On the one hand there is a body of propositions resulting from philosophical reflection on the 'cognitions of God' available to man on the basis of the natural powers of reason alone. Those propositions express a dispositional state of the intellect to which Aquinas gives the name of *scientia divina* or "Divine Knowledge." To that "science" are also given such names as "first philosophy," "metaphysics," "philosophical theology," and "natural theology."[1] In addition to *scientia divina* there is a dispositional state of the intellect called "faith"; to the "science" produced by faith, Aquinas gives the name of *scientia dei* or "Knowledge of God." The propositions which express that "science" result from a theological reflection on the 'cognitions of God' available to man on the basis of revelation (*sacra scriptura*).

The titles by which Aquinas refers to the two theological sciences are most significant. Natural or philosophical theology yields a form of knowledge which may be termed "divine"— i.e., related to divine matters—but which is *not* termed "knowledge of God." The term "knowledge of God" is restricted by Aquinas to that science which results from revelation, even though, as he claims, faith does not terminate here and now in knowledge or science.[2] The distinction between *scientia divina* and *scientia dei*, and the way in which each is 'about God,' forms the essential subject of this study. Since the thesis to be argued is somewhat radical—in the light at least of "traditional Thomism"—I have thought it best to state an essential part of that thesis, in its most radical form, before arguing it in any detail. A large segment of this chapter will

[1] Throughout this book those terms will be used synonymously.
[2] S. *T.*, II-II, 1, 5; *Ad Heb.*, XI, 1.

therefore consist of "promissory notes" almost entirely unredeemed by substantiating evidence.

Before presenting that thesis, however, which constitutes an interpretation of the relation between philosophy and theology—between *scientia divina* and *scientia dei*—in the works of Aquinas, a word must be said and a cautionary note issued concerning the single factor that unifies this rather schematic treatment of the thought of Aquinas: the problem of reference to God. If *scientia divina* is *divina* because it is knowledge related *to God*—if *scientia dei* is *dei* because it is knowledge *of God*—then either science is possible precisely as *divina* or *dei* if and only if it is possible to refer to God and to specify in what way the "sciences" of theology are *about* him. The cautionary note may be tersely expressed in the following *obiter dictum*: no language, no concept, no science can be 'about God' in anything like the way in which any other language, concept, or science is about its object. 'Referring to God' is a *most* peculiar thing to intend—in the first instance it seems impossible.

<h2 style="text-align:center">THE PROBLEM
OF REFERRING TO GOD</h2>

The subject of any science is that of which the science speaks.[3] There can be no knowledge of anything unless that knowledge can be expressed in words. That of which we cannot speak is that of which we cannot know. Theology, for Aquinas, is a "science"—a mode of knowing—and its object is God.[4] Theology is therefore defined as "talk about God" (*sermo de Deo*).[5] In order to talk about something, we must be able to refer to it in a meaningful way. Significant reference includes at least implicit predication. Both the referential and predicative aspects of "talking about" are included in Aquinas' term "to signify": a word may be used to signify an object or to signify a property; a proposition may be used to signify an object together with a property. Overt linguistic behavior (the sounds and marks of spoken and written language) are able to signify because they are the expressions

---

[3] S. T. I, 1, 7.   [4] *Ibid.*   [5] *Ibid.*

of *conceptiones intellectus* which are themselves significant—
which are themselves *about things*.[6] To have a significant concept of an object is to possess an *intention* of that object.
When a significant concept is used to *refer*, the user is said
to *intend* the object to which the concept refers. In order to
refer to God, it would seem that we must be able to intend
him—to have him 'in mind.' To have something 'in mind,'
however, is to have some notion of *what it is*. God, says Aquinas, is that 'being' concerning which we cannot know what
he is or how he exists.[7] It is not clear, then, that we can intend him or (intellegibly) intend to refer to him.

The problem of reference goes to the heart of any religious
action whatever. If an action is not to be regarded as an accident—or 'absent-minded' activity—it must be an 'intentional'
action.[8] To perform a *human* act is to act with intent. "Did
you intend to trip the waitress, or did you 'do it by accident'?"
means, "Was the tripping of the waitress *your* act, or did it
just happen in the order of things?" Intentional action is performed 'present-mindedly.' To 'intend' to trip the waitress is
to 'have the tripping of the waitress in mind' while or before
tripping her. If you 'had it in mind to stretch your legs' then
you accidentally tripped the waitress. All human action is
performed intentionally, whether or not it is performed 'voluntarily.' (One turns over his wallet to a thief *intentionally*,
but not *voluntarily*.) From time to time the 'intention' which
must accompany any *human* act is dispositional and not actual
(as when the worshipper signs himself with the cross 'absent-
mindedly'); but even the dispositional intention presupposes
the 'having in mind' of the act at some time. Some intentional
acts are also done 'on purpose' or with an end in mind; others
are done 'for no reason at all'; but both classes are intentional
acts if they are not pure accident (and therefore insignificant
to all but a psychiatrist, for whom they may *really* be inten-

[6] *Peri Herm.*, I, 2; cf. also, W. Sellars and R. Chisholm, "Correspondence," in *Minnesota Studies in the Philosophy of Science*, Vol. II (University of Minnesota Press, Minneapolis, 1958).

[7] *S. T.*, I, 3, Introduction.

[8] The use of single quotes here corresponds with a general distinction
made throughout the book. Terms in double quotes refer to *words*; terms
in single quotes refer to *concepts* or, as here, to *mental states* or *entities*.

tional after all). *What* one intends by his action is what he
'has in mind' when he performs it. Thus, the volitional sense
of "intending" presupposes a cognitive sense of "intending"—
nihil velle possumus nisi sit intellectum. I am only *free to do*
(as a *human* agent) that of which I can have an *intellectual
intention.*[9]

"Meaning" is a kind of "doing." To 'mean' something by
one's overt actions—linguistic or nonlinguistic—is to *use* one's
actions to *express* intentions. It is to 'have something in mind'
which is expressed by them. The words that we use are *significant*—our actions are meaningful—in part because they
are *about* things or make *references.* (This is not to say that
all language is referential or that bare reference supplies the
building blocks of meaningful discourse.) We could not use
language intentionally, if we did not 'have intentions'—if we
did not have ideas, concepts, or in general, 'mental-states'
which are themselves about things or are able to be used to
make references to things: "The problem of 'intentionality,'
[is] the problem of interpreting the status of *reference* to
objects and states of affairs, actual or possible, past, present
or future, which is involved in the very meaning of the 'mental-
istic' vocabulary of everyday life. Believing, desiring, intending, loving, hating, reasoning, approving—indeed, all charac-
teristically human states and dispositions above the level of
mere sensory consciousness—cannot be explicated without en-
countering such *reference* or *aboutness.*"[10] To some philosophers, intentionality is *simply* a characteristic of overt verbal
behavior (which stands in a kind of *physical* relation to the
actions or objects intended) and so-called 'thoughts' are
merely "hypothetical and mongrel hypothetical-categorical
facts" about observable behavior.[11] Behaviorism, including

---

[9] On the subject of the volitional sense of "intention," see E. Anscombe,
Intentions (Cornell University Press, Ithaca, 1950); on intellectual inten-
sions, see W. Sellars, "Empiricism and the Philosophy of Mind," in *Minn.
Studies in the Phil. of Science,* Vol. i (University of Minnesota Press,
Minneapolis, 1956); and, R. Chisholm, *Perceiving: A Philosophical Study*
(Cornell University Press, Ithaca, 1957).

[10] Sellars and Chisholm, *loc.cit.*

[11] The latter view is defended systematically in G. Ryle, *The Concept
of Mind* (Barnes & Noble, Inc., New York, 1949).

Rylean behaviorism, reduces 'mental-state' language to talk about overt verbal behavior, even if it is admitted that such talk is indispensable. We need not adopt a behavioristic interpretation of intentionality in order to state the problem involved in "significant religious action," verbal or nonverbal. Behaviorism seems, like positivism, to be dying a natural death among philosophers. Wilfred Sellars, for example, is quite willing to admit that overt verbal behavior is intentional only *because* it is expressive of 'thoughts' or 'inner events' that may be called intentional. "Meaning" for Sellars is an irreducible term referring to a characteristic of human language deriving not from its physical relatedness to overt action or external objects, but from its use by thinking animals.[12] That is in agreement with Aquinas, for whom the marks and sounds of overt linguistic behavior (*scriptura* and *vox*) are significant only because they express inner states—*intentiones* or *conceptiones*.[13] (Needless to say, Sellars and Aquinas ultimately attribute different characteristics to such 'inner events.') Significant intentions, however, cannot be generated willy-nilly by the human mind; men are mortal for all their thought, and they can only perform the humanly do-able. The question, "How can we *intend* a significant religious act—verbal or nonverbal?" ultimately reduces to, "To what is it humanly possible to refer?" If it cannot be shown that God falls within the range of possible referents, it follows that we *cannot intend* a significant religious act, whatever we may *think* we are doing at the time.

The point can be made in terms of the 'self-crosser.' The act of 'making the sign of the cross' can be shown to be intentional without necessarily being religious or *significantly* religious. Thus, if a 'self-crosser' were asked, "Did you intend to do that funny bit of business on your chest?" he might well reply, "Oh yes, I always do it when I kneel down." The further question is certainly in order, however, "But *what* did you intend by it? Did you merely intend to make a circular sweep over your breast—and if so, why?" The worshipper might reply, a bit abashedly, "I must be getting careless. What I

---

12 Sellars and Chisholm, *loc.cit.*
13 *Peri Herm.*, I, 2.

really intended was to make two straight movements over the breast, one horizontal and one vertical." We now know at one level *what* he intended—what he 'had in mind' when he performed the act. In answering the "why" question, however, he indicates that he had more in mind. He intended to describe a cross *in order to express or make a reference to* a particular historical cross of physical, tangible wood. So far, no one could dispute that he had such 'things' in mind, whether or not such a cross actually existed as and when he believed. It is possible to *intend* a reference to something like a physical object even if such an object has no existence and thus *cannot really be referred to.* The action would be viewed as a *religious* act, however, only if the agent intended something more: either, "I intended to express or confess the fact that on that cross the Son of God died for me," or, "I expressed my belief that through that cross I shall receive a new mode of existence—a new relationship to the Ground of my being." In any case, to qualify as a *religious* act in any interesting sense, an act must be performed with a *religious* intention in mind. All religious intentions make or imply references to a being or state which lies beyond the realm of things to which we can clearly and unquestionably make references in human community, the realm of the ordinarily observable. If the 'religious act' is not to be regarded as 'accidental' or 'absent-minded' precisely at the point of its religious interest, it must be possible to 'have in mind' the being or state to which the religious intention makes or intends to make a reference. This question ought not to be confused with the question of whether or not a religious reference succeeds—i.e., whether or not there really *is* a God. Whether or not there is a God, a reference to him could only be intelligibly *intended* if it were possible to have an intention *of* God. To have an intention of something is to know how it could be significantly referred to *if* it existed. If the 'believer' *simply* does not know what he 'has in mind' when he tries to intend to refer to God, then he is not even succeeding in *intending* to refer to God (successfully referring or not according to whether or not God exists). If the 'believer' does not *know* what he 'has in mind' then it would *appear* at first glance that he has nothing significant in mind. To ask, "What do you *mean* by 'God'?" is to ask, "What do you have in mind when you say 'God'?"

How do we state the meaning of *any* referential term? What kind of thing do we 'have in mind' when we use a word to refer? What does it *mean* to refer? In a paradigm case of reference, we pick out a particular aspect of 'that which is' and direct attention to it. Even in the simplest case of reference, such an act is immensely complex and presupposes a developed conceptual system. The common-sense notion that a reference to an object might be as simple as "pointing" to it was overturned with decision by Wittgenstein.[14] Merely pointing in a certain 'direction' may be an instance of referring to an object, its color, its shape, its texture or its total context—or it may not be a case of referring at all. Pointing to a jar and saying "jar" is a case of referring only if you have in mind what is *intended* by the word "jar." The logic of thing-words must be present 'in the mind.' If you point to a jar and say, "Red," I will only *take* you to be making a reference to the *color* of the jar if I understand the use of "red" to express the concept 'red'—to do that I must know the logic of color-words, which in turn implies that I know the logic of thing-words and a number of *other* sorts of words. To know what a color *is* is to know the kinds of things that have colors and the distinction between colors and the areas that are colored, and so on. Making a reference does not depend upon the direction in which a finger is extended but upon what is 'in the mind'—what is intended.

Upon what does *that* depend? How do we distinguish between the multifarious things and kinds and characteristics to which we may point? The answer would seem to be a paradox: we know that *this* is a separable part of our experience to which we may refer, because we *now* see that in the past it (or something *like* it) *was* a separable part of our experience to which we *might* have referred had we known it.[15] The ability to refer follows upon the recognition of repetition.

14 L. Wittgenstein, *Philosophical Investigations* (The Macmillan Co., New York, 1959), Part I.
15 Cf., P. Strawson, *Individuals* (Methuen & Co. Ltd., London, 1959), p. 31.

Identification is primarily *re*-identification. It presupposes empirical generalization, not as a self-conscious application of rules, but as the very form in which we come to think conceptually.

In a paradigm case of referring, therefore, similarities are distinguished within differences—we can refer to *a* thing because we can refer to that *kind* of thing. Reference is not just location in physical space, but in logical or intentional space. The intention we have of an object is part of a conceptual *system* with syntactical interrelations describing a kind of logical or intentional space. In a paradigm case of referring, we must know some at least of the general characteristics of that to which we intend to refer—something that it has in common with other things to which we could refer—as well as that which distinguishes it from fellow members of its universe of reference. To 'have a thing in mind'—to intend a thing—is to know what *kind* of thing it is. Everything to which we refer is, of course, unique in some way—even if only in the sense of not being any other particular thing. But nothing to which we can intentionally and significantly refer would seem to be *absolutely* unique in the sense of having *nothing* in common with anything else to which we can or could refer. To locate a thing *within* logical space is to imply that at some level of analysis it is a *sort* of thing—it belongs to at least one general class of real or possible referents. The name "God," however, is unique: God, says Aquinas, falls into *no general class.*[16] God cannot be located *within* the logical space in terms of which we make significant references. There can be no conceptually significant intention of what God is, how he exists, or how he is related to things of which we can have meaningful intentions.[17] It is not clear that we can have 'God' in mind when we say "God"—it is not therefore clear *what* we have in mind.

[16] S. T., i, 3, 5; and De Pot., 7, 3.

[17] It might seem premature to say that we do not know how God is related to the world. Is he not said to be the *cause* of the world, for example? I shall argue below that we use "cause" to name a relation that we do *not* know. It will suffice here to point out that, if we do not know what x is or how it exists, we can hardly *know* how x is related to anything else.

Some sense of the uniqueness of the word "God" may be conveyed by the very fact that the "existence of God" is so often debated. It is quite common to talk about *things*—it is not so common to talk about the *existence* of things. To ask, "Does God exist?" is not at all like asking whether or not something other than God exists. The kind of uncertainty that leads us to ask, "Does God exist?" is not, for example, the kind of uncertainty that leads us to ask (not so often), "Do unicorns exist?" or, "Do abominable snowmen exist?" In the latter cases—if we really mean the questions—there must be some ground for thinking that such things *might* exist—that there might be, among the many things *to which we already refer*, other sorts of things whose existence would also not be a *problem* if they really existed. There may be some *question* as to the existence of unicorns, but there is no essential *problem*. That is why the question of their existence is not very often debated—it is a mere matter of fact. Most of the times that we do raise questions as to the existence of an object, we are merely asking whether or not such an object is among those things whose existence we do not normally question. We do not ordinarily raise questions about the existence of something except in the context of references to *things* which unquestionably exist. We can discuss the *existence* of things because we can and normally do discuss *things* without discussing their existence.

If the question, "Does God exist?" is not like the question, "Do unicorns exist?" may it perhaps be like the question, "Do ghosts exist?"? Here it would appear that we are faced not only with a question but also with a problem. We appear to be asking whether or not there are 'things' radically unlike the kinds of things we ordinarily discuss without raising questions as to their existence. Any conversational reference to 'ghosts' is likely to elicit an immediate query as to whether or not such things could *possibly* exist, since the word "ghosts" seems to make a reference which cannot be handled on the basis of the intentional space in terms of which we conceive the world and refer to things. In fact, however, we know what kind of question is being raised by "Do ghosts exist?" precisely because the logic of personal reference *is* part of our intentional space. It is because we know how to use "Uncle John" to refer to a living man (concerning whom we did not raise the *question* of his existence while alive), that we are rather disturbed by the claim that Uncle John made a door slam after Uncle John died. The important logical point is that the question "Can we *continue* to refer to people after they are dead" obviously implies that we know how to refer to them under ordinary circumstances. The problem of the existence of ghosts is a queer one; it is the problem of whether or not successful references can be made under highly problematic circumstances to the *same beings* we were able to refer to under ordinary circumstances (i.e., under circumstances when the question of their existence did not arise). The question of the existence of God, however, is not a question of whether or not we can *now* refer to a being to whom we *could have* referred in a nonproblematic fashion some time ago. Reference to people may *become* a problem after they die—reference to God is always the same problem. God may—in the shallow jargon of existential theology—be dead; but he can never be dead the way Uncle John is dead.

Ordinarily, to raise the question "Does *x* exist?" is to *deny* that the object language in terms of which a reference might be made to *x* (if it exists) is normally used to refer to objects whose existence is a problem or concerning which the question of existence ought ordinarily to be raised. When we raise the question, "Does *x* exist?" it is because we know that the existence of *x* would not in itself be a *problem*. X may *not* exist, but we can easily conceive of circumstances in which it would clearly be true to say that *x does* exist. ("A ghost exists" only seems to be an exception when we fail to note that it really amounts to saying, "Uncle John *still* exists.") We know what kind of question "Does *x* exist?" is, because we know the kind of thing to which "*x*" refers, we know that logically similar things *do* exist, and we know that the question of the existence of such things does not normally arise. The question "Does God exist?" however, signals far more than an uncertainty as to whether or not the word can be used to refer to something in the general class of objects concerning which we do not ordinarily raise the question of their existence. The question of the existence of God is a *real* problem, which is probably why it is so often raised.

There are, of course, other ways of raising the question of the existence of *x*. Some of them begin to suggest the logic of "Does God exist?," but none of them is able to eliminate the essential uniqueness of the theological question. Thus, while "Does *x* exist?" *ordinarily* presupposes the possibility of referring to objects whose existence is in no way called into question, it is possible to make a problem out of the existence of anything. A person could conceivably ask, "Does that chair over there *really* exist?" Assuming that he does not mean anything as nonproblematic as "There seems to be a chair over there, but I am not sure," he might mean one of two things: either he is entertaining the essentially neurotic 'suspicion' that maybe *nothing* exists (an alternative more suited to psychoanalytic discussion than to philosophical discussion), or he is raising a peculiar question about the entire object language in terms of which he refers to 'what is.' It is important to note that he is not (if he is sane) denying the reality of what he *sees*. The word "existence" has rather taken on a highly specialized use dependent on the notion of an ideal description of 'what is the case.' To say, "Perhaps chairs do not *really* exist," is to say, "Perhaps there is a language in which a complete description of the world could be given, in which such molar terms as 'chairs' would have no use, in terms of which the concept 'chair' could not simply and without remainder be constructed or defined, and which I would commend as the best or 'ideal' language in terms of which to talk about 'what is'."[18] We do not have to believe that such a language is possible or that, if it is possible, it ought to be granted methodological priority over the physical-object language, in order to see that such a claim has nothing in common with raising the question "Does *x* exist?" "Does *that chair over there* really exist?" grants the existence of the chair in the sense in which we have been discussing "existence." It merely asks whether or not the language in terms of which we refer nonproblematically to existent objects has final ontological priority over

[18] Cf., Sellars, *Science, Perception and Reality* (Routeledge and Kegan Paul, New York, 1963), Chaps. 4 and 5.

other possible language systems. In a sense the question "Does God exist?" is related to the question "Does that chair over there *really* exist?" It certainly is *not* asking, "Is God to be found among those things whose existence we normally assume without question, and to which we refer in our object language?" It is *not* asking if God exists like "that chair over there." It is rather like asking, "Is there an ideal language in terms of which a complete and adequate description might be given of 'that which is' and in which the expression 'God' would occur referentially?" There are, however, two problems which make of the question a unique question: (1) When we ask, "Is there an ideal language in terms of which a complete and adequate account may be given of 'what is' and in which 'chair' would *not* occur referentially?" we clearly know the use of the word "chair" in the language we are using when we raise the question. We know what "chair" means and to what it refers. It is not clear, however, that we know what the word "God" means in the language we use to raise the question of his existence. (2) When we contemplate the possibility of constructing an ideal language in which "that which is" would be adequately described, we know (in our *chair* instance) what we mean by "that which is"—we are referring to *what we experience* when we say such things as, "There is a chair over there." In order for "God" to occur referentially in a language describing "that which is," however, the meaning of "that which is" must be extended to cover some 'reality' that we do *not* experience in ordinary referring contexts. We may conceive of the possibility of referring to what we now experience in terms of a rather different conceptual system, but it is not at all clear that we can conceive of the possibility of referring to that which we do *not* experience—unless we can state what that reality is *like*, or how it *might* be experienced.

It would appear, therefore, that however the question "Does God exist?" is to be interpreted, some notion of what God is or some notion of 'reality' beyond what we encounter in ordinary experience is required to state the meaning of the question. The problem of referring to God (even as a "possible entity") is once again seen to be intimately connected with

the problem of "intending God" or "having God 'in mind.'"
So long as the question "What is God *like*?" elicits the response,
"He is not like anything," or, "He is like nothing," the problem
of intending a reference to him appears insoluble. The problem of the existence of God is radically intertwined with the
problem of meaningfully predicating something of God. The
question "What could it *mean* to intend a significant reference
to God?" implies the question, "What could it *mean* to say,
'God exists'?"

An interesting question, of course, is what it means to say
of *anything* that it exists. It is tempting to oversimplify the
question in such a way that "exists" will have some straightforward import such as "can be encountered in the world" or
"may be experienced." One might even suggest that "exists"
means "occupies space." None of these definitions really succeeds. It may be debatable whether something may exist
without occupying space, but it hardly seems reasonable to
assume that "exists" *means* "occupies space." As for the "en-
counterability" of existent things, it is not an evident characteristic of electrons or molecules.

We could short-circuit the entire process, of course, by defining "exists" as "may be referred to." The problem is, however, that we refer in so many ways to so many kinds of
'things.' In one sense, nevertheless, it is a perfectly proper
definition, since we do in fact say that all sorts of things
"exist" because we can refer to them. Thus, numbers 'exist,'
ideas 'exist,' and possibilities 'exist' because we can locate
them in intentional space. Clearly, however, the meaning of
"exists" changes radically when the word is used not of chairs
but of numbers. Insofar as "may be referred to" *justifies* "exists," the *meaning* of "exists" depends upon the way in which
reference can be made. To say that numbers 'exist'—in *that*
sense—is not necessarily to manifest an ontological commitment; it is not to say that "numbers" refers to a *kind* of entity
which exist as well as or in addition to such things as chairs
and persons—and in the same general sense of "exists." To be
an interesting question, "What does it mean to say of anything
that it exists?" must be construed to mean, "What does it mean

to say of anything *real* that it exists?" In other words, we are currently interested in one *use* of "exists"—its use in making references to real entities or 'that which is.'

If "that chair *exists*" does not mean "that chair is spatial" or "that chair may be encountered in the world," what *does* it mean? One promising approach is to point out that saying "*x* exists" is not *predicating* something of *x*, but *doing* something with "*x*." In essence this is the suggestion of G. J. Warnock in his book on Berkeley.[19] For Warnock, to say "*x* exists" is not equivalent to describing *x* or claiming to "encounter" *x* in the present, past or future, but is rather equivalent to writing "*x*" on an index card and filing it in a drawer—a drawer called "The Contents of the Universe." On this point, Warnock reminds one of the scholastics, for whom "exists" is not just a predication among others, but the presupposition of all predication.

While philosophy is not primarily interested in making out the cards for such a catalogue, it *is* interested in how such cards do get made out and how they are filed away. Philosophy does ask on what principles we catalogue cards about what there is in the universe. It would be fair to say, I think, that the "common-sense existence catalogue" has grown up somewhat chaotically and arbitrarily. In shuffling through the cards in the "common-sense catalogue" a philosopher might come upon many that seem to have been stuffed in with no thought of their cataloguing value: they could not conceivably have a use in a catalogue describing the contents of the universe. The philosopher is not likely to claim that the cataloguer has made a factual error, but rather that he has made a categorial error. Thus, if at the back of the drawer there are a number of cards marked with 'names' such as "Borogrove" and "Brumph," something has gone wrong and the usefulness of the catalogue has been impaired. It would be simple, however, to make a categorical correction: for "Borogrove" and "Brumph" the philosopher will write " 'Borogrove' " and " 'Brumph,' " which refer to physical words or patterns which

[19] G. J. Warnock, *Berkeley* (Penguin Books, London, 1953), Chap. 10.

do exist in reality. Should the "God" card be changed to " 'God' "?

In order to answer that question, we must know something of the way in which a card comes to have a *significant* place in the catalogue. The direction in which the solution lies may be indicated by the addition of a second drawer to the catalogue.[20] If we label the first drawer "The Real Entity Drawer," we might call the second "The Intentional 'Entity' Drawer."[21] The I. 'E.' Drawer will contain a duplicate card for every entry in the R. E. Drawer, plus a number of other cards, such as 'Unicorn,' which are not cross-indexed with a card in the R. E. Drawer. To know the *significance* of filing a card in the R. E. Drawer—to know how to give it a significant *place* in the drawer—is to know the position or status of its duplicate in the I. 'E.' Drawer. Thus, to know the significance of filing a "chair" card in the R. E. Drawer is to know how the 'chair' card is cross-indexed with other cards *within* the I. 'E.' Drawer. To know the rather different significance of filing an "electron" card in the R. E. Drawer is to know how the 'electron' card is categorially differently cross-indexed within the I. 'E.' Drawer. (To have a metaphysics, by the way, is to have an instruction book which determines the *kinds* of I. 'E.' cards that could in theory be filed in the R. E. Drawer.) The entry on an I. 'E.' card which indicates that there is a duplicate in the R. E. Drawer must not be viewed as a *predicate* of the card. The claim that there is a duplicate of the I. 'E.' card in the R. E. Drawer does not say anything about the I. 'E.' card, but rather says something about the makeup of the catalogue itself.

On the other hand, we can introduce at this point a predicative use of "existence." Its purpose, however, will not be to say anything about I. 'E.' cards—it will not predicate "existence" of 'possibles'—but rather to define two classes of R. E. cards. I shall first discuss why "exists" is not a predicate when written on an I. 'E.' card. In the I. 'E.' Drawer will be found

[20] The interpretation of "exists" given in this chapter is schematic and provisional. A more systematic account will be given in Chapter Two.

[21] I put "entity" in single quotes because I do not believe that ultimately there are such things as 'intentional entities' or 'mental beings,' although I believe those terms may be used to *name* something real in men.

such cards as 'dog' and 'unicorn.' The former will contain an "existential" cross-reference to the R. E. Drawer, and the latter will not. If we assume that something—i.e., "existence" —is being predicated of 'dog' but denied of 'unicorn,' we must ask what the subject of that predication is. Since the expression "the I. 'E.' 'dog' card" means "the intention or idea of 'dog,'" to predicate "existence" of that card will mean that the intention or idea of 'dog' (or 'doggeity') exists. But the mere fact that there *is* a 'unicorn' card means that the intention or idea of 'unicorn' (or 'unicorneity') *also* exists and in the same sense. To say that an I. 'E.' card is in the drawer is to say that *it* exists as an intention or idea. To say that there really *are* dogs, but no unicorns, is not to say anything about the intention or idea of 'dog' or 'unicorn.' Suppose, however, that one of the cards in the R. E. Drawer is labeled "Abraham Lincoln." The duplicate in the I. 'E.' Drawer will contain a nonpredicative "existential" cross-reference to the R. E. Drawer. In addition, however, the card in the R. E. Drawer will *itself* contain a predicative entry: "Does not exist now." Existence in *that* sense—the sense in which "Ismael is no more"[22]—says something about the card on which it appears. That is to say, "Does not exist now" says something about Abraham Lincoln —not about the intention or idea of Abraham Lincoln. In order to know, however, that "existence" can be used of anything in this *predicative* sense, we must know on independent grounds that its subject card is in the R. E. Drawer—we must already know that the subject is a real entity, not merely a possible one. How do we know that? What does it mean to say "*x* exists" in the nonpredicative sense? When can one file an "*x*" R. E. card?

Short of introducing chaos into the R. E. Drawer—i.e., to safeguard its significance as a usable catalogue—several preliminary conditions must be laid down in the rule book: (1) The card must have a duplicate with a significant place in the I. 'E.' Drawer. Its I. 'E.' duplicate, that is, must be intelligibly cross-referenced with the other members of the I. 'E.' Drawer.

[22] For a discussion of predicative and nonpredicative uses of "existence" see, P. Geatch, "On What There Is," in *Proceedings of the Aristotelian Society*, Suppl. Vol., 1951.

(This is no more than the claim that the 'intention' of the object must be part of an intelligible conceptual system.) (2) The "existential" cross-reference on its I. 'E.' card must be justified either by a direct appeal to sense-experience or on the basis of a kind of cross-reference to other I. 'E.' cards which do contain "existential" cross-references justified by an appeal to sense-experience. This does *not*, of course, mean that the entity referred to must be perceivable in order to have a card in the R. E. Drawer. It means only that its intention must be part of a conceptual system such that certain states of the sensory system justify either the existential cross-indexing of that card or the interpretation of its conceptual context in such terms as themselves justify that cross-indexing. (The former mode of justification would hold for "chair," while the second would hold for "electron.") Proviso number 2 is simply the assertion that the world of sense-experience is the 'anchor' of our 'sense of the real'—sense-experience provides our 'reality principle.' All existential references—in order to be significant *for us*—must be justified by reference to our experience of 'the world.' Can we conceive of any significant and intelligible way of cross-indexing a 'God' card with I. 'E.' cards nonproblematically containing "existential" cross-references to the R. E. Drawer? Can we intelligibly relate 'God' to 'chair,' 'person,' 'electron,' or to the conceptual frameworks in which such intentions occur?

There have been, especially on the part of Thomists, horrendously naïve attempts to explicate the relation between 'God' and 'the world.' Most of this nonsense parades under the name of 'analogy'—the so-called 'analogy of proper proportionality.' It will be argued below that the radical error of interpretation which has led to generations of false claims is that of Cajetan. At the moment I shall simply outline the basic circularity of the all-too-popular move—a circularity which affects almost all attempts to specify in intelligible terms the relation between the logic of 'God' and the logic of 'things in the world.'

The normal move is to begin with the claim that God is the 'cause' of the world. On the basis of that relation, it is believed possible to predicate certain 'perfections' of God in a mode appropriate to the 'cause' of the world—the 'first cause,' as it is called. To exhibit the circularity of the move, we must immediately challenge the use of 'cause' in relation to God. If we ask how the Thomist is using "cause" he normally replies in terms of 'efficient causality'—that mode of causing a thing which explains that a thing is. In common terms God is the 'maker' or 'creator' of the world. The non-Thomist is likely to reply that he is only familiar with uses of "causing," "making," or "creating" which refer to ordinary occurrences *within* the world. He knows what it is to make or create something out of something else, and what it is for a state of affairs in the world to be the cause of another state of affairs; if by "God is the first cause," however, the Thomist means "God is the maker of everything that is, with the exception of himself," then the word "cause" seems to have lost its intelligibility—its explanatory power. We simply do not know what it would be like to 'make something out of nothing.' We can form the notion of 'nothing,' followed by the notion of 'something,' but we cannot conceive intelligibly of the means by which the transition takes place. We have never had the occasion to use the word "cause" or the concept 'cause' in such a way as to render the 'coming into being of something from nothing' intelligible. The notion of 'cause' was not formed to cover such 'happenings.' When we seek for intelligibility by asking the Thomist *how* God operates in such a way as to produce 'something out of nothing'—how, that is, the relation 'makes out of nothing' can be a *significant* and *intelligible* way to tie 'God' into the existential catalogue—he will reply in such terms as "God merely thinks and wills, and the existence of the world follows." When we reply that we fail to see how 'thinking and willing' are intelligibly related to 'coming into being from nothing,' the Thomist grants that he is using the words analogically—as, it turns out, he was using "cause." Of course, when *we* think or will—when indeed we think of thinking and willing in the only way we can conceive such acts —there is no reason to assume that such acts could conceivably lead to the 'coming into being of something from nothing.' *God*, however, 'thinks' and 'wills' in a way appropriate to God *alone*—and such 'thinking' and 'willing' is the intelligible cause of the 'coming into being of the world from nothing.'

Now, in order to understand what "thinks and wills in a way appropriate to God *alone*" means, we have to know what it is to be appropriate to *God*. We have to know what God is *like*. If the Thomist replies "in a way appropriate to the *creator*," the circle is already complete: "God is the maker of the world" was *supposed* to give us our notion of how God is related to the world; but in order to understand that definition we must know what it means to 'think' and 'will' in a mode appropriate only to the *creator*. We are hopelessly floundering in a sea of 'extended meanings' with no lifeline to the dry ground of ordinary meaning.

The circle, of course, can be enlarged almost indefinitely. The Thomist may say that God 'thinks' and 'wills' in a way appropriate to and possible only for a 'necessary and omnipotent being.' When we ask, however, what a 'necessary and omnipotent being' *is*, the Thomist replies, "A being who does not need to be made or created in the way in which the world *does*, and who is able to create out of nothing as God *has*." But those again are the very notions we were trying to comprehend! According to the "analogy-of-proper-proportionality" school *every* term used of God is used in a way appropriate to ✓ God *alone*—there are always two unknowns in a definition of "God": one in the *definiens* and one in the *definiendum*. In a way, the Thomist is correct to make that assertion. His mistake is generally to suppose that such 'analogical speech' gives us any 'intelligibility.' We cannot use analogy to tie God into the catalogue—to make *significant* and *intelligible* the relationship between 'God' and 'table.'

Such is the problem of referring to God. If it is impossible to have a significant and intelligible concept of *what God is*, and if it is impossible to have a significant and intelligible notion of how God is related to the world, the problem appears insurmountable. This much is clear: if we *do* succeed in getting some notion of 'God' and if we *do* succeed in defining a kind of relation between 'God' and 'what I experience,' both the notion and the relation will of necessity be unique. The way in which 'God' may be tied into an existence catalogue will be—if not impossible—by definition significantly different from the way in which anything else is tied into the catalogue. From which it follows that no language or science can be about God in the way in which any other language or science is about its object. We may now turn to our promissory notes regarding the relationship between those two "sciences" which Aquinas claims to be in some sense about God.

THE THEOLOGICAL USE OF PHILOSOPHY

The vast majority of contemporary philosophers, both Thomists and analysts, treat St. Thomas as though he intended to be a philosophical theologian in his own right. Large segments of his work are cited as examples of "Aquinas' philosophy" and are analyzed in total isolation from the distinctly dogmatic settings in which they occur. Such a procedure is misleading: (1) It implies that Aquinas was at times motivated by a purely philosophical intention. (2) It implies that the philosophical positions and arguments utilized within the theological treatises of Aquinas are his own positions and arguments, or ones with which he must necessarily agree. (3) It implies that philosophical statements remain unchanged in their essential nature when they are integrated into a theological framework. All of those claims are false.

Aquinas' sole intention in writing such works as the *Summa Theologiae* is the articulation of theological truth—he writes as *catholicae veritatis doctor*.[23] Even in the *Contra Gentiles* Aquinas self-consciously adopts a theological order, rather than a philosophical order.[24] The closest that Aquinas comes to manifesting a purely philosophical intention is in his commentaries on Aristotle. Even there, however, theological considerations color his interpretations, and there he articulates positions which are rejected in his basically theological writings. In the *Summa Theologiae* every article defines its problem from a radically theological perspective, and every response of Aquinas to a question is based upon an appeal to sacred doctrine. Thus, his primary response to the question, "Does God exist?" is, "Yes, for it is written in Exodus 3, as

[23] S. T., *prologus*.
[24] S. C. C., II, 5. See also J. Anderson, Introduction to Vol. II of *On the Truth of the Catholic Faith* (Image Books, New York, 1956).

from the very person of God, 'I am he who is.' "[25] His citation in the body of the article of "five ways" in which the existence of God can be proved cannot be understood apart from the preceding article in which he establishes *as a matter of faith* that "the existence of God is manifest from the things that have been created." Aquinas is convinced *on divine authority* that arguments terminating in "God exists" must be possible. It is therefore with an essentially theological concern that Aquinas quotes, with seeming approval, "five ways" in which philosophers have historically 'demonstrated' the existence of God. The arguments are not offered as *proofs* of the *theological* statement "God exists," or even of the *theological* statement "God's existence can be proved"—in matters of faith the authority of God suffices. Aquinas makes it quite clear that philosophical arguments are not needed to establish the truth of revealed propositions (including those that in theory *might* be proved apart from revelation); in the context of theological reflection on revealed propositions, philosophical arguments may be cited only as *external* evidence with *probable* authority.[26] Since, in the *Summa Theologiae*, the propositions "God's existence can be proved" and "God exists" are taken as revealed and certain, the philosophical arguments which occur in conjunction with them are offered by Aquinas as external and probable only. If Aquinas in the *Summa* (or anywhere else for that matter) were engaged in his own version of philosophical theology—what he calls "first philosophy"—he would have to establish his philosophical positions with more conceptual rigor, clarifying his principles (*rationes*) and arguments (*viae*) in greater detail. He knows that *in philosophy* demonstrations of matters concerning God are possible only "after a long time and with much effort"[27] and with inevitable admixture of error! Since, however, Aquinas is doing *theology*, he can effortlessly *quote* the positions of philosophers, referring briefly to their principles and arguments, depending upon the *authority* of the philosophers or traditions he quotes to provide the external and probable evidence admissible in theology. All of Aquinas' arguments

25 S. T., I, 2, 3.   26 S. T., I, 1, 8, ad 2.   27 S. T., I, 1, 1.

· 23 ·

are from authority: he recognizes, in descending order, the authority of *scriptura*, the *sancti*, and the *philosophi*. Only the first of these is both necessary and sufficient to establish the truth of any position taken in the *Summa Theologiae*.

It is therefore misleading to refer to "Aquinas' philosophy." When philosophy occurs in Aquinas' theological treatises, it occurs on the authority of some one other than Aquinas. Nevertheless it is true that Aquinas does not *normally* quote a philosophical argument unless he takes it to be philosophically in order.[28] Thus, he quotes most extensively from 'The Philosopher' because he believes that Aristotle has the highest authority in philosophy (since he was then invading the philosophical faculty of Paris?). It is not always true, however, that Aquinas agrees with *every* philosophical position he quotes as probable evidence for a theological statement. He often quotes, for example, the positions and even the *viae* and *rationes* of the Platonists on such matters as participation, without assenting to them, or even while explicitly rejecting them.[29] At such times he either 'throws in' the Platonic argument for good measure,[30] or introduces it because he agrees with the proposition emerging from it while rejecting the "way" in which the proposition was argued.[31] For Aquinas to say, "There are five ways in which the existence of God may be demonstrated," is not for him to say, "There are five ways in which *I* can demonstrate, on the basis of *my* philosophy, that God exists." It is merely to say that there are five ways in which philosophers have traditionally proved the existence of God. It happens to be the case (as will be argued below) that the *rationes* on which the five *viae* are based are mutually inconsistent. They could not all be arguments in a single philosophy—even Thomism. It happens further to be the case (also to be argued below) that none of

28 *De Trin.*, II, 3, ad 8.

29 On this entire subject, see the important work of R. J. Henle, *Saint Thomas and Platonism* (Martinus Nijhoff, The Hague, 1956). This work calls into question the excessive ontologism of Geiger and Fabro on the subject of participation.

30 See, for example, his use of Platonic epistemology in S. T., I, 76, 2.

31 This, I believe, is what occurs in the 'fourth way'; it is also obvious whenever Aquinas uses the language of participation while rejecting its ontological roots.

the five ways as they now stand is compatible with Aquinas' understanding of the logic of 'God.' Such an observation would not disturb Aquinas in the least. The theological point that he wishes to make is that the mind of man is ordered to its Creator as to One Unknown. Aquinas expects to find indications of that ordering in all philosophical traditions, regardless of the nature of their *rationes* or starting points. The "five ways" are arguments quoted on philosophical authority as external and probable evidence of the truth of the *theological claim* that the mind of man is ordered to an Unknown God and can reflect on that order. Whether or not Aquinas believed any or all of them to succeed, the "five ways" are *not* "St. Thomas' proofs for the existence of God"!

Aquinas has another use also for philosophical statements. Not only are they adduced as external and probable evidence for the truth of theological claims—although they can only be recognized as evidence in the light of faith—but they are also used as conceptual material for the articulation of theological claims. That is, philosophical categories are used as the medium through which theological 'propositions' are expressed. The basically Aristotelian analysis of the powers of the human soul, which occupies such an astounding amount of space in the *Summa*, is there in order that Aquinas may use, for example, the vocabulary of "act" and "disposition" in expressing the teachings of sacred doctrine on faith, hope, and charity. With regard to that analysis, it is clear that, while it is not Aquinas' own creation, he takes it to be correct. As we shall see, it is possible that another analysis of the 'human soul' is more suitable to make the same theological claims. At any rate, when the Aristotelian analysis is used in a theological framework it ceases to function in a purely philosophical manner. It is used to express essentially non-philosophical intentions. Aquinas puts it rather bluntly: it might be thought, he says, that the use of philosophical statements in expressing the faith will result in the "watering down" of the faith; rather, he replies, when philosophy is used in the light of theology "water is turned into wine"— philosophy *becomes* theology.[32]

[32] *De Trin.*, II, 3, ad 5.

Treating Aquinas as a philosophical theologian has resulted in two radical mistakes. On the one hand, most traditional Thomists, such as Garrigou-Lagrange and Maritain, have assumed that it is possible to abstract from the writings of Aquinas a consistent philosophy which can be seen to be purely rational and uniquely 'Thomistic.' In order to get anything more than "second-hand Aristotle," they have found it necessary to introduce either non-Aristotelian positions cited by Aquinas (usually resulting in a weird mixture of Aristotle and Plato) or radically theological concepts, as part of Aquinas' "unified and philosophical system." Forcing such radically different conceptual parents into miscegenation has led to the most bizarre babies (all rather different, but all duly baptized under the Christian name of "Thomistic Philosophy"). On the other hand, Thomists such as Gilson, who have clearly seen that Aquinas' own thought cannot be understood without a primary and basic reference to his theological position, have assumed that the wedding of theology and philosophy has resulted in the birth of a new kind of *philosophy* —"Christian Philosophy"—which remains philosophical even though constituted in part by the therapeutic insights of revelation.[33] Gilson refers to Aquinas as a "sleight-of-hand artist" and a "magician"[34]—and so he would be, if Gilson were correct, for according to Gilson, Aquinas manages to produce philosophical rabbits out of theological hats.

It is not quite clear what a 'Thomistic Philosophy' or a 'Christian Philosophy' might be. The suspicion of most non-Thomists is that it could only be a kind of 'un-philosophy' dependent upon gratuitous theological propositions. This suspicion is not greatly dissipated by the esoteric devotion of Neo- and Paleo-Thomists to jargonized 'first principles' whose 'self-evidence' escapes all but themselves and God. It would appear simpler—and more in accord with the statements of Aquinas—to acknowledge the fact that when philosophy appears in the theological treatises it has been so integrated into

[33] E. Gilson, *The Spirit of Medieval Philosophy* (Charles Scribner's Sons, New York, 1940), Chap. 2.
[34] E. Gilson, *The Christian Philosophy of St. Thomas Aquinas* (Random House, New York, 1956), p. 136.

a theological structure as to lose its independent philosophical character. Philosophy, when read with the eyes of faith, becomes something more than philosophy and thus ceases essentially *to be* philosophy.

A refreshing exception to the traditional Thomistic approach is the treatment inflicted on Aquinas by Walter Kaufmann in his *Critique of Religion and Philosophy*.[35] While providing us with a purely analytic refutation of the 'proofs' as philosophical arguments for the God of religion, he goes on to imply that their status in Aquinas' work cannot be understood without reference to a key theological concept which controls the entire *Summa*. For Kaufmann, that concept is the reality of Hell, which justifies almost any devious means to bludgeon man into acceptance of the faith: "But it would be a grave mistake to suppose that his argument in support of the Inquisition was an incidental all-too-human shortcoming which the saint shared with his age. Not only is it presented in exactly the same logical form as everything that has gone before, but *what has gone before cannot be fully understood apart from the question 'Whether Heretics Should Be Tolerated?'* The reader might mistakenly suppose that Thomas considered his many arguments self-sufficient, when in fact he realized that Aristotle and even Scripture could also be cited by way of proving very different conclusions from his own. He was not so naïve as one might suppose. . . ."[36] In his merciful concern to bring men into the Fold and thus save them from Hell, Aquinas fudges patently irregular arguments, hoping to deceive the naïve into Salvation!

It is difficult to know which picture of Aquinas is more distorted: the rational philosopher undergirding the Faith with rigid bands of unaided reason, or the saintly cynic correcting philosophy with inquisitorial conviction. As in all credible distortions there is an element of truth in each interpretation. In an ironic sense, however, Kaufmann is closer to the truth. Whatever integrity the seemingly philosophical sections of the *Summa* may have, they cannot be understood or evaluated

[35] New York, Harper and Brothers, 1958.
[36] *Ibid.*, p. 106.

except in the light of a basic theological principle, which has, however, more to do with Heaven than with Hell.

No passage in the *Summa*, no claim to possess a 'cognition' of God, can be understood apart from Aquinas' eschatological understanding of the intelligibility of God. In this life God is radically *unintelligible*.[37] Only in the Beatific Vision does man 'see' God with the 'eyes' of the mind. All that man 'sees' (or understands) in this life is the world, which is, for Aquinas, a mixture of partial intelligibility and radical absurdity.[38] The precise purpose of Aquinas' 'philosophical' discussions of God is to drive home again and again the fundamental claim that man *cannot know* God in this life even by the most intense application of his higher intellectual faculties. Aquinas stands firmly in the tradition of Augustine, Pseudo-Dionysius, and their later heir, Nicholas of Cusa. To claim to know God in this life is to confess a mode of nonknowledge or learned ignorance: "God as an unknown is said to be the terminus of our knowledge in the following respect: that the mind is found to be most perfectly in possession of knowledge of God when it is recognized that His essence is above everything that the mind is capable of apprehending in this life: and thus, although what He is remains unknown, yet it is known that He is."[39]

The theological ground of Aquinas' astounding negativity is clear and straightforward. No action, no thought, no intention or decision of man possesses the slightest soteriological value apart from the grace of God.[40] The conformity of the mind to God is an aspect of salvation. Thus, there can be no *movement* of the mind toward God apart from the initiative of God himself. There can be no natural power of *coming to*

[37] Cf., *De Ver.*, ii, 1, ad 9; *De Pot.*, vii, 5, 2; and, *De Trin.*, i, 2, ad 4: "And thus he seems to be called intelligible more by way of remotion than by positive affirmation."

[38] The ambiguous expression 'radical absurdity' will receive an interpretation in Chapter Three.

[39] "Commentary on the *De Trinitate*," in *The Trinity and the Unicity of the Intellect*, trans., Sister Rose Emmanuella Brennan, S.H.N. (B. Herder, St. Louis, 1946), i, 2, ad 1, p. 31.

[40] *S. T.*, i-ii, 109, 5 and 6.

know God.[41] In ignoring this fundamental claim of Christian theology, the traditional interpreters of Aquinas have attempted to utilize his 'philosophical theology' as a conceptual conveyance to carry man "part of the way" toward God. The 'philosophical theology' of Aquinas, however, takes us nowhere; it leaves us where we began, facing a world of partial intelligibility and radical absurdity. It adds to that context nothing but the explicit claim—implicit Aquinas feels in the very tendency of the mind to seek intelligibility in its own terms—that there *is* an area of reality to which the mind cannot carry us. It illuminates the frustrating fact that man's mind is ordered to know that which it cannot discover. Paradoxically, the arguments quoted by Aquinas prove the existence of God only by concurrently proving that we cannot know what we have proved. Even the expression "prove the existence of God" is misleading, since the identification of that unknown "which all men call God" with the God of revelation is a function of *theology*, not of philosophy. Those 'pagans' who "prove the existence of God" as an unknown cannot be said to believe in God, since the 'God' of the proofs is the name of a human frustration, not the name of the one who revealed himself in Christ.[42] Nonetheless, Aquinas is concerned to argue that philosophy lays bare a *real* ignorance—an ignorance of that which *is*. It is thus important that he be able to argue that man's conceptual categories do *not* exhaust the nature of the real. He must prove (by philosophical authority) that God *exists as unknown*—that man's apprehension of partial intelligibility is but a partial apprehension of reality.[43]

Two distortions of metaphysics are possible. The one would argue that the mind can attain to the entity postulated in the proofs—that philosophy can describe in intelligible terms not only the limits encountered by man in his search for understanding, but also the kind or sort of being whose existence

[41] Such 'cognition' of God that philosophy can produce is merely the clarification of what was there all the time—a felt ignorance.

[42] S. T., II-II, 2, 2 and 3.

[43] It will be an important part of this work to indicate why the obligation to argue that philosophy reveals the real ignorance of man is a *theological* obligation.

would render reality entirely intelligible here and now.[44] The other would argue that empirically derived categories of understanding exhaust the nature of the real—that philosophy cannot postulate the existence of that which it cannot conceive in intelligible terms. Aquinas is concerned to argue the reality of an unknown lying beyond the scope of human conceptual power. The underlying shock of Aquinas' use of the proofs has been too strong for both his defenders and his detractors, neither of whom have generally taken seriously his explicit denial of any attempt to tell us what God is like or how he exists.[45] They have failed to note that the proofs are not valid *unless* their conclusions are specifications of an old ignorance and not items of a new knowledge. The purpose of 'natural theology' is not to convey information about God, but rather to empty the mind of any pretension of possessing concepts in terms of which to judge the nature of the "final intelligibility" of reality—the intelligibility of God. It does not attempt to render man's experience intelligible here and now, but to draw conclusions from the nonintelligibility of that experience.

Walter Kaufmann, then, has failed to see that the proofs are not soteriological; human assent to the proofs is in *no* sense a step away from Hell. If man is to be saved, God must do it, not metaphysics. Only faith can recognize the referent of the proofs, since only faith conforms the mind to the being of God. Kaufmann and others have presumably mistaken a logical presupposition for a psychological propedeutic. If the claims of theology are true, it follows logically that man's understanding does not exhaust the nature and extension of the real. In that way only does revelation presuppose the truth of natural theology. For Aquinas, assent to the proofs in no way *contributes* to the reception of faith, and failure to follow and accept the proofs is not an impediment to election by God.

In part the difficulty arises from the fact that modern man views faith in a wholly different light from the theologians of the middle ages. For medieval man, the real question is not

---

[44] That is the assumption of all speculative metaphysics.

[45] Among the exceptions are Sertillanges, Victor White, Karl Rahner, and, in general, the continental theologians who utilize the categories of phenomenology or existentialism to interpret Aquinas.

"Does a god exist?" but "What is salvation?" To prove that there is an unknown entity which *might* turn out to have soteriologically interesting features would be to prove the commonplace. Natural theology was not itself a cause for rejoicing. In the modern world, on the other hand, a basic source of anxiety is the underlying suspicion and fear that the mind of man has in fact exhausted the nature of the real. To prove that it does not—to hold out the *logical* possibility of a God who might care—is tantamount to psychological salvation. In the twentieth century, natural theology, if believed, might have a soothing effect on the nerves; but to the thirteenth century, salvation was not a state of the nerves. It was not a product of what I *might* believe on the basis of probability judgments. Salvation was seen as the end product of faith— the conformation of the mind by God to himself. To that conformation, natural theology contributes nothing whatever except bare, passive material to be turned into theology.

Such a judgment must appear rather extreme in the light of Aquinas' many references to "the things concerning God which reason investigates" and "cognitions of God attained by the natural light of reason." To investigate things which have to do with God, however, is not necessarily to obtain *knowledge* of God—what he is like or how he operates. The truths about God available in theory to the unaided reason—that he is and that he is one, simple, and so forth—are logically peculiar if not unique among human truth claims. They involve the claim that certain propositions, e.g., "God exists," are true; but they do not involve the claim that we know in what way these propositions predicate intelligible characteristics of an intelligible subject. They posit the truth of propositions the only intelligible content of which is simultaneously denied of the subject of attribution. As Father Victor White maintains, Aquinas gives us not so much proofs of the existence or unity of God, as arguments for asserting the proposition "God exists" or "God is one."[46] He argues that a proof of the existence of a being must produce some concept of the *esse* of that being, and that a proof of the unity of an entity must produce

[46] V. White, O.P., "The Unknown God," in *The Unknown God* (Harvill Press Limited, London, 1948).

a notion of the kind of unity asserted. The conclusions of
natural theology, however, are notable for their utter lack of
specific content—for their sentential vacuity. To investigate,
on the basis of reason alone, things which have to do with
God, is to investigate the world and to attribute it to an
unknown source.

"Cognitions of God," then, are not necessarily instances of
intelligible knowledge of God. The ordinary word for "know"
in Aquinas is *scire*, which is never used in connection with
cognitions of God through natural reason. *Cognitio* and *cognoscere* are the broadest possible generic terms, referring to any
state of mind connected with the apprehension of reality. To
have a 'cognition' of God is to be in a state of mind that *in
some way* takes account of God. To believe on the basis of
external evidence that there is something inside of a closed box
is to have a cognition of that which is in the box, even though
one cannot say anything more about it than that 'it' is in the
box. To believe on the basis of external evidence that the
world is related in some fashion to an extrinsic and unknown
principle is to have a cognition of that principle, even though
one cannot say anything more about it than that it is not like
anything else in existence. It is *not*, however, to have 'science'
or knowledge, strictly speaking, of that principle. In "first
philosophy" one has knowledge of the world and knowledge
of the fact *that* the world is related to an unknown principle,
but one does not have knowledge of that principle. Thus
Aquinas maintains that in that 'theology' pursued by philosophers (*scientia divina*) God is *not the subject* of the science.[47]
In the context, however, of theology proper (*scientia dei*) the
unknown referent of philosophical theology becomes the subject of the 'science.' As a result, those philosophical arguments
concerning God which are quoted in theology can be seen by
faith to have the God of theology as their referent. Theology
in some way makes manifest what natural theology was *trying*
to do. In the context of faith, philosophy ceases to be merely
philosophy, for it begins to be *about* the God of revelation.
Theology, founded on faith, allows the language of philosophy
not merely to point beyond itself, but to point to God.

[47] *De Trin.*, v, 4.

Questions 1 to 26 of the *Summa Theologiae* are often regarded as instances of "natural theology" or "first philosophy."
In order to sustain such a patently false interpretation,
Thomists have had to explain away Aquinas' constant appeal
in those questions to sacred doctrine,[48] his dependence on
premises drawn from revelation,[49] and his repeated claim that
the omnipotence and providence of God (attributes supposedly proved in his "natural theology") can be known only
by revelation.[50] It will be argued below that Questions 1 to 26
are in fact Aquinas' *theological reflections upon* natural theology, that they manifest Aquinas' *use* of philosophical statements to express theological claims which are not contained
in those philosophical statements, but for which those philosophical statements may be seen as external and probable
evidence. It will be argued, for example, that the philosophical
demonstrations of the existence of 'god' quoted in I, 2, 2, do
not terminate in the God whose existence is theologically
asserted in the same article—that the 'goodness' of 'god'
philosophically defined in I, 7, is in no sense identical with the
Goodness of God theologically asserted in the same question
—that the philosophical statements of 'love,' 'mercy,' 'justice,'
and 'power' as attributes of 'god' are nothing but vacuous and
negative implications of the claim that there is an unknown
external principle of the world, and are thus not statements
of God's Love, Mercy, Justice, and Power as those attributes
are theologically conceived by Aquinas. It will be argued, in
short, that Aquinas is always in the *Summa* operating *qua*
theologian, and that the philosophy quoted in his theology is
neither necessary nor sufficient to establish the meaning or
truth of any assertion made by Aquinas, from "God exists" to
"God is Three Persons in One Substance." In each question
Aquinas interprets philosophy—gives it a new meaning or
intention—by examining it in the light of faith.

The paradox involved in such a claim is a paradox em-

[48] In the *sed contra* of every article.
[49] As in S. *T.*, I, 12, 1.
[50] Cf., *De Ver.*, 9, ad 8: "But the unity of the divine essence such as
is conceived by the faithful, that is *together with omnipotence and providence over all*, and the other attributes of this kind, *which cannot be
proved*, makes up the article of faith." Cf. also S. *T.*, II-II, 1, 8, ad 1.

bedded in Aquinas' own statements on philosophical theology: the arguments of philosophy are not formally about God himself—God is not their subject—and yet they may be said to make in some fashion a reference to God which is recognized and articulated in theology. Since philosophical discourse is merely the self-conscious refinement of natural discourse, it is not surprising to find that Aquinas believes that *all* men make opaque references to God—references which do not differ in kind from those of philosophy.[51] Philosophy makes reflexive the manner in which all men opaquely refer to God in seeking understanding and satisfaction. The relationship between philosophy and theology (between *scientia divina* and *scientia dei*) is but a special case of the relationship between theology and all human intellection. By examining the logic of philosophical references to God and their relationship to the references of faith, we shall be able to ascertain the relationship that Aquinas wishes to establish between the noetic of faith and the noetic of ordinary experience. The first half of this study will examine the logic of "natural theology" as Aquinas theologically construes it; the second half will examine the referential claims of theology in the light of a provisional "Thomistic" epistemology.

[51] S. *T.*, I, 2, 1, ad 1.

CHAPTER TWO

EPISTEMOLOGY REFORMED AND A

CAUTIONARY NOTE REISSUED

INTRODUCTION **A**NY philosophical analysis of the problem of significant reference in the writings of Aquinas is in danger of falling prey to the temptation already rejected of treating the seemingly philosophical passages of those writings in isolation from the dogmatic settings in which they occur— as though the theologian says what he does about God (or even about what he says about God) as a result of what he independently holds to be true of language in general. If our discussion of what Aquinas says concerning the significance of language about God is based entirely upon his discussion of Aristotelian epistemology, it might be thought that, had he held another philosophical view of meaningful language, he might have made other claims regarding the status of theological language. While such an assumption cannot be proved wrong, it would entail the peculiar notion that theological truth might be judged *by a theologian* on the basis of philosophical truth. On that issue, Aquinas has clearly declared his mind: "In the use of philosophy in sacred Doctrine there can be an error by using truths of philosophy in such a manner as to include under the measure of philosophy truths of faith, as if one should be willing to believe nothing except what could be held by philosophical reasoning; when, on the contrary, philosophy should be subject to the measure of faith. . . ."[1] Nonetheless, Aquinas utilizes the categories of Aristotelian epistemology *to make* his theological claims concerning the status of language about God. It is therefore necessary for us to see what is essentially entailed by his espousal of that epistemology and how it is related to the theological substance of his own teaching.

[1] *De Trin.*, I, 2, 3. I have again used the translation of Sister Rose Emmanuella, "Commentary on the *De Trinitate*" in *The Trinity and the Unicity of the Intellect.*

Simply to repeat the Aristotelian terms utilized by Aquinas will not provide us with a critical or even comprehensible version of 'Thomistic epistemology.' I shall therefore translate the epistemological doctrine of the *Summa Theologiae* into a fairly contemporary mode of discourse highly dependent on the insights and terminology of Wilfred Sellars.[2] From time to time I shall modify or reformulate certain aspects of Aquinas' stated position, eliminating what I take to be superfluous or contradictory elements. The justification for such modification is twofold: (1) Aquinas adopts the epistemological position that he does because he takes it to be the position of "The Philosopher," whereas a modification of Aristotle might be better suited to the theological intent and the explicit theological claims of Aquinas himself. (2) I am not interested only (or even primarily) in what Aquinas thought—as a matter of historical curiosity—but in what can be made at the present time of the *methodology* of Aquinas in explicating the status of natural language about God and its relation to revealed language. By modifying Aquinas while remaining true to his theological intent, it may be possible to develop a tentative 'Thomistic epistemology' with more evident viability in the contemporary world than that possessed by the more traditional "Thomistic epistemologies" which depart from the theological intent of Aquinas with equal or gayer abandon.[3]

Having discussed (and reformulated) Aquinas' epistemology, I shall draw a number of general conclusions about the kinds of references to God which are by definition *impossible* according to such an epistemology. In each case I shall indicate from the text of the *Summa* the way in which Aquinas rejects the same sorts of references. Included will be all attempts (both ontological and cosmological) to make of the proposition "God exists" a *per se nota* truth. The tentative epistemology formulated in the first half of the chapter will form the basis for a discussion in Chapter Three of Aquinas'

[2] I have used especially the essays in *Science, Perception and Reality*. It would be ungracious of me to imply that Sellars would agree with my interpretation of Aquinas or with my use of his own terms. It will be clear from time to time that I reject certain of Sellars' conclusions.

[3] I shall, of course, make it clear when I *think* I am doing more than merely translating Aquinas into different terms.

understanding of 'natural theology' and of the peculiarly negative mode of analogical predication that enables him to 'refer to God' without including God in his significant conceptual system.

A SYNTACTICAL INTERPRETATION
OF INTELLIGIBILITY

While Aquinas' doctrine, "Nothing in the intellect unless first in the senses,"[4] has led many commentators to emphasize the empirical basis of his interpretation of cognition, it would be a mistake to think of him as an "empiricist" in the contemporary sense. "Conceptual empiricism" reduces all meaningful ideas or concepts to the status of language about the particulars of sense experience or their immediately observable common characteristics. Whether the particulars of sense experience are said to be 'sense data,' 'appearings,' 'impressions,' or 'objects,' they are construed by empiricists to be immediately given or noninferentially cognizable. Our meaningful ideas are basically names or systems of names for those particulars and their observable characteristics. Thus, the concept 'red in general' or 'redness' is analyzed either as a generalized use of a remembered 'red impression' or as a concept whose empirical 'object' is the "straightforward resemblance between the things whose color we call 'red.' "[5] 'Humanity,' in order to be a significant concept, must be a concept *of* something. Since there are no "universal entities," 'humanity' must in some fashion be a concept of or about particulars. 'Humanity' is thus either a generalized use of 'man' or it is a concept of that which is directly apprehended to be common to more than one man. In any case that which can be *signified* is that which is *given* in sense experience.

It is notorious what such a doctrine, if rigorously held, will do to the language of theoretical entities in science.[6] It is

---

[4] S. T., I, 84, 7.

[5] A. J. Ayer, *The Problem of Knowledge* (Penguin Books, Middlesex, 1956), p. 11. The first view is, of course, that of Hume.

[6] For an interesting discussion of the ontological status (or cognitive meaning) of theoretical entities according to the schools of empiricism, see E. Nagel, *The Structure of Science* (Harcourt Brace & World, Inc., New York, 1961), Chap. 6.

obvious what it would do to the language of theology. In the stricter versions of empiricism, the concept 'electron' is not the concept of something *real*, but must be analyzed as a way of speaking *about* what one experiences directly in perception —what can be stated in protocol-like 'observation language.' To say that a number of electrons are behaving in a certain way is *merely* to say that a certain observation will be possible under conditions specified in the experimental language. Those nonpositivistic empiricists who desire to assert the reality of electrons must nevertheless assert that the *meaning* of the claim that electrons are 'doing things' in the world can be determined by ascertaining what generalizations in the observation language the claim is supposed to organize and explain in theoretical terms. Whether we construct upward in the direction of 'universals' or analyze downwards in the direction of electrons, the *meaning* of our statements and concepts is either translatable into the observation language in terms of which we report without embroidery on the *given* contents of sense experience, or derivable by means of coordinating definitions from general statements *in* the observation language. "God" is not a concept of or about the particulars of sense experience; nor is "God" a theoretical means of organizing and explaining generalizations in the observation language—be those generalizations ever so general. If Aquinas were an empiricist in the contemporary sense, he could not use the word "God" in even the guarded way that he does.

It must be admitted that there is a prima facie similarity between the dogmas of empiricism and the claim of Aquinas that no meaningful act of the understanding can take place without reference to 'phantasms' or remembered images of the objects of sensation.[7] The doctrines, however, are not identical. I shall argue that Aquinas has no doctrine of an immediately given or noninferentially *cognizable* content of sense experience and that his notion of a meaningful concept—be it of a particular thing or a general characteristic—cannot be reduced to statements about the particulars of sense experience.

A preliminary indication of the divergence between Aquinas

[7] S. T., I, 84, 7.

and the empiricist may be found in a rough analysis of the act of cognition as Aquinas understands it. To begin with, sensation is, for Aquinas, an act of the 'composite'—an act involving the physical organism *and* the intellect.[8] While I think that Aquinas underplayed the role of the physical alteration of the sense organs in the process of sensation (especially in his analysis of seeing),[9] he is quite clear in claiming that sensation is rooted in and dependent upon the organic or physical sensory system.[10] Thus we may say that for Aquinas the first element in an act of cognition may be termed a physical state of the sensory system. The physical state of the sensory system is not itself a "conscious" state, nor is it that of which the 'mind' is conscious. Correlated with the physical aspect of sensation is the 'mental image' or intention of the 'sensible form' of the *object* of sense experience.[11] While I shall later argue against the notion that there are such things, we may simply note that the 'mental image' is *intentional* in nature—it is *immaterial* and *of* an object. The important point, however, is that the 'image' or 'form' of the sensible object is not merely a *given* of sense experience, but is *produced by the soul itself* and is *ordered to* the operations of the intellect.[12] The sensible form by means of which the 'mind' knows or apprehends the object is a result of the 'mind' *taking* its experience in a particular way. At the very first moment of conscious cognition there is an intentional interpretation of the object of experience, ordered to the intelligible categories of the mind.

I shall say little more about the 'sensible forms' themselves since they do not play as crucial a role in concept formation

[8] S. *T.*, I, 77, 5, *sed contra*: "The sensitive power is in the composite as its subject."

[9] Cf., S. *T.*, I, 78, 5: "Sight, which is without natural immutation in either its organ or its object. . . ."

[10] S. *T.*, I, 78, 1; and I, 77, 8.

[11] S. *T.*, I, 78, 3: ". . . an *intention* of the sensible form is effected in the sensile organ. . . ." An 'intention,' for Aquinas, is a mental or nonmaterial representation.

[12] S. *T.*, I, 78, 1: "There is an operation *of the soul* which is performed through a corporeal organ. . . ."; and I, 77, 7: "The senses are a certain imperfect *participation* of the intelligence; thus, by natural origin, they proceed from the intelligence as imperfect from the perfect."

as another sort of intentional 'image' in Aquinas' epistemology
—the 'phantasm.' In reality the 'phantasm' is simply the
'sensible form' as *retained* by the imagination.[13] It is *logically*
identical with the intentional or mental image and equally
problematic; from this point on, I shall use the terms 'mental
image' and 'phantasm' interchangeably.

The first moment of cognition, then, is the production by
the 'mind' of an intentional image of the object of sense
experience. In the second moment of cognition, the agent
intellect is said to make intelligible that which is potential in
the phantasm by abstracting from it the 'intelligible species'
or 'form' of the object of sense experience. Since the agent
intellect is the source of the categories to which the phantasm
has already been ordered, it is not entirely clear what the
process of abstraction really is. The first step, however, is
entirely clear: on the basis of memory the intellect 'abstracts'
the common elements of several phantasms of identical objects
by merely discounting what is *not common* to them. If one
depends entirely upon I, 85, 1, ad 1, of the *Summa*, it would
appear that that is *all* that is necessary to produce the
'intelligible form' of the object. Since Aquinas maintains,
however, that the phantasm contains or represents, not the
object itself, but only the sensible accidents of the object,[14]
it is not clear how a multiplication of the contents of phantasms will amount to a concept or intelligible species of a
substance or *object*. I believe that Aquinas means to say that
the phantasms supply all of the *matter* that is necessary to
formulate an 'intelligible species' of the object itself, but that
the agent intellect must produce the form or concept which
makes the matter abstracted from the phantasms actually
intelligible.[15] As Aquinas puts it in the *De Veritate*, "The
intellect *forms within itself* likenesses of things, inasmuch as

---

[13] S. T., I, 78, 4: "For the retention and preservation of the [sensible]
forms, the phantasy or imagination is appointed."

[14] Not, that is, 'what the object is' (its quiddity), but the object *as*
sensible.

[15] Note I, 84, 6: "Since the phantasms cannot by themselves affect the
passive intellect, and require to be made actually intelligible by the
active intellect, it cannot be said that sensible knowledge is the total and
perfect cause of intellectual knowledge but rather that it is a *kind of
material cause*."

by the light of the agent intellect the forms *abstracted from* sensible things *are made* actually intelligible. . . ."[16] Merely paying attention to the common elements of one's sense experience is not to have a meaningful *concept* of the object of sense experience, although it may be all that is materially necessary in order to produce or form such a concept. The intelligible form which the 'agent intellect' impresses on the 'passive intellect' (i.e., brings consciously to mind) is not simply identical with the common aspects or material similarities of one's sensations; it is rather the *conceptio intellectus* (the intelligible notion) that the intellect forms of the object on the basis of the contents of sense experience. The intellect creates its own intelligible notion of what the object of sense experience really *is*.

The content of the phantasms is used to refer the intellect to the external object, but the *concept* of the object is not merely that which is 'in the senses.' In some way the intellect creates out of the common matter of the phantasms (already 'ordered to' the categories of the understanding) *and* out of its own conceptual powers, a new kind of 'form'—a form appropriate to the conceptual order and not merely to the order of conscious perception. I shall attempt below to make some sense of Aquinas on this point; at the moment, however, I shall merely claim that for Aquinas what is 'in the mind' concerning reality is there *because* there has been something in the senses, but what is 'in the mind' is not formally identical with or reducible to that which is in the senses. The concept is not merely a way of referring to the common elements of one's sensations. Thus, Aquinas is not an empiricist in the contemporary sense.

There has been some confusion relating to the role of the intelligible form in Aquinas' epistemology—a confusion which is evident in the writings of Thomists and their critics alike.[17] Within Thomism the debate has taken the form of asserting

---

16 *De Ver.*, x, 6. Note that the forms *already abstracted* from sensible things must still be 'made actually intelligible.' Mere abstraction, in the sense of ignoring differences, is not sufficient to produce an intelligible form or species.

17 Sellars criticizes the 'Thomists' for holding the view that I here reject.

or denying that the mind (in possession of the intelligible form) 'takes a look at the world.' The positive party asserts that the intelligible form received by the passive intellect is to be interpreted as the result of the *external object informing* the mind.[18] Thus 'chair' or 'man' exists in the mind because the 'real form' of the external object (the form that the object 'really' has) makes its way into the mind by way of the senses and 'informs' the mind by impressing itself on the mind. The 'real form' of the external object thus causes the mind to form a mental version of that which, formally speaking, is 'really out there.' The only role that the intellect plays in this procedure is to change the status of the 'form' as it is instantiated in the physical object and received by the senses into a 'nonmaterial' version of 'the same thing.' Any further action on the part of the mind in interpreting the contents of sensation must, they assume, lead to some sort of scepticism with regard to 'what is really there.' The schools of Maréchal and Lonergan,[19] however, have correctly seen that such a minimalist interpretation of the role of the agent intellect in the creation of the 'intelligible form' fails to do justice to Aquinas' language. They claim that Aquinas is to be taken seriously when he says that the 'agent intellect' must "make actually intelligible" that which is abstracted from the 'phantasms' by simply ignoring certain aspects of the sensible species; understanding involves a real creation of a *new form* by the conceptual powers of the mind itself, so that the concept of 'what the object is' (its true nature) is never merely "given" in sense experience. The 'real form' of the external object does not inform the intellect—the intellect *informs itself*, on the basis of sense experience, of that which sense experience does not actually contain—the nature of the external object. There is, therefore, a risk in "knowing," or making epistemic claims: it is theoretically possible to re-

[18] That includes all of the 'traditional' commentators. Among the more notable exceptions are Père Sertillanges and the followers of Maréchal.

[19] See the *Cahiers* of Père Maréchal, esp. *Le point de départ de la métaphysique* (Louvain, 1926), and B. J. Lonergan, *Insight: A Study of Human Understanding* (London, 1958).

conceive the natures of things.[20] Why I agree with the latter, "dynamic," school of Thomistic interpretation may become clear below.

Two questions arise from such a bare analysis of Aquinas' epistemology: (1) What is to be understood by 'intelligible species or form'? (2) Why does Aquinas introduce the notion of intentional modes of sensation (the phantasms or mental images)? I shall address myself to the first question, answer it in part, and then turn to the second before returning finally to the first.

Wilfred Sellars has pointed out[21] the seeming paradox that, in order to have any concept, one must in a sense have them all. One cannot have a concept without having a conceptual *system.* The 'agent intellect' is Aquinas' theoretical (we might even say "mythical") locus of the 'first principles'—logical axioms and rules of inference—from which an intelligible conceptual system might be generated. The 'agent intellect' might be described as a natural disposition to use the 'first principles' in the course of rendering intelligible the contents of human experience. If there is any real paradox in philosophy, it is that the rules of inference that we *use* in all 'valid' argumentation cannot be validated by arguments. The existence of that real paradox ought not to be interpreted, however, as a *problem* for philosophy, since any attempt to call the 'first principles' of valid argumentation into question depends itself upon their validity. "What if it is the case that *p* and *not-p* are simultaneously true" conveys meaning only if one assumes that *p* and *not-p* *cannot* be simultaneously true— otherwise we could not arrive at a notion of how "*p*" is being used in the question. Indeed, "What if the rule of noncontradiction were a mistake?" can only mean, "What if there were no meaningful propositions?" If that *were* the case, it would mean nothing to claim it—indeed neither it nor anything else could ever be "claimed."

A *reductio ad absurdum,* of course, is not an instance of

20 Cf. W. Sellars, *Science, Perception and Reality,* esp. Chaps. I, IV, and v.
21 *Ibid.,* p. 148.

arguing *from* axioms, rules of inference, and premises *to* a new proposition (in this case a rule of inference itself). We cannot by definition construct an argument from which the rules of inference we must use to construct *any* argument emerge as implications. Nonetheless we *know* that the 'first principles' are in order. As Aquinas puts it, we cannot have *science* of 'first principles' (although there might be a science *about* the first principles), but we naturally know that they are valid.[22] The 'first principles' are the very *form* of thought—they are the "light of reason" within which intelligibility can be recognized. The closest that we can come in Aquinas' own words to understanding what he means by the 'intelligible form' of an object is to say that the 'intelligible form' is what emerges when the contents of sense experience are seen in "the light of reason."

It is possible, I believe, to offer an interpretation of Aquinas which—while it might never have occurred to him—will express what he intended. At the very least it will not be inconsistent with what he does say. The attempt involves a momentary abstraction of the notion of a conceptual system from the notion of an *empirically* significant language. It is interesting to note that, while Aquinas correctly assumes that man could not possess an actual conceptual system if he were not having sense experiences, he maintains that an angelic intellect possesses a complete conceptual system from the first 'aeviternal moment' of its being. I shall, for the moment, treat man like a temporal angel.

To possess a conceptual system without the ability to refer to external objects is to possess a language with purely syntactical or logical 'meaning.' Such a conceptual system would be based on axioms and operational rules (rules of inference, formation, transformation, et cetera) on the basis of which one could derive statements which are true *ex vi terminorum* within the system and statements which are well-formed but not true *ex vi terminorum*.[23] The 'meaning' of any concept or

[22] *In Meta.*, III, 5, 290.
[23] "True *ex vi terminorum*" means "true within the system by virtue of the significance of the terms." This is not to be confused with "analytic" —it will be maintained, with Sellars, that there are some statements which are *synthetic* but true *ex vi terminorum*.

statement which could be formed within the system would be nothing but the syntactical role played by that concept or statement within the system. To say of any term that it expressed a concept of the system would be to say that the term possessed an intelligible or specifiable syntactical status in the system—e.g., that it could occur in certain sorts of statement-forms in the place of certain kinds of variables, but not in other statement-forms or in the place of other kinds of variables. Thus, a certain term (or family of terms) could occur in certain ways in certain statements (or families of statements) but not in others. The concept 'biffeity' might occur in statements of the form '. . . is a general characteristic of . . .' ('Biffeity is a general characteristic of biffs') but not in statements of the form 'All . . . are . . .' ('All biffeities are brown'). The latter is simply not well formed within the the logic system. Similarly, 'the wands of biffs are brown' might be in order while 'the wands of biffs are loud' would be ill formed.[24] The syntactical meaning of '. . . is a general characteristic of . . .' or 'all . . . are . . .' would in turn be determined by the syntactical status within the system of the statements in which they occur. Thus we must ignore their ordinary meaning in our language. Their status would be governed purely by the axioms and operational rules of the system. Such a system would be entirely formal—it would have no material content. We may speak of the terms which occur in the system as 'elements' or 'forms' of the system. The *ratio* of a form could be expressed in terms of the syntactical role of the form within the system. Thus the *ratio* of 'unicorn' could be expressed in the following manner: "Given the axioms and operational rules of the system, it can be shown that 'x is a unicorn' implies 'x is a four-legged animal with a single horn.'" Once again, we must forget the "ordinary meaning" of the terms within single quotes. 'Four-legged' means only what can be expressed by showing the syntactical status of the term within the system. To give the syntactical

---

[24] The rules determining that certain terms can occur in certain syntactical relations with certain terms, but not with others—e.g., 'wands of biffs' with 'brown' but not with 'loud'—would in fact duplicate the topology of perceptual terms and 'sensible characteristics.'

(formal) meaning of *any* term, reference need not be made to anything other than the elements, sentences, axioms, and operational rules of the system itself. In such a language a term would have 'significance' if it could be shown to play a role within the system—a role that could be entirely described in terms of the axioms, rules of operation, and well-formed statements (both 'necessary' and 'contingent') already unquestionably part of the system.

The rules of the system are such that they define the following sets of elements (among others): The K-set consists of elements of the form 'K$_1$', 'K$_2$' . . . 'K$_i$'. The I-set consists of elements of the form 'a', 'b', 'c', and so forth. It is part of the logic of such elements that they can occur in statements of the form 'a is a K$_1$', 'b is either a K$_2$ or a K$_3$', et cetera. Using 'x' for "a member of the I-set," we may say that, for any 'x', 'x is either a K$_1$ or a K$_2$ . . . or a K$_i$.'[25] A third set, the P-set, consists of elements of the form 'ϕ_1', 'ϕ_2' . . . 'ϕ_i'. It is part of the logic of these elements that they can occur in statements of the form 'ϕ_1a', 'ϕ_2b' or, in general, 'ϕ_ix'. When such statements occur, the member of the I-set may be said to 'have' that which is signified by the member of the P-set. When a member of the I-set 'has' that which is signified by certain subsets of the P-set, it follows on the basis of the rules of the system that it 'is' an instance of a certain member of the K-set. If, for example, 'ϕ_1a and ϕ_2a . . . and ϕ_na' then 'a is a K$_1$'.[26]

---

[25] We should not be misled into assuming that such a language, with purely syntactical 'meaning,' contains the notion of 'that particular thing there'—such a notion, of course, depends upon the matter of sense-experience. Our syntactical language would manifest, not knowledge of particulars, but the logic or syntax of individual variables. The logic of specific terms (thing-kind terms) presupposes the *logic* of instantiation or individuation. Conversely, the *sort* of thing that could possibly count as a particular individual is determined by the sorts of thing-kind terms that occur in a conceptual system. We might say that our syntactical language would not contain the notion of particular individuals, but rather the *formal* notion of specific individuals (the logical notion of members of a class).

[26] We may give a misleading interpretation of those statements in terms of ordinary language: If something *has* the qualities signified by "red," "roundish," "solid" . . . (plus a number of other specified characteristics) then it must be said *to be* an apple. Such a 'translation' is mis-

Conversely, if a member of the I-set 'is' an instance of a specified member of the K-set, it follows immediately that it must 'have' that which is signified by a specific subset of the P-set (plus that which is signified by other, unspecified, members of the P-set). If 'a is a K_1', then '$\phi_1 a$ and $\phi_2 a$ . . . and $\phi_n a$, and either $\phi_{n+1} a$ or $\phi_{n+2} a$ . . . or $\phi_{n+m} a$'.[27] It is important to note that such 'implications' are justified purely by the axioms and operational rules of the system. They are not definitions. '$\phi_1 a$ and $\phi_2 a$ . . . and $\phi_n a$' *justifies but does not mean* 'a is a K_1'.

The members of these sets are subject to an operation which we may call 'assertion.' To 'assert' is to underscore. Since the members of any one of the three sets are defined in a categorially different manner from the members of the other two sets, it follows that the 'assertion' operation will have categorially different implications when applied to members of different sets. The 'syntactical meaning' of '$\_$' is categorially different in the expressions 'a', 'K_1' and 'ϕ_1'. Nonetheless, these 'meanings' are interrelated by means of the following definitions and justified implications:

1) To 'assert' a member of the K-set is to *mean* that some member of the I-set is 'assertable' and 'is' of the kind signified by the 'asserted' member of the K-set.

2) To 'assert' a member of the P-set is to *justify* the implication that some member of the I-set is 'assertable' and that it 'has' that which is signified by the 'asserted' member of the P-set.

Combining these rules with those already discussed, we may summarize the interrelationships of the members of the

---

leading because the ordinary meaning of such terms derives in part from sense experience. The important point is that a purely syntactically defined language might well duplicate the 'logical topography' of such ordinary terms.

[27] Misleadingly translated into ordinary language: If something *is* an apple, it must *have* the qualities signified by "roundish," "solid" . . . (plus a number more) and *may have* the qualities signified by "red," "green," "sweet," et cetera. It is clear that we have schematically defined the logical topography of "substance terms" (both 'first' and 'second' substance) and of "property terms" without essential reference to sense-experience.

three sets in the context of the assertion operation in the following terms:[28]

1) $'K_1' = {}'$x and x is a K_1'.

2) $'\overline{K_1}' \supset {}'$x and $(\phi_1 x \cdot \phi_2 x \ldots \cdot \phi_n x)$ and $(\phi_{n+1}x \vee \phi_{n+2}x \ldots \vee \overline{\phi_{n+m}x})'$.

3) $'\phi_1' \supset {}'$x and $\phi_1 x'$.

4) $'\overline{\phi_1 \cdot \phi_2 \ldots \cdot \phi_n}' \supset {}'$x and x is a K_1'.

And, from $\overline{1)}$ and $\overline{4)}$:

5) $'\underline{\phi_1} \cdot \underline{\phi_2} \ldots \cdot \underline{\phi_n}' \supset '\underline{K_1}'$.[29]

It is crucial that one aspect of the system be again emphasized. While 'x and x is a K_1', and thus 'K_1', may be immediately justified on purely syntactical grounds by '$\phi_1 \cdot \phi_2 \ldots \cdot \phi_n$', it does not follow that '$\phi_1 \cdot \phi_2 \ldots \cdot \phi_n$' is logically equivalent to 'K_1'; similarly, '$\phi_1 a \cdot \phi_2 a \ldots \cdot \phi_n a$' justifies but does not mean 'a is a K_1'. The meaning of 'K_1' (and thus of 'K_1' within the system) is determined not only by its syntactical relation to 'ϕ_1', 'ϕ_2' ... 'ϕ_n' but also by its relation to *all other* elements in the system; the meaning of 'K_1' is determined by its total role within the system, and it plays a categorially different sort of role from either 'ϕ_1' itself or any combination of elements from the P-set. That '$\phi_1 \cdot \phi_2 \ldots \cdot \phi_n$' justifies '$K_1$' (or 'x and x is a K_1') is a purely formal truth of the system and cannot be reduced to an intensional identity of the two assertions. It is a *truth of the system* and not merely a truth deriving from a definitional relation between members of the S-set and members of the P-set.

Since the relation between 'K_1' and '$\phi_1, \phi_2 \ldots \phi_n$' is not explicitly definitional, it is also not arbitrary. While the word

[28] I use '=' for "means," '⊃' for "justifies on the basis of the rules of the system," '∨' for "or," and '·' for "and."

[29] Continuing the misleading use of ordinary terms, and using 'here-now' for the assertion operation: 'Here-now-apple' means, not 'Here-now-apple-kind,' but 'Here-now-something which is an apple.' 'Here-now-apple' justifies but does not mean 'Here-now-something that has the qualities of redness, roundness, solidity, et al.' 'Here-now-red' justifies but does not mean 'Here-now-something that has the quality of redness.' 'Here-now-red-round-solid-et alii' justifies but does not mean 'Here-now-something which is an apple,' or, more simply, 'Here-now-apple.'

(token) "apple" is merely conventional, and thus arbitrarily related to the words (tokens) which express the properties of an apple, the relation between the *concept* 'apple' and the *concepts* 'roundish,' and 'solid,' et alii, is *not* arbitrary. In the system I have schematized, therefore, the relation between 'K_1' and '$\phi_1, \phi_2 \ldots \phi_n$' is not arbitrary, but determined by the system as a whole. Within the system it is *intelligible* to move from '$\underline{\phi_1} \cdot \underline{\phi_2} \ldots \cdot \underline{\phi_n}$' to '$\underline{K_1}$'—rather than to '$\underline{K_2}$' or '$\underline{K_3}$'—because it is a priori a *correct* move, given the axioms and rules of the system. *Intelligibility is a formal or syntactical matter.*

We are now ready to introduce the element of empirical experience into the account. We must assume that the man-angel already possesses a completely developed conceptual system with such characteristics as have been schematized. The problem is to relate that system to his empirical experience.

With no explanation, we will simply assume that the mind of the man-angel has an interesting characteristic in addition to its system-generating capacity: it behaves rather like an intentional movie screen! Images of a rather peculiar sort are projected onto it from a *hidden* (theoretical) projection-booth, roughly identifiable with the entire sensory system—including, of course, the imagination. The mind does not *look at* the projected image, for the image is projected *on* it. Rather, the mind *has* the image. The nature of the image results from two operations within the 'projection-booth' of the sensory system: (a) The information which is eventually to be projected on the mind-screen enters the booth by means of an electrical "reading" of the material alterations of the receiving organs of the sensory system—alterations caused by the impact on the organs of objects (in the broadest sense) outside the theater. Those alterations are (but are not *known* to be) isomorphic with aspects of the state of affairs outside the theater at any time. The 'common-sense'[30]—a physical computer—combines the various kinds of information blocks entering the booth through the various organs into a single electronic state isomorphic with all of the sensible aspects of the external world (with all those aspects or events which register on the receiving organs). (b) The image-projector (Aquinas' "power

[30] On the 'common-sense,' see S. *T.*, I, 78, 4, ad 2.

of the imagination") then takes over. It is naturally programmed in such a way that it projects on the mind-screen only such regularly repeated patterns of the state of the sensory system as are isomorphic with elements within the conceptual system of the man-angel's intellect. In projecting, it translates those patterns from their electrical-state mode to a mode of representation proper to an intentional image. Once again, isomorphism is all that is required. In such a way it projects only such patterns as can be isomorphically related to a subset of the *P-set terms* of the conceptual system. When various imaginal patterns isomorphic in some respects with the physical state of the sensory system and also isomorphic with elements in the conceptual system are continuously projected onto the mind-screen of the man-angel, he learns to note the isomorphism between elements of the images and certain members of his P-set, and he 'asserts' the relevant elements.[31] Now, however, '$\phi_1 \cdot \phi_2 \ldots \cdot \phi_n$' has not only its syntactical sense, but a *new* sense that may be called *semantical*. (This is an idiosyncratic use of 'semantical.') '$\phi_1 \cdot \phi_2 \ldots \cdot \phi_n$' is now *used* to assert 'Out-there-now-$\phi_1 \cdot \phi_2 \ldots \cdot \phi_n$'. The *meaning* of, e.g., 'ϕ_1' is now a function *both* of its status in the conceptual system *and of its use in referring* to 'that which is' outside the theater. Included in its meaning is an element provided by sense-experience.

Suppose, then, that the man-angel, as a result of the kinds of mental-images that have been projected on his mind-screen, notes in the 'phantasms' thus projected repeated and similarly interrelated elements that are isomorphic with the logical interrelationships of such P-set terms as 'red,' 'roundish,' 'solid,' 'sweet,' 'moist,' et alia, and asserts 'Out-there-now-red-roundish, et cetera.' Once the elements of his conceptual system (with their defined syntactical interrelationships) have been plugged into a semantical or referential use, the conceptual

---

[31] How the man-angel learns to 'note' repeated patterns of the phantasm presents a problem that ultimately uncovers a fatal flaw in the story: the phantasm cannot be an 'intentional image' possessed 'by the mind.' Sensation cannot be a conscious state until the contents of sensation (physical states of the organism) are 'informed' by the intellect. That 'information' cannot be a self-conscious comparison of two isomorphic 'given' elements.

system takes over. Apart from the newly discovered semantical use of the forms of the system, the man-angel is still in control of the old syntactical status of the P-set terms used in the referential statement. 'In the light of the reason'—i.e., on the basis of the rules of the syntactical system—he knows that he is justified in moving from the assertion of 'red,' 'roundish,' et cetera, to the assertion 'something which is red, roundish, et cetera,' and thus to the assertion 'apple.' (This is merely a special case of the formally justified move from '$\phi_1 \cdot \phi_2 \ldots \phi_n$' to '$K_1$'.) He thus asserts 'apple'—produces the $\overline{formal}$ concept out of his own conceptual system and relates it to the assertion of 'red,' 'roundish,' et cetera. In doing so, he plugs 'apple' into the semantical use of language and uses it to *refer*. The move from 'Out-there-now-red-roundish-et cetera' to 'Out-there-now-apple'—like any other move of the form 'Out-there-now-$\phi_1 \cdot \phi_2 \ldots \cdot \phi_n$' therefore 'Out-there-now-K_1'—is justified *only and sufficiently* by the syntax of the conceptual system (by what is intelligible in *its* terms). The move is *not* a matter of checking again to see if 'apple' is *also* represented in the intentional image, but of checking the conceptual system and its formally justified inferential rules. The 'intelligible form' of the *external object* is not given in sense experience, but is known through the sensible 'accidents' of the object by the application of the "rules of the game." To assert that a red apple exists 'out there' is to assert that *what one has experienced* through the sense organs has in reality a structure isomorphic with the syntactical structure of the concept 'red apple.'

The expression "isomorphic" has been used throughout the story with no specific definition. The alterations of the sense organs were said to be "isomorphic with aspects of the state of affairs outside the theater"; patterns within the projected mental-image were said to be "isomorphic with the physical state of the sensory system and with elements in the conceptual system." The intellect interprets the mental-image as a representation of that which exists, and thus posits a relationship of "isomorphism" between its own formalized representation of the mental-image and the external state of affairs. The use of the term "isomorphic" in explicating the dynamics of perception was suggested by Sellars' use of the term in *Science,*

Perception and Reality.[32] It appears to me to be a useful way
of stating the implications of Aquinas' view that the act of
knowing is analogical in its mode of representing or understanding 'that which is.' Aquinas maintains, for example, that
it is a presupposition of the act of knowing that there exists
in reality a counterpart of the logical form constructed by the
intellect of the intended object (that is part of the meaning
of "know")—he denies, however, that we can know *in what
way* the real form of the external object parallels that which is
'in the intellect.'[33] It would be insane to argue, for example,
that the *redness* of the object 'out there' is related to the *shape*
of the object in just the way that our *concept* 'red' is related
to our *concept* of the shape of the object. Our concepts are
syntactically interrelated—the order of reality is not a syntactical order. It is essential to note that we do not 'take a
look' at the world, *see* how it is *really* ordered, and then
create a conceptual order isomorphic with what we apprehend
or notice. As Aquinas maintains, concerning the adequation
of the intellect to its object:

> The intellect is able to be cognizant of its own conformity
> with the intelligible thing; but it does not apprehend that
> conformity by knowing of anything *what it is*; rather, when
> the intellect *judges that* the thing itself *corresponds to* the
> form that the intellect apprehends concerning it, then it
> knows and speaks the truth.
>
> [Intellectus autem conformitatem sui ad rem intelligibilem
> cognoscere potest: sed tamen non apprehendit eam secun-
> dum quod cognoscit de aliquo quod quid est; sed quando

[32] Chap. 2.
[33] S. T., 1, 85, 5, ad 3: "The likeness of a thing [*similitudo rei*] is received in the intellect *according to the mode of the intellect*, and not
according to the mode of the thing. Therefore *something* corresponds to
the composition and division of the intellect on the part of the thing; but
it does not exist [non se habet] in the same way in reality as it does in
the mind." This is an important statement of Aquinas' analogical view
of knowledge. It must be coupled with the claim that we only know the
thing by having the (mental) similitude. (See 1, 85, 2.) The act of intellectual cognition is not transitive—it is immanent.

iudicat rem ita se habere sicut est forma quam de re appre-
hendit, tunc primo cognoscit et dicit verum.][34]

We perceive reality (perceive *consciously*) in terms of our
categories of understanding—we do not create our categories
of understanding on the basis of what we already know reality to be like. To know what reality is like *is* to judge one's
experience in terms of one's conceptual system. There is no
means of short-circuiting the process and 'taking a look' at the
world *in its own terms*.

We may now give a tentative interpretation of Aquinas'
claim that the intellect "abstracts the intelligible species from
the phantasm." To abstract the intelligible species or form
which is potentially present in one's experience—to make
one's experience actually intelligible—is to express the isomorphism that exists between one's experience and one's conceptual system by *utilizing* that system as a means of consciously perceiving and informing that which one experiences.
While Aquinas does not suppose that a man could possess an
explicit conceptual system *apart from* experience, he also does
not believe that the formal significance of a conceptual system could be given *in* experience or merely abstracted *from*
experience by simply ignoring the 'nonformal' or 'material'
elements of experience. For Aquinas, the formal significance
of our descriptions of reality derives from the power of the
'agent intellect' or the 'light of reason.' When our sense experience is interpreted in the 'light of reason'—when we introspect our experience in terms of the formal rules of our conceptual system—we are able to use the formal elements of
that system to 'note' or 'become aware of' repeated patterns
within our experience and to interpret them in intelligible
terms. The forms by which we judge experience are not learned
from experience, but result from the natural tendency of the
mind to use the 'first principles of the intellect' in interpreting
experience. In this general claim I believe that Aquinas is
correct.

It is true, of course, that we do not actually conceive the

[34] S. *T.*, ɪ, 16, 2. Another crucial question.

formal notion of 'red' prior to all experience of "red things." Since we are not angels, it is not clear how we might entertain such a purely formal notion of 'red' (the status of 'red' in a bare, syntactical language). The man-angel must be demythologized. Sense experience is, of course, the *occasion* for the actual development of a conceptual system. It would be a mistake, however, to suppose that the *meaning* of "red" is purely a function of the contents of our sense experience. We do not *first* 'notice' or 'become aware of' an identity of content within several experiences and *then* coin a word or form a concept to refer to that which is identical within the experiences. In order to 'notice' or 'become aware of' the fact that I am having an experience of *the same thing again*, I must *already* have the concept of that thing.[35] In order to know that I am having an experience of "red" again—in order to know that it is the same *sort* of experience as the past experience—I must already possess the concept 'red' and all other concepts necessary to the understanding of that one. To have the concept 'red' is already to understand the logic of color-words and the logic of object-words. The *logic* of those words is not given in experience, but is rather a function of the role played in my conceptual system by the concepts they express. We may say that the *formal significance* of the language we use to describe reality derives from the rules and principles of the conceptual system we find ourselves using to interpret experience, while the referential or semantical content of that language (the 'matter' of the language) derives from the experience on the basis of which we use the language to refer to reality. That is the explanation, I believe, of Aquinas' claim that the world as (nonintentionally) experienced is only *potentially* intelligible and must be made *actually* intelligible by the judgments of the intellect. To say that 'being' is 'intelligible' is to say that ultimately 'that which is' can be measured in terms created by

---

[35] Cf. Sellars, *op.cit.*, p. 176: "For we now recognize that instead of coming to have a concept of something because we have noticed that sort of thing, to have the ability to notice a sort of thing is already to have the concept of that sort of thing, and cannot account for it."

intellect, not that intellect is measured by norms discoverable in 'that which is.' It is because of the natural power of the 'agent intellect' to create intelligible forms that we are able to understand that which we experience. It is not merely because the world is the way that it is.

While I shall criticize the entire notion of a 'phantasm' or 'intentional image,' it is important to see that even in Aquinas' own terms *conscious* perception or sense *awareness* is not itself a mere matter of 'taking a look at the world.' The 'redness' which is 'in the mind' when the imagination forms an image of the object of sense experience is not the 'redness' of the external object itself. It is only that which we 'have in mind' when we make the judgment, "There is a red object over there." Although Aquinas maintains that the phantasm images or represents the sensible qualities of external reality, he nevertheless maintains that those qualities *as imaged* have already been ordered to the intelligible concept of, e.g., 'red.' *Consciously* to perceive is *already* to interpret reality in terms of the intelligible forms produced by the agent intellect. Conscious perception is a matter of what we *take* to be the case— and 'taking' is a mode of 'informing.' We notice or become aware of those aspects of our experience to which we have already given form—which we have already interpreted in intelligible terms.

I do not think, however, that we need to speak of "images" in order to understand perception. The notion that there *are* such things as 'phantasms' or 'intentional images' suffers from analysis. Aquinas, it will be recalled, maintains that the phantasm is an intentional representation of the object of sense-experience, and that it contains conceptually significant representations of the 'sensible qualities' of the object. Thus, there might be 'in the phantasm' an imaginal representation of 'blue,' but there could not be an imaginal representation of 'table.' Clearly the word "image" is being oddly used—how can the 'blue' be imaged unless the substance which *is* blue is also imaged? The oddity of the word becomes clearer when we note that the intentional image must contain representations of such nonvisual qualities as 'rough,' 'soft,' 'sweet,' et

cetera. Clearly, the 'image' is not a *picture*.[36] The odd status
of the 'phantasm' is also implied by the claim made—in
the context of the man-angel story—that the mind *notices* an
isomorphism between the contents of the phantasm and its
own P-set terms. Even when we re-emphasize that the 'phantasm' is not a picture at which the mind 'looks' but rather a
representation that the mind 'has,' there are problems: If the
'imagination' had already 'ordered' the contents of the phantasm in such a way that the 'blue' of the conceptual system
was already to be found *in* the phantasm by some sort of noninferential cognition, there ought to be no need to speak of
isomorphism. If, on the other hand, the 'imagination' had *not*
so ordered the phantasmagorical matter, how can the phantasm be described as *intentional* (a possession of the mind)?
Aquinas denies the first alternative by claiming that the 'phantasm' must be "made actually intelligible" by the intellect.
According to the second alternative, however, the 'phantasm'
must be, not an intentional image, but a material state. Aquinas seems to define the 'phantasm' in such a way that it must
be both intelligible and nonintentional—both material and (in
some sense) mental. I shall attempt to show that the very
notion of a perceptual mental image which is 'blue' prior to
the operation of the intellect is self-contradictory.

Beginning with the intelligible notion of 'blue,' it is clear
that its primary and ordinary usage is to refer to 'blue objects
out there.' That is the reason that we cannot have the concept
'blue' without knowing the logic of object-words. In that sense
of blue, the sense in which we say that a physical object is
blue, Aquinas is able to say that the 'eye' (or the physical
sensory system) does not "become blue" in sensing a blue object.[37] Thus, while Aquinas admits that sensation is rooted in
physical organs, and that sensation presupposes a physical

[36] K. Rahner, in *Geist in Welt* (Kösel-Verlag, Munich, 1964), also
argues against the notion that the 'phantasm' is an *intentionales Bild*. He
argues that 'intentional' for Aquinas does not imply 'mental inexistence'
and is not opposed to 'real' or 'physical' being. The 'phantasm,' he argues,
is a material being, produced by the efficient causality of the sensible
object, and thus a formal aspect of the sensible object itself. See esp.
Chap. 2.
[37] S. T., I, 78, 3.

modification of the sense organs, he does not think that the 'qualities' sensed by sight are 'in the organs' in a material way. Just as the 'eye' does not "become a stone" in sensing a stone, so also it does not "become blue" in sensing a blue sensible. If the 'eye' does not become blue in sensing a blue sensible— if 'blueness' as a characteristic of physical objects is not 'in the sensory system'—how does the 'blueness' of a sensible object come to consciousness? Aquinas' "solution" is to maintain that sensing, however much it may presuppose a physical altera- tion of the sense organs, is not a purely physical process. 'Blueness' or 'blue' is 'in the senses' in an *intentional* mode.[38] Aquinas seems to speak as though the senses themselves were powers of *knowing*—as though "*A* senses an *x* which is *B*" makes an *epistemic claim* about that which *A* knows. Surely, such a claim is unintelligible, for *knowing that x is B* presup- poses a conceptual judgment which the senses are not able to make. Aquinas speaks as though the senses know that *x* is *B* before the intellect forms the intelligible concept of *either x or B*.

Aquinas must see the problem in such a claim, since he does see that the contents of the phantasm or mental image are not intelligible:

Nothing corporeal can make an impression on the noncor- poreal. And therefore, according to Aristotle, in order to cause an intellectual operation, the mere impression of a sensible body does not suffice, but there is required some- thing nobler. . . . The higher and nobler power which he calls the 'agent intellect' . . . *makes the phantasms* received from the senses *actually intelligible*. . . .

[Nihil autem corporeum imprimere potest in rem incorpor- eam. Et ideo ad causandam intellectualem operationem, se- cundum Aristotelem, non sufficit sola impressio sensibilium corporum, sed requiritur aliquid nobilius . . . illus superius et nobilius agens quod vocal intellectum agentem . . . facit phantasmata a sensibus accepta intelligibilia in actu. . . .][39]

[38] *Ibid.*   [39] *S. T.*, I, 84, 6.

There are a number of points made in the quotation which will, on closer analysis, lead us toward an understanding of what Aquinas is about, and why his analysis is both interesting and interestingly false. First, however, it must be pointed out that Aquinas has apparently smuggled into his epistemology a new and unjustified use of 'blue.' We have said that the concept (i.e., the *intelligible* notion) 'blue' is used to refer to 'blue objects out there.' The intentional 'blue' which is 'in the phantasm' and which supposedly *images* the blue of the object is not the intelligible notion 'blue.' The 'blue' of the phantasm cannot "make an impression on the mind" until the agent intellect creates the intelligible form or concept 'blue,' or renders the 'blue' of the phantasm intelligible. If the 'blue' of the phantasm cannot 'get into the mind' or come to consciousness until it is made intelligible by the intellect, how can the phantasm itself be called "nonmaterial" or "intentional"? If the 'blue' of the phantasm is not that 'blue' that we 'have in mind' when we say "That object is blue," how can the phantasm be said to be an intentional image of the 'blueness' of the object? It is no solution merely to claim, with no explanation, that sensation is ordered to the intellect or is a kind of participation in the intellect.

To see clearly the proportions of the problem, we may note that Aquinas, in the quotation cited, treats the phantasm as though it were both material and immaterial. Thus, a "mere impression of a sensible body" cannot make an impression on the mind since "the corporeal cannot make an impression on the noncorporeal." The 'physical object out there' cannot directly impress the mind. We need an intermediary between the world and the mind, and that intermediary is the 'phantasm.' Presumably, the 'physical object out there' can "make an impression" on the senses, since the senses are rooted in material existence. The 'phantasm' is the 'intentional image' of the impact of the physical object on the senses. If the impact of the physical object on the sense organs is able to give rise to an 'intentional image,' why can it not be said to "make an impression on the mind"? The reason is that the 'phantasm,' while supposedly 'intentional,' is also part of the physical system, since its organ (the 'imagination') is rooted in the body.

Thus, the 'phantasm' must itself be "rendered intelligible" (i.e., fit for the conscious mind) by the agent intellect, even though it is declared in the previous breath to be 'intentional' and a kind of participation in the intellect. Aquinas cannot have it both ways. Why does he want it both ways? Why does he treat sensation as an intentional process while denying that the contents of sense experience are themselves intelligible enough to "make an impression on the mind" without the agency of the intellect?

I would suggest that half of the answer derives from the fact that Aristotle (whom Aquinas uses) saw the *problem* of epistemology and covered it over with a myth.[40] The problem is a matter of the interpretation of perception, which *seems* to be a process involving both 'the body' and 'the mind.' The problem is raised by the very fact that Aquinas uses such expressions as "material" and "immaterial." To say that a 'material object' cannot make an impression on an 'immaterial object' is simply to say, in rather misleading terms, that we can never get 'mental-state' or 'intentional' language out of 'physical-state' or 'extensional' language. The behavioristic attempt to reduce the former to the latter, as well as the idealistic attempt to reduce the latter to the former, has failed ignominiously. We are currently "stuck with" our two irreducible languages, as were Aristotle and Aquinas. In order to account for our experience, we need *both* a language which describes or refers to 'physical states' *and* a language which refers to 'mental states.' The problem of epistemology (and of perception) is how to find a satisfactory mode of ingress and egress to and from the 'mental-state' language system from and to the 'physical-state' language system.

One way of accomplishing that feat is to invent an 'entity' which is 'both-and'—a doorway, as it were, between the world of the physical and the world of the mental. Such mythical entities normally have no substance—they are two-dimensional—but they have the interesting logical characteristic that looked at from one side they are in the 'physical order' and looked at from the other side they are in the 'mental

[40] The other half (a theological concern with the unity of body and soul) is discussed below.

order.' (Note, e.g., the logic of 'mental *image*.') Phenomenalism is itself such a myth. Using 'sense data' or 'appearings' as the radical physico-mental building block, the phenomenalist attempts to construct *both* language systems out of that single mythical entity. Unfortunately, phenomenalism is unable to reconstruct *either* language without implicitly assuming *both*. The only alternative (a form of positivism) is to lop off a great number of seemingly intelligible statements in both languages in order to safeguard the integrity of the myth.[41]

Phenomenology starts, as it were, from the other end: in order *not* to exclude by mythical definition any of the sorts of statements we find ourselves making in *both* languages, the phenomenologist extends the doorway 'between the two worlds' in such a way as to get both 'worlds' into the doorway. *Reality itself* is physico-mental. 'Being' is already significant with a significance that escapes the polarity of 'subject-object' by including within itself both poles. The 'physical-state' and 'mental-state' language systems are both *abstractions* from the immediate object of cognition—'reality'—which is itself a unity of the objective and the intentional.

Both of these myths—phenomenalism and phenomenology —are radically misleading in that they purport to *solve* the problem of the two languages by giving us here and now a unified or neutral language. I would maintain that they are correct in their *desire* to find such a language, but wishing does not make it so. The *problem* of the two necessary and incommensurable language systems is indeed a *problem*; but it is one with which all epistemologies are currently "stuck." A mythical way of handling the problem does not solve it.

Platonism succumbs to an opposite temptation: it does not attempt to solve the problem but rather ontologizes it. Granting that we have and need to have two language-frames, Platonists draw an unjustified metaphysical conclusion. We must and ought to use two kinds of languages because there are in our experience two kinds of *entities*—man is 'body *plus* soul.' So to ontologize the language-split creates insurmountable problems for the Platonist. There cannot be a *tertium quid*

[41] My all-too-easy dismissals of rival epistemologies must simply be taken as *obiter dicta* justified if at all by the chapter as a whole.

which is both-and or neither-nor physical and/or mental. Thus, the Platonist wavers back and forth between regarding sensation as a pure act of the body (in which case it is difficult to see how sensation affects the soul) and treating sensation as an act or state of the soul (in which case it is difficult to see how it can be of bodies). Platonism petrifies the problem and offers *no* mythical solution.

Aquinas' mythical 'phantasm' differs in interesting ways from its counterpart in any phenomenalistic epistemology. It is, of course, similar in several ways: (a) it has a foot in 'both worlds'—it is rooted in the physical order but present to the mental order; and, (b) it is severely limited in content. It does not, however, play the role that the immediately cognized contents of sensation play in phenomenalism—it is not the means of reducing either language system to the other or both to a third. Aquinas keeps both languages separate and distinct. The 'phantasm' is *simply* Aquinas' method of getting from one language to another—or, in his own terms, of indicating how the physical may affect the 'mental.' Granting, as I think we must, that it is an impossible entity—a self-contradictory *tertium quid*—we must ask what its logical importance might be for a corrected epistemology.

The most crucial aspect of the 'logic of phantasms' is that the 'phantasm' is produced by a kind of pre-judgmental and pre-conceptual automatic causality. The 'imagination'—that power which supposedly creates the 'image'—is a theoretical power that operates according to the physical laws of the sensory system: "The action of the imagination is caused by the action of the senses."[42] Nevertheless, the form that the 'image' actually takes is dictated by the presence 'in the mind' of conceptual powers and categories. All that Aquinas can really be saying is that our *conscious experience* of, e.g., 'blue objects' is a result *both* of that which occurs in the physical sensory system when we sense a blue object, *and* of the production by the intellect of the formally significant concept 'blue.' *There are no 'phantasms.'* Or, to put it differently, the notion of a 'phantasm' is a *theoretical* notion which results from reflection on the completed act of *conscious perception*;

[42] S. T., I, 84, 7.

it postulates an isomorphism between the physical state of the sensory system and the external cause of sensation, and it draws attention to the operational unity of sensation and intellection in the act of perception. The notion of a 'phantasm' does not refer to an 'intentional image' but rather to the entire organic process by means of which we perceive and thus know the objects of sense experience.

The meaning for us of the word "blue" when we say, "That object is blue," is a function both of the state of our sensory systems and of the syntax of the concept 'blue' as determined by our conceptual system. The reality (the 'external sensible quality') that we *name* when we say, "That object is blue," is neither 'in the senses' nor 'in the mind,' any more than the object itself is 'in the senses' or 'in the mind.' It is a presupposition of the very notion of 'perceiving external reality' that the states of our sensory systems and the logic of our referring expressions isomorphically or analogically represent reality to us; but it does not follow that we must know *how* they do so. We do not need to apprehend directly in some noninferential fashion the 'true' or 'inherent' nature of sensible reality and compare it with the intelligible forms by means of which we experience reality, in order to be said to perceive that which exists in reality (the very notion is self-contradictory). To have conscious experience of that which exists in the external world is to use the intelligible forms of our conceptual system to introspect and inform the states of our sensory systems. Not even in terms of 'sensible qualities' such as 'blue' do we take a direct and immediate look at the world as it exists in itself.[43]

The word "introspect" could be highly misleading. I do not, of course, mean that we *look at* the states of our sensory systems with an inner 'mental eye.' I mean only that perception (*conscious* experience of external reality) arises *jointly* out of the nonintentional contents of sensation and the forms of conceptual thought. The most valuable aspect of Aquinas' myth of the 'phantasm' is that it reminds us that man is not 'two

[43] There is, of course, a perfectly correct use of the expression 'take a look at the world.' In sensation we may be said simply to 'see' what is before our eyes. Sensation in that sense, however, is not an intentional or conscious process, but a material act.

things'—"a body *plus* a soul"—but *one* thing—"a rational animal." Sensation, says Aquinas—and he means *conscious perception*—is not an "act of the body" or an "act of the soul," but rather an "act of the composite." There *is* no problem of how 'physical states' or 'states of the sensory system' *get into* 'the mind.' There are simply certain processes or acts of the total rational animal that we can describe purely in terms of the 'physical-object' language, and other, quite crucial processes or acts of the total rational animal that involve us necessarily in the 'mental-state' language. We do not know exactly how the two *languages* are to be syntactically interrelated—and thus all contemporary epistemologies must be tentative—because we do not as yet have a language in terms of which to express clearly and completely the manner in which man—"body-and-soul"—is *one thing of nature.*

We have now argued that the intelligibility both of our object-words and of our predicate-words (including those which express *sensible* predicates) derives from their syntactical status in a conceptual system, while their semantic or referential *content* is a function of the nature of our sense experience. It is further a consequence of Aquinas' description of sensation and rational judgment that the intelligible *unity* of the object of perception is not given in experience. The sensible characteristics of external entities do not include the *subsistence* of objects—the manner in which the objects of experience exist as unified or single things in their own natures. The unity that we *attribute* to the objects of our experience (that we *judge* them to have) is the unity expressed by an *intelligible form* (an element in our conceptual system), and that is a *logical* or *conceptual* unity. Of course we *know* that there must correspond to that conceptual unity a mode of existential or substantial unity in reality, but we do not *see* or noninferentially *experience* the unity that things 'really' have. It is the lack of *perceived* substantial unity (or, better, of immediately cognized *natural* unity) and the role of conceptual unity in describing and referring to 'that which is' that underlies Aquinas' view that "unity," like all of the transcendentals, is essentially analogous. Real substances or existent entities have that mode of 'unity' that is appropriate to

the world (the *ordo rerum*); we are immediately or noninferentially aware only of that mode of 'unity' that is appropriate
to the order of intentionality or conceptual forms: to say that
we can use the latter to refer to the former, or that the 'unity'
that things actually have is represented to us in the 'unity' of
our concepts, is to say that 'unity' is an analogous concept,
which is but a special case of saying that 'existence' is itself
an analogous concept.

In explicating that claim, we may begin by relating the
logical operation of 'assertion' ('—'), as it was defined in the
man-angel's conceptual system, to the use of "exists" in our
language. It would, of course, be misleading to say that '—'
actually *meant* "exists" even before the man-angel began to
use the conceptual system to introspect or inform his experience. The move itself had no "existential force"—no reference
to reality. The conditions governing the lawful use of '—' are,
to be sure, formally similar to the laws which govern our use
of "exists." Thus, not every element in the system could be
asserted ('—')—only those related in specifiable ways to members of the I-set. Even those elements that could in theory be
asserted could be actually asserted only under specified conditions (e.g., if certain other elements were also assertible).
The logic of '—' does define the *logic* of "exists" and prede-
termines the *kinds* of entities that *might* be said in our language to exist, *whatever* the nature of the contents of sensation. To put it another way, the lawful and significant use of
the word "exists" is governed by the syntactical rules of our
conceptual system. We can therefore say that, when the conceptual system of the man-angel is used to refer, '—' *means*
"exists."

At another level, however, '—' cannot be interpreted as the
concept of 'existence' or 'being.' The full-blown 'syntactical-
semantical' significance of "existence" or "being" is not *merely*
a function of the logic of '—' and the nature of our sense experience. The entire conceptual system takes on 'existential
import' when *the system as a whole is used to refer* to that
which is not 'in the mind' or 'in the senses.' Using the system
to refer is not itself to *mean* or to *assert* something—it is the
precondition of meaning or asserting *anything* about the 'real.'

To use the system to refer is to have a meaningful notion of 'reality.' (The notion of the *Vorgriff* in phenomenology might be usefully called to mind.) Thus, *to have the concept of 'existence' or 'being' is to be naturally disposed to use one's conceptual system to refer to the objects of experience.* The concept 'being' is not an element *in* a conceptual system, but a dispositional tendency to compose or bring together the formal intelligibility of a conceptual system and the contents of sense experience in order to use the resultant forms to refer to that which is not immanent in human consciousness. To have the dispositional concept of 'being' is naturally to construct an intentional and analogical representation of the world and to judge it to be a mode of knowing objective reality. "Exists" expresses a natural or dispositional judgment that there is a relation of isomorphism between the forms of the intellect and the real world. That judgment is not a factor *in* our conscious experience, but a presupposition *of* our conscious experience. (Thus it is a Vor*griff*.) The ability to make such a composition and to refer by analogy to reality is presupposed by all empirically significant language and thus by all consciousness. In that sense, 'existence' or 'being' is the "first concept of the intellect"—the primal concept.

Such an interpretation should put to rest any of the more naïve objections to Aquinas' doctrine that "being is the first concept in the intellect." It does not mean, for example, that if only parents would stop talking baby-talk to babies—if babies were left on their own to explain what is on their minds—they would utter "Being-being" before "Da-da." Nor does it mean that "Something *is*" is the first truth that the mind comprehends or entertains. It means only that knowing how to use conceptual systems on the basis of experience to refer to the objects of experience is a presupposition of empirically significant language or thought—and that having that dispositional 'know-how' is having the concept of 'reality' or 'existence.' It is crucial to note that internal sensory states plus significant conceptual systems do not themselves add up to the notion of 'really existent objects of experience.' The intelligible forms which result from the introspection of experience in terms of the conceptual system must be *used* to refer—must be judged analogically to represent what *is* 'out there'—before we have the notion of 'reality' or 'being.' The very notion that there *are* things is an analogous notion. It is not, however, a notion that we must *learn*—we are naturally disposed so to judge. The concept of 'being' is *naturally* the first concept of the mind.

The natural disposition of the mind to use the intelligible forms of the intellect to refer to the objects of experience is the source of the intentionality of the mind (the intentionality of speech and thought). The contents of a conceptual system do not themselves possess an element of 'aboutness'—they do not *signify* objects or states of affairs unless they are used to do so. An uninterpreted logical calculus signifies nothing except its own syntactical 'meaning.' Similarly, the organic states of the sensory system are not significant or intentional in their own right. Sensory states signify or represent experienced states of affairs only because we take them to do so. It is the primal dispositional concept of 'existence'—the natural tendency of the mind so to use conceptual systems and so to take sensory states—that accounts for the fact that our words and thoughts are about reality. Intentionality is a function of our radical concept of 'being.'

'Being' by this account is an analogous term in more than one sense. Firstly, its use as an interpretation of '—' is analogous by what the Thomists would call 'analogy of attribution.' The conceptual move '—' has a rather different logical status when used with members of the P-set than it has when used with members of the I-set (keeping always in mind that a member of the I-set must 'be' of a kind signified by a member of the K-set). Thus, we could say that an existential claim concerning a property (P-term) is a claim that it 'of-exists' with regard to a substance (an x of kind K_1). The traditional term would be 'in-exist.' In a case of the 'analogy of attribution,' the notion of the prime analogate (in this case the 'substance') is *placed in* the definition of the other analogates (the properties). Similarly, the meaning of '—' as used of members of the I-set is 'placed in' the meaning of '—' as used of members of the P-set. This is not a matter of *explicit* definition (arbitrary usage) but of *implicit* definition, justified by the axioms and rules of the system within which the analogates are elements. Thus, once the syntactically justified move is made from '$\phi_1 \cdot \phi_2 \ldots \cdot \phi_n$' (in its referential use) to 'x and x is a K_1', we may say that 'K_1' is 'placed in' the definition of '$\phi_1 \cdot \phi_2 \ldots \cdot \phi_n$'. That is why, for Aquinas, a proposition uniting a substance and its properties is a form of *per se* truth. The notion of 'apple' is placed in the notion of 'red and roundish and moist et alii,' not by arbitrary definitional fiat, but by the "rules of the conceptual game." In the 'analogy of attribution,' the definition of the secondary analogates in terms of or by reference to the prime analogate is a form of *per se* truth (it is true *ex vi terminorum*) although it is not a matter of explicit definition (it is a synthetic move).

'Being' in our construction, however, is analogical in a more profound sense. In its role as naming a disposition to use a conceptual system to inform experience and refer to sensible reality, it may be said to be *essentially* analogous by what Thomists call 'analogy of proper proportionality.' There is no a priori means of excluding the possibility that there might be *other sorts* of intelligible conceptual systems from those that we use, in terms of which 'reality' could be equally well or more adequately represented and understood. Different sorts of axioms and operational rules might generate conceptual systems with radically different sorts of primary elements from those of the K-, P-, and I-sets of our 'object language'— indeed, such systems already exist to some extent in contemporary physics. It is in theory possible that such a conceptual system be used to inform the contents of sense experience and thus produce radically different sorts of intelligible forms from those with which we now make our judgments concerning 'that which is.' If such a system were used to inform the contents of sense experience, the person would *perceive* (*consciously* experience) quite different things from what we now perceive (although he would, in the nonintentional sense, be *seeing* the very same thing); and he would assert the analogical reality of different sorts of 'entities' or 'realities' in the world. Wilfred Sellars seems to feel that science may well create such a conceptual language in the future. There is certainly no way of excluding his claim a priori.

It might *even* be said, as Chisholm has claimed, that another kind of apprehension than that programmed through the physical sense organs might *in theory* be possible. Such 'experience' would have to be rendered intelligible by a vastly different sort of conceptual scheme from ours, and would generate a different sort of existential claim about 'that which is'—an existential claim that could only be called 'analogous' to ours by the 'analogy of proper proportionality.' 'Being' may well have different modes—the concept of 'being,' that is, not *reality itself*. In each case, the mode of 'being' would be determined by the mode of signification—i.e., by the manner in which a *kind* of conceptual system informing a *kind* of experience would be used to signify a *kind* of 'entity' or 'reality' in the world. An instinctive awareness of such possibilities might explain why we understand such questions as, "*Is* there anything of which we could not in theory conceive?" Those metaphysicians are wrong, however, who assume that, because we are aware of the "analogy of 'being' " (because we know what it means to say that 'being' may have modes), we therefore possess an intuition of 'being' that goes beyond our current empirically significant conceptual system. Because we know that 'being' is essentially analogous, it does not follow that we have an 'intuition' of "Being Itself."

Three senses of 'being' are implied by the analysis thus far presented: (1) To have the concept 'being' is to be disposed to use a conceptual system to refer on the basis of experience to the external objects of experience. (2) Within the conceptual system there is a syntactically defined move ('__') which determines the syntax of "exists." (3) When the system as a whole is actually used to refer to what is experienced, the syntactically defined move is used to assert that something "exists in reality"—a purely logical *move* is used analogically to represent real existence. In the first sense of 'being' the concept is essentially analogous by the 'analogy of proper proportionality'—the concept of 'being' would be possessed by a rational being whatever kind of conceptual system he might use to refer to whatever sort of experience he might have. In the second sense of 'being' we find an 'analogy of attribution' in terms of which several interrelated uses of '___' are implicitly co-defined by reference to a primary usage. The third sense of 'being' (its ordinary use in our language) shares in both kinds of analogy: it utilizes the logic of "exists" as defined by the conceptual system, but with the implicit understanding that in theory 'that which is' could be experienced in a rather different way and judged by different forms of intelligibility. There might be other logical moves by means of which the real could be analogically signified—logical moves which would not justify the assertion that reality consists of *objects with properties.*

A major question, of course, is what such a revision of the traditional Thomistic epistemology implies for the thought of Aquinas himself. I shall argue that it is more clearly consistent with Aquinas' *theological* reading of the epistemology he actually adopts than is the traditional version. That which follows epistemologically from the revision is only a slightly more radical statement of that which follows from Aquinas' own formulation of Aristotle. It follows that reality is *entirely* reconceivable. Not only the intelligible forms of substances (defined in terms of sensible properties) but also the intentional forms of sensible qualities result from the conceptual powers of the intellect and not from what is merely given in experience. Our experience of the accidents of objects has no more direct claim to being veridical than our judgments about the natures of things. Our knowledge of the world is entirely analogical. It is that strong claim that can most readily be related to Aquinas' theology.

Granted that the contents of (nonintentional) sensation might remain unchanged whatever conceptual system we might find ourselves using to describe reality, why do we use the conceptual system that we do? Why do we find ourselves referring to "objects," "substances," "properties," and so on? The question is particularly crucial when we realize that our language of *persons* (our references, for example, to 'mental states') is necessitated by the failure of the 'physical state' language to render our experience wholly intelligible, and that the very *meaning* of our language of persons is correlative with, indeed dependent upon, the meaning of our 'physical state' language. What it means to be a person with 'mental states' could not be known unless it were also known what it means to see or refer to such things as 'physical objects.' Aquinas realizes that all men do in fact use the same conceptual system to interpret their experience of reality: all ordinary human languages are intertranslatable within the limits of the porosity of concepts. All men do talk about "objects out there having sensible properties"; the 'object language' and its correlative 'person language' are naturally common to all men. It would be tempting to say that all men use the same kinds of concepts to refer to 'that which is' because all men *see* that 'that is the way things are.' We have shown, and Aquinas knows, that such is not the case. If it *were* the case then either positivism or some form of conceptual empiricism would be in order. Aquinas' 'solution' to the problem is to maintain that all men form the same kinds of concepts about reality because all men possess *by nature* a common power of conceptualization—the *intellectus agens*. The 'agent intellect' is the source of our intelligible notions of 'that which is,' and the 'agent intellect' is the same in all men.

Given that Aquinas believes that 'the way that we are' results from the creative intention of God, it would again be tempting to assume that God made us this way—possessed of a common mode of conceptualization—because he wanted us to 'come up with' a *correct* conceptual picture of the world. We conceive the world in the way that we do because God *knows* how the world really is and has programmed our minds in such a way that we conceive it as it really is. Aside from the fact that there is some evidence that we do *not* conceive the world as it really is (witness for example the unfortunate bifurcation of our language into incommensurable 'physical-state' and 'mental-state' language frames), such a theory overlooks elements in Aquinas' own discussion of the status of our knowledge vis-à-vis the real state of nature.

It would be correct to say, I believe, that Aquinas holds that all men possess the kind of conceptual powers that they do because God willed it so, and it would be correct to say that God willed it so because such conceptual powers result in a mode of conceiving reality that is *appropriate* to the status of man *in via*—'on the way' to God. Aquinas would not say that we *falsely* conceive the world. For a man 'on the way' *correctly* to conceive the world is for him to conceive it in the way that we do. Aquinas does not maintain, however, that we directly or nonanalogically *know* the true natures of things.[44] To know reality in terms of a human conceptual system—or even in terms of an angelic conceptual system—is to know reality by a kind of "evening knowledge."[45] It is to know reality by analogy with created thought forms. The only way to know things *as they really are* is to know them in God—by what Aquinas calls "morning knowledge." The 'intentional' existence that things have for God is a true, ideal, and completely adequate expression of what things really are in their own being.

To convert that claim into our vocabulary of "languages," we might say that our 'subject-object' language is appropriate to and adequate for our status in this life. It is a correct language for *man* to use in describing 'that which is.' It is *not*, however, a *theoretically ideal* language. There may be other languages, based on other conceptual systems, which could also and more adequately be used to express the nature of 'what there really is.' Aquinas' claim is that *God's* language is the only *completely* adequate expression of what really is the case. The real nature of things is intentionally expressed only in the language or "Word" of God.

Whatever we make of Aquinas' theological claim, it is clear that the epistemological correlate of that claim is quite consistent with our revision of the traditional Thomistic epistemology. The language we now use—based on the conceptual system we now possess—is not ideal or completely adequate to express the nature of things. Reality is in theory completely reconceivable. It would appear that there is some evidence that such a claim is correct. We are now "stuck with" the bifurcation of language into 'physical-state' and 'mental-

[44] S. T., I, 16, 2.
[45] For a discussion of "morning and evening knowledge" see S. T., I, 58, 6 and 7.

state' language frames. We find it impossible to explicate completely and intelligibly how those language frames are related
to one another. As a result, all of our epistemologies are tentative—they utilize either mythical or theoretical means of
bringing epistemological unity out of the manifest dualism of
reflective human experience. The epistemological 'theories' of
the linguistic analysts are but the de-mythologized fragments
of metaphysics. They *also* do not tell us what is going on at
the other end of the references made by 'mental-state' terms.
They cannot tell us in intelligible terms how syntactically to
relate the language of 'physical states' to that of 'mental
states.' Epistemology cannot tell us what it really is to be *a*
"thinking animal." Unlike the metaphysicians, however, the
analysts at least do not try, which on the whole prefer-
able. Some, like Sellars,[46] assume that one day science will tell
us in intelligible terms what we are referring to when we say
"The mind," and they await the eschatologically perfect theoretical language of next-century's neuro-physics with the
same myth-making expectation that Aquinas reserves for the
Beatific Vision. But the point is that *now*—whether we mean
the *now* which is previous to the first coming of the Good
Scientist or the second coming of the Good Shepherd—we
do not know how we know or how what we know is related
to how things 'really' are.

Such a statement is intimately related to Aquinas' famous
claim that we cannot directly and noninferentially know what
the mind is—what *we* are as persons.[47] We only know the
nature of the intellect—the essential actuality of a man—by
inference from the *acts* of the intellect.[48] What we are is
known adequately and intelligibly to God alone. The essence
of man is expressed only in the intentional being—the "Word"
—of God. One thing appears certain: the 'mind' as we have
represented it by analogy with the acts of the thinking animal

[46] *Science, Perception and Reality*, Chap. 1.
[47] S. T., I, 87, 1: " 'The intellect understands itself in the same way
that it understands other things.' But it understands other things not by
their essences, but by their similitudes. Thus it does not understand itself
through its essence."
[48] *Ibid.*: "Therefore the intellect knows itself not through its essence
but through its acts."

(and I, with Sellars, would maintain that we do not know the acts of the thinking animal apart from an examination of overt verbal behavior)—that 'mind' does not exist. The notion of "intentional stuff" over against the "physical stuff" of bodies is manifestly an analogy and serves only to *express* the unresolved "Mind-body problem," not to solve it. What it really means to say that man is a *thinking* animal—that he has a mind—is known only to God (and perhaps to the neurophysicist of the future). It follows that we do not *know* precisely what is going on 'in the mind'; there may be operations of the 'mind' or 'soul' of which man, in his linguistic and conceptual self-awareness, knows nothing. Such a claim will have immense significance in our final resolution of the problem of the language of faith. We must now draw some general conclusions from our tentative epistemology as it affects the logic of 'natural theology' or 'references to God intended on the basis of natural human experience.'

"GOD" AND THE TRUTHS
OF THE SYSTEM

Our tentative epistemological findings to date may be summarized as follows:

1. We find ourselves using a conceptual system to inform our experience, and we find ourselves using the resultant intelligible forms to refer to 'that which is.'

2. Upon reflection it appears that the intelligibility of our knowledge of the world is a function of the logic or syntax inherent in the conceptual system we find ourselves using.

3. That logic or syntactical order—the source, that is, of the intelligibility of our experience—does not derive either from the nature of our sense experience (the states of our sensory systems) or from the way that things really are, since we cannot know or be aware of either our experience or the way that things are except in terms of our conceptual system.

4. The fact that our conceptual system leads us inevitably to construct a language which is subject to a radical bifurcation into a 'physical-state' and a 'mental-state' language frame, and the fact that it has proved impossible to indicate coherently and intelligibly how the two 'languages' are to be

syntactically united, may be taken as evidence that our language and thus the conceptual system upon which it is formulated are inadequate and misleading.

5. Upon further reflection it appears a priori possible that there might be other conceptual systems in terms of which the same experience might in theory be informed and thus in terms of which 'that which is' might be described or named; and it appears a priori possible that there might be other modes of experience (other sorts of inner states) which, in combination with other conceptual systems, might generate radically different sorts of intelligible forms in terms of which a different kind of 'entity' or 'reality' might be describable or namable.

6. It is therefore possible that there might be an ideal language based on a new mode of conceptualization in terms of which that which we now experience might be more adequately known and described; and it is therefore possible that there might be another mode of apprehending or experiencing which, in conjunction with a new mode of conceptualization, would provide a more adequate way of knowing and describing what we now experience and which would enable us to experience and describe other sorts of things that exist in reality but which we do not now experience. "Existence" is a radically analogical word.

7. The contents of sense experience (the states of our sensory systems) are nonintentional and therefore lack the essential quality of 'aboutness' that is presupposed by significant reference. The forms of a syntactically significant conceptual system are referentially neutral unless they are *used* to refer, and therefore do not themselves possess the intentionality essential to significant reference. We must therefore assume that the 'intellect' is itself the radical source of the intentionality of human speech and thought. The 'intellect' may therefore be analogically described as "radical intentionality" or "essential aboutness"—a natural tendency to manifest an openness to reality by utilizing the intelligible forms which result from informing experience in terms of a conceptual system as analogical similitudes of the real. That tendency is expressed in the existential judgment.

It might be objected that the tentative epistemology thus far adopted treats the categories of human understanding in too Kantian a fashion. As Gilson said of Durantel[49] we seem to be claiming that the very form in which we experience reality is a universally given (or even God-given) fact about human rationality, and possibly unrelated to the true nature of that which is experienced. To assume that a conceptual system is logically independent of the contents of experience and merely used 'after the fact' to *inform* experience, appears to say that the intelligibility that we *impose* on reality is in no sense the intelligibility that things really *have*—and this is true even if it be admitted that experience is the *occasion* for the creation of a conceptual system. Our judgments concerning 'what is' may be *irrelevant* to 'what *really* is' (shades of the noumena) whether or not we insist that nature 'must' be analogous with our conceptual judgments.

My very choice of the word "analogous" suggests that I do not believe our conceptual judgments to be irrelevant to that which we experience in sensation. On the other hand, the isomorphism between our judgments and reality (an isomorphism presupposed by the very notion of a conscious awareness of reality) cannot be *exhibited* as such. The very demand that we be able to *exhibit* the isomorphism between our existential judgments and reality would make sense only if reality were assumed to be inherently and actually intelligible apart from the application of norms deriving from the intellect itself, and could thus be noninferentially cognized *together with* its inherent norms of intelligibility. The notion, however, of a material state of affairs (the world) containing in itself norms of intelligibility seems to me to be self-contradictory. To say that reality is intelligible is rather to say that we are in fact able to utilize *our* norms of intelligibility to inform our experience—that the world is amenable to understanding according to *our* forms of intelligibility. Gilson's annoyance at being told that the mind contributes the forms of intelligibility and that the world itself—apart from the judgments of the human intellect—cannot be *seen* as an actually intelligible

[49] E. Gilson, *The Christian Philosophy* . . . , p. 472n.

order reminds one of the annoyance of a farmer who is told that, while he can put eggs into neat boxes of twelve each, his hens are not mathematicians.

The question that ought rather to be raised concerns the source of the appropriateness or *relative* adequacy of the conceptual system that we in fact use. Granted that our conceptual system is not 'ideal'—that it leaves a lot unexplained—it is nevertheless true that man has managed on the basis of that conceptual system to acquire a great deal of intelligible understanding of reality. If the formal structure of that conceptual system—the source of the intelligibility of our experience—is not dictated by any 'given' or noninferentially cognized elements of direct experience, from where does it derive? I find no substance in the claim that *God* sees to it that our intellects produce conceptual systems that are in fact appropriate to our mode of life in the world, however true it may be that the intellect itself, and thus the ability to conceive, is a creation of God. There seems to be little convincing ground to accept Aquinas' notion that the 'agent intellect' together with the axioms and operational rules of the conceptual system we actually use is naturally common to all men—an essential aspect of a universal human nature. Aquinas himself remarks that the *per se nota* statements generated by the 'agent intellect' *arise from* experience, even though sense experience cannot formally account for them.[50] It seems most reasonable to assume that the specific form taken by our conceptual system—the axioms and rules of operation that determine the fact that 'objects with predicates' are the primary 'entities' of our conceptual system—is determined by the pragmatic or survival value to human community (with its socially defined goals) of that particular mode of informing experience and intending reality. The 'object language' generated by our conceptual system has value in enabling us to 'get around in the world' and in allowing us to preserve and communicate the cultural values and norms of society.[51]

It is therefore possible to agree with Sellars that the *ma-*

[50] S. T., I-II, 51, 1.

[51] Cf., S. Hampshire, *Thought and Action* (The Viking Press, New York, 1960), Chaps. 1 and 2.

terial moves which form a basic part of our *humanum*—the "stimulus-response" patterns of behavior that we learn through experience in community—are *in some way* determinative of the mode in which we conceive reality.[52] The problem is that we do not know *how* the pragmatic concerns of society-in-the-world determine or influence our mode of conceiving. We do not know the *mechanism* which relates the nature of things and the culturally defined concerns of society to the operative conceptual system that we find ourselves using. We do not know what 'inner state of affairs' causes or produces our conceptual system (although we can certainly say that it is a *natural* state of affairs and thus in theory open to scientific investigation).

Such a decision regarding the source of our conceptual system, with its inherent intelligibility and consequent problems, could have interesting theological overtones. If the mode of conceptualization universally in use among men is even in part determined by the pragmatic concerns and goals of human society-in-the-world, it would seem to follow that the extension and limitations of the operative human conceptual system are not entirely unrelated to the natural disposition of the human will or appetite.[53] That which is intelligible to man may be determined at least in part by that which man dispositionally finds appropriate as an end or goal of existence. If the theological notion of 'original sin' refers not to an actual decision of each and every contemporary individual, but rather to a state of deranged volition in fact universal in man as we know him, then an Augustinian notion of a 'fallen intellect' might appear theologically attractive. The theologian need not say that 'sin' has corrupted the natural *powers* of the intellect (and thus the very nature of man) but only that the derangement of the will has produced a *specification* of those powers (an operative conceptual system) which distorts man's *conscious* apprehension of the nature of the real, and destroys his natural ability to apprehend in intelligible fashion the essential reference of the world to God. In addition to a *Vor-*

[52] *Science, Perception and Reality*, Chap. 11.
[53] Here "natural" does not mean "inherent in human nature," but only "to be found in men as they actually are."

griff, it might be meaningful to speak, with Helmut Kuhn, for example, of a *schöpferische Wahl*[54]—a radical disposition of the human will which operates in actuality like a constantly renewed decision of man, although it is not at any moment consciously *made*. For our purposes, it suffices to note that the actual form taken by our conceptual system is in some sense determined by the pragmatic concerns of human society-in-the-world.

However our conceptual system is *causally* related to 'how things are' and to the cultural concerns of society, it is *not* the case that the intelligible forms of our concepts are merely derived from experience. Our mode of rendering our experience intelligible is *logically* independent of the experience we have and of how things are, since intelligibility is a formal or syntactical matter and the syntax of our conceptual system can never be got out of any so-called 'given' elements of our experience or noninferentially cognizable aspects of reality. There must therefore be something (which we name 'intellect') that accounts for that syntax. A Kantian (or Neo-Kantian) interpretation of the status of the 'first principles' is inevitable. Just as inevitable, however, is the claim that the "similitudes of the thing," which are created and possessed by the intellect, are the intentional analogues *in* which or *by* which *reality is in fact known*. Thus, Aquinas correctly says both that we *do not know* 'the natures of things' and that we *know* the thing in the similitude,[55] since we judge (and must judge) that there is an existential analogue 'in reality' of that which we intend 'in the mind.'

A sense of what is implied by such a statement may be developed by a further analysis of Aquinas' remarks concerning the "morning and evening knowledge of angels." The angels, Aquinas says, know the same things in two ways. They know the primordial natures of things as they are in the "Word" or intentional being of God. That is called "morning knowledge." Secondly, they know the same things as they subsist in them-

[54] H. Kuhn, *Begegnung mit dem Sein* (J. C. B. Mohr, Tübingen, 1954), Chap. 5.
[55] S. T., I, 16, 2; and, S. T., I, 85, 2.

selves. That is called "evening knowledge."[56] Insofar as it is
the *same things* that they know in the two modes, neither
"knowledge" is inferior to the other. According to Aquinas,
the "nobility" of one's knowledge is determined primarily by
the "nobility" of the *object* of knowledge, not by the quality
of the act of knowing. Since, however, to know things by
"morning knowledge" is to know things in the very intelligible
forms by which *God* knows them, and since to know things
by "evening knowledge" is to know them in the immanent or
created intelligible forms by which *angels* naturally know
them, the latter form of knowledge is inferior—it does not so
adequately or clearly represent the true natures of those
things which are nevertheless known by it.[57] If it were not
possible for the angels simultaneously to know things in both
ways—if they had to drop their own form of knowing when
they knew things in God—then we would say that their
natural analogical mode of knowing things is 'irrelevant' to
the true natures of things—or simply false.

To apply that judgment to our linguistic account of human
knowledge, if the possession of a theoretically ideal language
(based on a radically different mode of conceptualization)
were to lead to the complete abandonment of our current
'object language,' or if the continued use of the 'object language' could not be seen, in the context of the ideal language,
to be a mode of describing the 'same things'—however inadequately—then it would be correct to say that the 'object language' that we currently use is irrelevant to the true natures
of things—or simply false. According to Sellars, when, in
adopting a new referential language system, we simply cease
to use the old one, then a statement previously made in the
old language ought not to be said to be "true in its own context" or "true in the old language," since the adoption of the
new language implies the denial of referential truth status to

[56] S. *T.*, I, 58, 7.
[57] *Ibid.*: "If it be called evening knowledge, in that through innate ideas
they know the being that things have in their own natures, then the
morning and evening knowledge differ. Thus Augustine seems to understand, when he calls one inferior to the other."

the old one. Thus, such a statement would be declared to be simply *false*.[58] It would seem, however, that if an account could be given in the new language of the *relative* adequacy and appropriateness of the old language, then the statements in the old language could not be said to be *false*, but only *inadequate* or *misleading*. Aquinas' claim would seem to be that the ideal language which is constituted by the "Word" or intentional being of God is such that it contains an adequate representation of the *same things* inadequately represented in our language, and could thus account for the relative success of our language in enabling us to 'get around in the world.'[59] The major (logical) distinction between Aquinas' "ideal language" and Sellars' "ideal scientific language of the future" is that the intentions of things in the "Word" of God are *not analogical* in the sense in which we have been using the word (*mere* isomorphism), while the language of science will always be analogical—even if by a most adequate analogy. This distinction, which touches on the very problem of the *esse* of things, is, as we shall see, crucial to the notion of 'natural theology.'

Before turning to what 'natural theology' is, however, it might be helpful to determine broadly the kinds of things that 'natural theology' *cannot be*. Our negative thesis is that any argument that presupposes or purports to demonstrate the intelligibility of "God" is illegitimate by virtue of Aquinas' epistemology. To support that thesis we shall examine in some detail the claim that intelligibility is a purely formal or syntactical matter.

In a passage that remains shocking in spite of its traditional place in medieval theology, Aquinas declares that all intelligibility is a function of necessity:

The intelligible precisely as intelligible is necessary and incorruptible, for necessary things are perfectly knowable by the intellect.

[58] *Science, Perception and Reality,* Chap. 11.

[59] *S. T.,* I, 58, 7, ad 3: "Nor is there any inconsistency in knowing a thing through two mediums, one of which is more perfect and the other less perfect."

[Intelligibile in quantum intelligibile est necessarium et in-
corruptibile; necessaria enim perfecte sunt intellectu cog-
noscibilia.][60]

Hoenen, in his study of the judgment in Aquinas, correctly
maintains: "It is always the necessary and only the necessary
which is intelligible and knowable."[61] It is almost inevitable
in the twentieth century—inflicted as it is by the dogmas of
empiricism—that such a statement will be interpreted as claiming that all significant or intelligible propositions are analytic
or logically true. The distinction between necessary and contingent propositions (analyzed truth-functionally) has been a
fruitful one in the history of philosophy, but it has led to a
disastrous lack of sensitivity to the elements of formal necessity which are to be found in the most contingent statement.
It is understandable that doctrinaire empiricism would have
no need of the notion of formal necessity in the analysis of
contingent propositions. If the meaning of significant referential concepts is derivable *tout simple* from the *given* or noninferentially cognizable contents of sense experience, then
the syntactical form of contingent propositions is merely a
conventional means of expressing that which is given in experience—i.e., that which happens to be the case. Whether
the idea of an object is a construct of qualitative sense data,
or itself a result of direct acquaintance with objects, the entire
meaning of an objective existential judgment can be exhaustively stated in terms of *bare reference* to the contingent contents of experience.

Aquinas, on the other hand, maintains that every contingent
judgment contains an element of necessity which constitutes
its intelligibility.[62] It is important to understand the analogical status of "necessity" in any Thomistic (and in any reliable)
epistemology. Perhaps the easiest way of explicating the meaning of "necessity" as a ground of intelligibility is to analyze
Aquinas' theories on the nature of a *per se* proposition (not

[60] *C. G.*, II, 55.
[61] P. Hoenen, *Reality and Judgment according to St. Thomas* (Henry
Regnery Company, Chicago, 1952), p. 126. Chapter 4 contains an excellent account of *per se* propositions.
[62] *S. T.*, I, 86, 3.

to be confused with a *per se nota* proposition). In terms of our analysis of the syntax of a conceptual system, we may say that a *per se* proposition is a proposition which expresses or makes an inferential move justified entirely and sufficiently by the axioms and rules of operation of a syntactically significant conceptual system (this is the same as expressing an *implicit* definition). Aquinas maintains, as I have argued, that a proposition expressing the relationship between an 'object' and its 'properties' (its *proper* predicates) is a *per se* proposition.[63] Aquinas correctly refuses to call such a proposition *per se nota* (*roughly* equivalent to "self-evident" or "logically true") since it is not a *merely* (explicitly) definitional matter indicating an identity of intension. It is a synthetic move (a 'composition') justified, not contingently (through observation), but syntactically—by the rules of the conceptual game. Thus, the *contingent* existential judgment, "That is an apple," presupposes a process of intellection through which an intelligible form or *ratio* is produced "in the light of reason"— by following the formal rules of a conceptual system. The actual *utterance* of the proposition may indeed be justified by a purely contingent matter—the state of the sensory system— but the *intelligibility* of the proposition, the fact that it enables us to understand or comprehend 'that which is,' is a formal or syntactical matter—a matter of the necessities or exigencies of our conceptual system.

It is a further characteristic of a contingently justified (and formally intelligible) existential judgment that it is either itself *per se nota* or derived through *per se* judgments from a *per se nota* judgment.[64] Aquinas' use of "per se nota" cannot be comprehended if "self-evident" is our *only* translation of the phrase. A literal translation is more informative: a *per se nota* proposition is a proposition whose truth is *known through itself* and not *per aliud* or *through another*.[65] Granted that our 'knowledge' of an existential state of affairs is not noninferential (or given) as empiricism would have it, it is nevertheless

[63] *Post. Anal.*, I, 10, 2.
[64] *De Log. Arist.*, VIII, 7.
[65] See, R. J. Deferrari, *A Lexicon of St. Thomas Aquinas* (Catholic University of America Press, Baltimore, 1948).

the case that *in the order of existential judgments* certain propositions are known to be true without appeal to other propositions. When asked, "How do you know that *that* is true?" we do not *always* reply, "Because I know that something *else* is true, and that something else implies that *that* is true." Some existential judgments at least must be justified or affirmed merely by the natural tendency of the 'mind' to *take* certain informed states of the sensory system as true analogical representations of 'that which is.' While any single *taking* of reality may be in theory corrigible, we cannot simultaneously call *all* of our *takings* into question.[66] In fact, therefore, certain of our existential judgments must be—at any particular time—unquestioned criteria on the basis of which we support or criticize *other* existential claims. They must be *per se nota* or justified without essential reference to other existential judgments.

If an existential judgment is not itself *per se nota*, it is only intelligible (i.e., part of a unified view of reality) if its truth can be derived from other existential judgments which *are per se nota*. Such an inference must utilize *per se* judgments—inferential moves justified by the formal structure of the conceptual system. The class of *per se* judgments which relate *per aliud nota* existential claims to *per se nota* claims may be roughly characterized as 'causal.' It is a correlate of Aquinas' epistemology that all intelligible causal statements are *per se* or based upon *per se* causal statements.

From the time of Hume until quite recently, it was thought to be impossible or arbitrary to grant to a causal statement a *per se* status. To say of a causal statement that it is *per se* is to say that it is not merely an empirical generalization, but a 'truth of the system.' The move from the assertion of the cause to the assertion of the effect (or vice versa) is justified, not by reference alone to the contingencies of experience, but by reference also to the formal rules of the system. A *per se* causal statement is, to put it bluntly, a kind of synthetic a priori judgment.

An understanding of Aquinas' doctrine on the *per se* causal

[66] Cf. R. Chisholm, *op.cit.* The thesis runs through the book.

statement is crucial to an understanding of his own 'causal' language about God. At one level, there is a surprising parallel between Aquinas and Hume with regard to the genesis of a causal statement. The first moment in the formulation of a *per se* causal statement is the experience of constant conjunction.[67] The essential difference between Aquinas and Hume on the nature of the constant conjunction is that, for Hume, the conjoined elements are *given* impressions, while, for Aquinas, they are intelligibly informed events or states of affairs. From sense experience, memory and conceptual judgment, the notion of 'A→B' is impressed on the passive intellect.[68] (In Aquinas' own example, the cessation of a particular ailment is experienced regularly to follow the taking of a certain drug.) In the absence of counter examples, it would obviously be possible to formulate an empirical generalization on the basis of such experience. Aquinas maintains, however, that the intellect *takes* the constant conjunction as the experiential ground for maintaining that 'A' is *naturally* productive (in normal circumstances) of 'B.' He introduces, that is, the modal expression "natural necessity" and utilizes the resultant causal statement as a first principle of a specific science.[69] That is to say that the causal statement becomes unconditionally assertable in the explanatory framework of that particular science. When that logical move has been made, an *inference* is justified from either the cause to the effect or from the effect to the cause. 'Natural necessity' is a postulated existential correlate of a mode of logical or intentional necessity. When an empirical generalization, then, takes

[67] *Post. Anal.*, II, 20, 11: "From sense there comes about memory . . . but from memory made many times concerning the same thing . . . experience comes about. . . . For example, when someone remembers that a certain herb has many times saved from fever."

[68] I use the arrow symbol for the 'if-then' of material implication.

[69] *Post. Anal.*, II, 20, 11: "Reason does not terminate in the experience of particulars, but from many particulars of experience, it grasps one common thing, *which is confirmed by the mind*, and considers it without reference to the particulars upon which it was founded; and this common thing it takes as the principle of the art and science. . . . Just as from memory experience comes about, so also from experience, or even more from the universal form coming into the soul (which form is taken *as though* it were the same in all as it was in experienced instances. . . .")

on crucial importance for the success and fecundity of an entire explanatory system, the definition of the cause is 'placed in' the definition of the effect, and the causal relation becomes a truth of the system. Such a step is never taken *in vacuo*: it forms part of a formally interrelated *system* of such judgments, such that one *per se* causal proposition cannot be given up without a more or less radical reformulation of the entire system.[70] Thus, not *every* empirical generalization becomes a *per se* causal principle (although all could in theory so function). When, however, one is using such a system of *per se* judgments, and when there is not sufficient empirical ground for abandoning the *entire system* or adopting *another* such system, seeming counter-examples to one of the *per se* causal statements may be judged *by definition* to be erroneous or irrelevant. Once the move is made from an 'empirical generalization' to a *per se* causal principle, nothing counts as an instance of either the cause or the effect *unless* the causal implication is instantiated in observation.

A fictitious example will illustrate the kind of logical move made in a *per se* causal judgment (although the example is too crude to actually occur in a scientific context). In the science devoted to the properties of solvents, there might come to the attention of the scientist a sort of solvent—'wondralyte'—whose essential experimental characteristics are 'ϕ_1, $\phi_2 \ldots \phi_n$'. It is discovered that whenever diamonds are placed in known specimens of 'wondralyte' the diamonds are dissolved. If the other experimental characteristics of the solvent (summarized as 'ϕ_i') are so related to other elements and statements in the theoretical language of solvents that the property of "diamond-dissolving" ('ψ') in conjunction with them allows the whole explanatory framework to be more widely used in intelligibly organizing, describing, and understanding the natures of solvents, then that characteristic may be placed in the definition of 'wondralyte': '$\phi_i w \rightarrow \psi w$' becomes unconditionally assertable, and no substance (even if one should be found) with the characteristics 'ϕ_i', but without the characteristic 'ψ', would any longer count as 'wondralyte.' More than likely, it would be tentatively assumed either that

[70] A good example, as discussed below, is the speed of light.

the new substance will turn out ultimately *not* to have the characteristics 'ϕ_i' or to have some other *unknown* characteristic that accounts for the absence of 'ψ'. In any case, it would not be *allowed* to count against '$\phi_i w \rightarrow \psi w$'. The 'cause' and the 'effect' are implicitly co-defined.

The entire procedure may sound, thus barely stated, most arbitrary. Such moves, however, are essential to intelligible explanatory systems. The *intelligibility* of a causal statement—the aspect of a causal statement that enable us to *understand* what we experience—is precisely the *formal license* to move mentally from the cause to the effect and vice versa.[71] A mode of intelligible necessity—or formally justified inference—is crucial to an intelligible explanation.

An interesting parallel to Aquinas' account of *per se* causal statements is found in the writings of Sellars. In a discussion of induction, he maintains that we may move from the generalization "In my experience, all ϕ's have been ψ," to the mediate position, "It is probable that all ϕ's are necessarily ψ," to a final decision that "all ϕ's *are* necessarily ψ": "We decide to adopt—and teach ourselves—the material move from 'x is ϕ' to 'x is ψ'. In other words, we accept 'All ϕ's are ψ' as an unconditionally assertable sentence of L, and reflect this decision by using the modal sentence 'ϕ's are *necessarily* ψ'. This constitutes, of course, *an enrichment of the conceptual meanings of 'ϕ' and 'ψ'.*"[72] Sellars feels no compunctions in calling such propositions "synthetic a priori." His definition of "analytic" is as follows:

> In the narrower sense, a proposition is analytic if it is either a truth of *logic* or *logically true*. By saying of a proposition that it is logically true, I mean, roughly . . . that when defined terms are replaced by their definientia, it becomes a substitution instance of a truth of logic. And a truth of logic may be adequately characterized for our present purposes as a proposition which occurs in the body of *Prin-*

[71] On causal statements as providing inferential license, see W. Sellars, "Counterfactuals, Dispositions, and the Causal Modalities," in *Minnesota Studies in the Philosophy of Science*, Vol. ii (University of Minnesota Press, Minneapolis, 1958).

[72] Sellars, *Science, Perception and Reality*, p. 357.

cipia Mathematica, or which would properly occur in a *ver-mehrte und verbesserte Auflage* of this already monumental work. If we now agree to extend the convenient phrase 'logically true' to cover truths of logic as well as propositions which are logically true in the sense just defined, we can say that an analytic proposition in the narrower sense is a proposition which is logically true.[73]

All propositions, then, that are not 'logically true'—in the sense defined—are "synthetic."

An a priori proposition may be briefly characterized as a proposition that is true *ex vi terminorum.* To qualify as *synthetic a priori* a proposition must be true *ex vi terminorum,* not by virtue of an *explicit* definition (which would lead to an analytic proposition), but by means of an *implicit* definition: "In rough-and-ready terms, a number of predicates without explicit definition are said to be implicitly defined if they appear in a set of logically synthetic general propositions which are specified as axioms or primitive sentences by the rules of the language to which they belong. To say that these propositions are axioms or primitive sentences is to say that they are specified to be *unconditionally assertable* by syntactical rules of the language."[74] By such a definition, the proposition "A straight line is the shortest distance between two points," is 'synthetic a priori' when actually affirmed *within* the Euclidean system (whose axioms are logically synthetic general propositions). On the other hand, the proposition, "In Euclidean geometry, a straight line is the shortest distance between two points," is analytic.[75] If a person possessed and used only the Euclidean conceptual system as a means (analogically interpreted) of informing his experience and describing reality, he would be using synthetic a priori statements in his existential judgments. Because any synthetic a priori statement of the form 'ϕ's are necessarily ψ's' is justified by the rules of a logically nonanalytic conceptual system (a system with axioms or primitive sentences which are synthetic), it is in theory possible that one might stop asserting such synthetic a priori statements—but *only if* one gives up

[73] *Ibid.,* p. 298.   [74] *Ibid.,* p. 303.   [75] *Ibid.*

the entire conceptual system in which they play the important role of unconditionally assertable 'truths of the system.' The speed of light in contemporary physics provides a good example of a "necessary" synthetic a priori truth. To give up that truth would be in effect to give up the whole of contemporary physics.

One of Sellars' more fecund synthetic a priori propositions is that every event definable in our conceptual scheme (the object language) must have a cause.[76] We may say that the *formal* relationship of causal entailment happens to be, in our conceptual system, a source of intelligibility, while the formally isolated 'brute fact' happens to be nonintelligible. A 'brute fact' does not allow the mind to move in any intelligible direction—to 'get anywhere' with the fact. To adopt a conceptual system is to be committed—for as long as one uses the system—to the a priori demands of the system. Since the formal exigencies of the system itself determine what can count as an 'event' or 'entity,' the intelligibility of such events must equally well be that which is demanded by the system. Intelligibility is *entirely* a formal or syntactical matter—a matter of a kind of necessity. The formal intelligibility of the system takes on existential import when the system is used to refer—when the judgment is made that reality is analogically represented by the syntactical moves of the system.

A completely intelligible causal statement is based, Aquinas holds, upon a mode of *propter quid* demonstration.[77] In a *propter quid* demonstration, the nature of an event—to be explained—is deduced from the formal definition of its cause by means of a *per se* judgment—by utilizing the inferential license issued within the explanatory system. To know *how* a cause explains its effect is to know *that* the mind is justified by the syntactical rules of the language in moving from the formal definition or *ratio* of the cause to that of the effect. The *ratio* of the cause is 'placed in' the *ratio* of the effect by means

---

[76] W. Sellars, "Counterfactuals . . . ," *Minn. Studies.*, pp. 305f.

[77] This follows from a series of propositions supported *passim* in the *Commentary on the Posterior Analytics*: 1. Science is of necessary things, which alone are intelligible. 2. Only those things that are known *per se* are intelligible and necessary. 3. Only *propter quid* demonstrations terminate in *per se* knowledge.

of implicit definition. Both the cause and the effect, therefore, must be intelligibly definable within the system.

A *quia* demonstration, on the other hand, is not based on a *per se* intelligible causal relation. It begins with an event that has *not* been integrated into a *per se* causal statement and *postulates* a cause of such a nature that, if it were known, the nature of the effect *could* be deduced from it by means of a *per se* judgment. Such a demonstration is not, for Aquinas, a *formal* but a *material* move.[78] It postulates but does not *make* a formally justified inferential move. In a *quia* demonstration, therefore, the formal *ratio* of the cause is not known; it is not known precisely what the cause is like. It is nevertheless possible to state the sorts of things that must be true of the cause if it is to function as an *intelligible* explanation of the known effect. A proper cause is postulated, the *ratio* of which *could* in theory be formally defined within the language in terms of which the effect itself and the rules of intelligibility are defined. It follows that a normal *quia* demonstration could in theory give rise to a *propter quid* demonstration. It is assumed that when the cause is discovered its *ratio* can be placed in the *ratio* of the effect by means of implicit definition within the system.

The only exception to that general rule concerning *quia* demonstrations is a *quia* demonstration of God. It is in theory *impossible* that we might ever have in our language a *propter quid* (or intelligible) demonstration of God "through his effects."[79] For that reason Aquinas denies that God can be *known* by means of causal arguments:

Nor [can divine things be known] by way of causality, since those things which are found to be the effects of those substances in inferior beings are not effects adequate to the power of the causes, so that it might be possible to succeed in knowing what the causes are.

[Neque etiam per viam causalitatis; quia illa quae ab illis substantiis inveniuntur effecta in inferioribus, non sunt effectus adaequantes eorum virtutes, ut sic perveniri possit ad sciendum quod quid est de causa.][80]

[78] *Post. Anal.*, I, 23ff.   [79] *S. T.*, I, 2, 2.   [80] *De Trin.*, VI, 3.

God is incommensurable with those objects the *ratio* of which can be expressed in human conceptual terms. Whatever unexplained events might be defined in terms of human language, it is in theory impossible that God could function in the *same* language as their intelligible explanation. The *ratio* of God cannot be co-defined by implicit definition with the *ratio* of events or entities definable in our language. As we shall see below, that means, by implication, that the nature of the problem that the postulated agency of God is meant to answer could not itself be expressed in terms of the intelligible forms of our conceptual system. There is no 'effect' whose *ratio* precisely *as* an 'effect of God' could be intelligibly expressed in our language. That is to repeat the claim that we do not know the true natures of things—the natures of things as intended and created by God. For the moment, however, we may simply say that for Aquinas any argument which terminates in the judgment "God exists," and which presupposes or purports to give an intelligible account of "God" in our language, or which attempts to make the relationship between God and the world intelligible—subject to expression in a *per se* intelligible causal judgment—is logically impossible, since the concept 'God' can never intelligibly occur within our conceptual system. We can never know of God what he is or how he exists.

In addition to ruling out *ab initio* any scientific or intelligible proof of God by way of causality, Aquinas also rules out *ab initio* any attempt to arrive at the proposition "God exists" on the basis of *per se nota* judgments.[81] Since for Aquinas *all* intelligible argumentation begins with *per se nota* judgments and arrives at intelligible conclusions by means of *per se* implications,[82] there can be in theory no intelligible argument which produces knowledge of that which is asserted by the existential judgment "God exists."[83] All such arguments reduce God to an intelligible form of the system. For us to know

---

[81] S. T., 1, 2, 1. [82] *Post. Anal.*, 1, 35.

[83] This is not to deny that God could *in abstracto* be demonstrated on the basis of human reason alone. That is *de fide*. It is merely to deny that he can be intelligibly demonstrated in terms of the conceptual system actually in use among men.

what God is in terms of the analogically significant conceptual system by means of which we refer to reality would be for God to be a *kind* of thing, a being essentially conditioned by his relationship to contingent beings, and, indeed, a contingent being in his own right. Anything with a *ratio* definable in terms of the *rationes* of things in the world is logically part of the genus of created or contingent things:

> Created immaterial substances are not in any common natural genus with material substances, since there is not in them the same *ratio* of potency and matter; they are, however, in the same logical genus, since immaterial substances are in the predicament of Substance, whose quiddity is not their existence. But God is not like material things, either according to natural genus or according to logical genus, for God is not in *any* general class. . . . Thus, through the similitudes of material things something affirmative may be known of angels according to a common *ratio*, even if not by virtue of a specific *ratio*: but in no way is that possible with God (*de Deo non nullo*).[84]

What God is can never be defined or rendered intelligible in any affirmative judgment utilizing intelligible *rationes* definable by the rules of our syntactically significant and referentially interpreted conceptual system. We naturally know *only* the formal reality of *material* things.[85]

How that judgment affects various attempts to prove the existence of God on the basis of causal judgments will be discussed in the next chapter. For the rest of this chapter we shall consider the way in which the epistemology of Aquinas rules out any version of the ontological argument—any claim, that is, to know the truth of the proposition "God exists" on the basis of a *per se nota* judgment of truth. We shall turn first to the two versions of the ontological proof as they appear in the *Proslogium* of Anselm.[86]

[84] *S. T.*, I, 88, 2, ad 4.
[85] *S. T.*, I, 84, 7.
[86] What follows is not a detailed and reliable critique of Anselm's own intention in writing the *Proslogium*, but only of the traditional interpretation of that work, which Aquinas certainly shared.

The first version of the ontological argument may be summarized as follows:

A. God is a being than which nothing greater can be conceived.[87]

B. "A being than which nothing greater can be conceived" can be understood.[88]

C. A being than which nothing greater can be conceived exists in the understanding of one who understands "A being than which nothing greater can be conceived."[89]

D. That which exists in the understanding can be understood to exist also in reality.[90]

E. A being which exists in reality as well as in the understanding is greater than a being which exists only in the understanding.[91]

F. That being which exists in my understanding when I understand "a being than which nothing greater can be conceived" must be understood to exist also in reality, since, if it were understood to exist only in my understanding, I could conceive of something greater, namely, *the same thing* as existing also in reality.[92]

The paradoxical nature of the argument is evident in the conclusion. That which is understood to exist in reality must (if Anselm's argument is to succeed) be the *same thing* as that

[87] Anselm, *Proslogium,* II: "Thou art a being than which nothing greater can be conceived."

[88] *Ibid.*: "But at any rate this very fool, when he hears of this being of which I speak—a being than which nothing greater can be conceived—understands what he hears. . . ."

[89] *Ibid.*: ". . . and what he understands is in his understanding, although he does not understand *it* to exist."

[90] *Ibid.*: "It is one thing for an object to be in the understanding, and another to understand that the object exists."

[91] *Ibid.*: "Suppose *it* exists in the understanding alone: then *it* can be conceived to exist in reality: which is greater."

[92] *Ibid.*: "Therefore, if that than which nothing greater can be conceived exists in the understanding alone, the very being than which nothing greater can be conceived is one than which a greater can be conceived."

which is understood to exist in the understanding. Thus, the *same thing* is understood to have two modes of being ('real' and 'intentional'), and to be a "greater being" when it exists in the real mode than when it (the same thing) exists in the intentional mode alone. The notion that a single thing can be greater than itself (according to its mode of being) is an odd notion deriving from an epistemological blunder expressed in proposition C. of the argument. It is a category mistake to speak as though the existence in the understanding of a concept implies the existence in the understanding of the *being* signified by the concept. Anselm's Platonic reading of 'intentional being' generates a set of entities which are the objects or contents of concepts.[93] The intentional object or content is taken to be 'that which exists' in the real order when that of which we conceive really exists. It is true that in ordinary discourse we might say that unicorns *exist* only in the mind: and, if there really were unicorns, we might say that unicorns exist both in the mind and in reality. But it is philosophically disastrous to assume that 'the same beings' exist in the mind and in reality. What exists in the mind is *not* unicorn, but 'unicorn' (the concept or notion *of* unicorns) or 'unicorneity.'

Once we grant that understanding expressions of the form "a being such that . . ." means that such a being exists in the understanding we are open to the most extraordinary paradoxes. Does it follow, for example, that understanding "the only cat in the world" means that the only cat in the world exists in the understanding? Surely understanding "the only cat in the world" means only that 'the only cat in the world' exists in the understanding. The concept 'the only cat in the world' is not the concept of a *cat*, but the concept of what it would be like for there to be only one cat in the world. Would it, incidentally, be 'greater' if 'the only cat in the world' existed not only in the understanding but also in reality? What would it *mean* to say, " 'The only cat in the world' exists not only in the understanding but also in the real order"? Unless revised in a crucial way, it could only mean that a *concept* exists in the *ordo rerum* as well as in the intellect. It could be revised

---

[93] On this concept, see, W. Sellars, *Science, Perception and Reality*, Chap. 2.

to mean that the conditions really exist in which "There is only one cat in the world" is true. Some of us would be happier if there *were* only one cat in the world, but does it follow that such a cat would be a "greater" cat? And a greater cat than what? Certainly not "greater than the cat which is in the intellect when 'the only cat in the world' is in the intellect and it is not true that there is only one cat in the world." For 'the only cat in the world' to exist in the intellect is not for a *cat* to exist in the intellect, but at most for 'a cat' to exist in the intellect. To say that a cat is a greater cat than 'a cat' is nonsense. "Better to be a live dog than a dead lion" perhaps. But, "To be a dog is to be a greater dog than to be a 'dog,'" makes no sense.

The entanglements which ensue when it is assumed that having a concept means having an object in (the) mind may be illustrated in the following parable:

A man is led into a large room with two doors in the opposite wall. He is told that behind each door there is a room which contains a desk. He is asked to open each door in turn, examine the two desks, form a 'concept' of each and report on which he takes to be the 'greater desk.' Upon opening the first door, he finds a dark brown walnut desk, five feet long and three feet wide. He notes that it is impressive in appearance and convenient in dimension. Upon opening the second door he finds, not a desk, but a man on a chair, with a furrowed brow and a contorted posture. Our hero returns and reports that he has found only one desk—that there *is* no desk in Room Two. He is informed, however, that there is indeed a desk in Room Two, since the man in the chair is *thinking* of a desk—there is a desk in his understanding. The task is to evaluate the real desk and the intentional desk, and decide which is the greater desk. Now, of course, the furrowed brow and contorted posture of the man in the chair are understandable, for he is trying to lean on the desk in his mind and write a letter. The hero is tempted to think that he has solved the problem. Of course the desk in Room One is the greater desk: one can sit at it, rest on it, write on it, and look authoritative behind it. As for the desk in the mind, one looks a fool if he tries to do *anything* with it. Just as our hero is about to blurt out his decision, however, a fiendish suspicion crosses his mind. He asks the man in the chair, "What is the desk *like* of which you are thinking?" Of course the answer is, "Why, it's a dark brown walnut desk, five feet long and three feet wide. It is impressive in appearance and convenient in dimension." Is it any longer clear which is the greater desk? It remains true, of course, that the desk in Room Two cannot be leaned on—or does it? Our hero asks, "Pardon me, but is it possible to lean on the desk of which you are thinking?" "Why yes," replies furrowed-brow, "as a matter of fact the desk of which I am thinking is in the next room; you can go lean on it if you wish." Now it is logically impossible to answer the initial question, "Which of the two is the greater desk?" since there is only one desk. The desk which is in Room Two (intentional mode) is also in Room One (real mode).

It might be thought that the parable plays directly into the hands of Anselm: "Ah, of course, in your story there is but *one* desk, which exists both in the understanding and in reality. It is therefore a greater desk than one which exists in the understanding alone." But let us continue the parable:

Our hero is slightly exercised at being made a fool—at being made to attempt the impossible. He therefore sneaks quietly back into Room One, breaks up the desk, makes a bonfire and burns the pieces to ashes. With a diabolical smile, he walks back to Room Two and asks the man in the chair (who is still contorted), "Has anything at all changed in this room?" "No." "You still thinking of that desk?" "Yep." "It hasn't changed at all? It's still as great as ever?" "Oh, yes indeed." "You mean that the very same desk that existed in your mind before still exists in your mind and is neither greater nor lesser?" "That's right!" It is evident that the 'desk in Room Two' still exists as it did before and is neither greater nor lesser. But our former conclusion was that there was only *one* desk, and that 'it' existed in both rooms. The desk in the mind *was* the desk in Room One, but *that* desk no

longer exists—there is no 'desk in Room One.' The man is
no longer thinking of a desk that exists—he is thinking of a
desk that does *not* exist but which he *thinks* exists. Oddly
enough, it is one and the same thing to think of a desk that
exists and to think of a desk as existing. In neither case does
one have the concept of a greater desk. Whether or not the
desk exists is contingently related to its 'intentional being.'
In the realm of existence, thinking can never make it so.

To understand "that than which nothing greater can be conceived" is to have the concept 'that than which nothing greater
can be conceived.' To understand that-than-which-nothing-
greater-can-be-conceived to have 'intentional existence' *only*,
is to understand that that-than-which-nothing-greater-can-be-
conceived does not in fact exist. To understand (or to think)
that that-than-which-nothing-greater-can-be-conceived exists
in the real order is not to conceive something greater than that
which one conceives if he does *not* understand (or think) that
that-than-which-nothing-greater-can-be-conceived exists in the
real order. In each case the *concept* is the same: 'that than
which nothing greater can be conceived.' Whether we are
thinking of something that really exists or are thinking of
something that really does not exist, we are conceiving 'the
same thing.' Whether we think of something as existing or as
not existing, we entertain the same concept. It may be "greater"
to be God than to be 'God,' but to be 'God' is to be 'God'
whether or not God exists.

It is for that reason that Aquinas rejects the first version of
the ontological argument. Whether or not one understands
God to exist in reality, the content of 'God' ('that than which
nothing greater can be conceived') remains the same; if one
thinks that God exists, the content of 'God' is the same whether
or not he really exists; if one thinks of God *as* existing, the
content of 'God' is the same whether or not one *believes* that
God *really* exists. In no case does one have a concept of a
"greater being." Thus, Aquinas can reject the argument with
a straightforward observation:

Nor can it be argued that [that which is signified by "that
than which no greater can be conceived"] exists in reality,

unless it is granted that there is in reality something than which no greater can be conceived: which is not granted by those who deny that God exists.

[Nec potest argui quod sit in re, nisi quod sit in re aliquid quo maius cogitari non potest: quod non est datum a ponentibus Deum non esse.][94]

Nonetheless, it might be thought that Aquinas grants to Anselm some points that we have rejected in theory. It would appear, for example, that Aquinas has a notion of 'intentional inexistence' (the notion that *things* may have intentional existence in the mind). He, like Anselm, can raise the question of whether something which has 'intentional being' in the intellect might *also* have 'real being' in the *ordo rerum*. His argument against the first version of the ontological argument seems, in fact, to grant that point:

Even if someone understands this name 'God' to signify what was said—namely, 'that than which nothing greater can be conceived,' it does not follow that he understands that which is signified by the name to exist in reality, but *only in the apprehension of the intellect.*

[Dato etiam quod quilibet intelligat hoc nomine *Deus* significari hoc quod dicitur, scilicet illud quo maius cogitari non potest, non tamen propter hoc sequitur quod intelligat id quod significatur per nomen, esse in rerum natura, sed in apprehensione intellectus tantum.][95]

This could be construed as meaning that one who understands "that than which nothing greater can be conceived" *apprehends a being* or an object than which nothing greater can be conceived. That would imply that one apprehends or knows something distinct from the act of conceiving—something which must then exist. That existent object might be the 'content' of the concept or that to which the concept is related as subject to object. In either case, Anselm's argument could once again get off the ground.

[94] S. T., i, 2, 1, ad 2.
[95] *Ibid.*

While it is true, however, that Aquinas uses the "ordinary language" of "things existing in the mind" and of "nonexistent things apprehended by the mind," he rejects the epistemological theory upon which such language seems to be based. Anselm's reading of 'intentional being' is dependent upon a Platonic epistemology rejected by Aquinas. For 'something' to have intentional existence in the mind is not—in Aquinas' thought—for there to be an *entity* which is related to the mind as object or content. For 'something' to have intentional existence in the mind is for the mind to have a *concept*. That concept is defined, not by a *relationship* to an object or content, but by its own intrinsic structure or *ratio*. Aquinas does not object to the "ordinary language" which underlies the Platonic mistake: he will speak of 'something having intentional existence in the mind' and of 'something having real existence in the *ordo rerum*.' He would not rule out of court the common questions, "Does x really exist or does it exist only in the mind?" He is quite clear, however, that if x really does exist, what exists is not the *concept* in another mode of being.

The difference between Aquinas and Anselm may be understood in terms of the way in which a concept has 'significance' —or 'signifies something.' For Anselm, as for the Augustinian and Platonic traditions—a concept has significance because it *signifies an entity*. Some concepts signify (refer to or are related to) 'logical entities' which could not in theory have 'real existence.' Other concepts signify (refer to or are related to) 'possible entities' which can 'exist' in either an 'intentional' or a 'real' mode. In the latter case, if that which is signified by the concept exists *in re*, it is assumed to be the same entity or being that exists in the intellect and in the *ordo rerum*. For Aquinas, on the other hand, a concept has significance because it has a *ratio* or intelligible structure (we would say "a syntactical role") in terms of which its semantical status (or meaning) can be understood.

The notion that a significant concept—especially a concept like 'unicorn,' which could in theory be used to refer to real objects—is meaningful because of its syntactical status within a conceptual system, and not because of its relation to a being or object, might be disconcerting at first hearing. It ought *not* to be disconcerting, however, when it is pointed out that its status as a 'possible entity' (as a concept which could in theory be used to refer) is a function of the syntactical relation between the elements of its *ratio* ('animal,' 'four-footed,' 'single-horned,' et cetera) and the *rationes* of other concepts which we possess, which have syntactical meaning within the same system, and which we are *already* able to use to refer to real objects. Thus, while the concept 'unicorn' has significance because of its syntactical relationship to other concepts, its referential status is determined by its syntactical relationship to concepts with semantical content derived in part from the contingent fact that they may be used to refer to real objects in the *ordo rerum*. Thus, the *semantical* status of 'unicorn' is, as Aquinas insists, a function ultimately of its syntactical relationship to language about sense experience—the basis upon which concepts are used to refer. Its significance as the concept 'unicorn,' however, is not a function of any relationship to an object which *is* that which 'unicorn' *expresses*—whether that object be an 'intentional unicorn' or 'subsistent unicorneity.' It remains, of course, true that part of the syntactical significance of 'unicorn' is that it *might* (contingently) be used to refer to a real object.

A concept which *is* used to make references to real objects is such that it may (according to Aquinas) be said to render 'intentionally present to the mind' the very physical objects to which it refers. When one uses a meaningful concept in order to make a reference to a thing in the *ordo rerum*, Aquinas is willing to say that that thing is 'intentionally' in the mind. When, however, I refer to "that chair over there"—using referentially the concept 'chair'—it is the *particular* chair that has 'intentional existence' in my mind. It is clear that this is a distinct usage of 'intentional existence' from that which enables Aquinas to say (in "ordinary language") that unicorns have existence 'only in the mind.' When one merely *has* the concept 'chair' and is not using it to refer to a particular chair, then it may be said that 'chair' or 'chairness' has intentional existence in the mind. It is because 'chair' has significance apart from its actual use to refer to *a* chair that it is able to *signify* a chair when used referentially—a *referent* can be 'intentionally in the mind' because a *concept* is already 'intentionally in the mind.' The Anselmian tradition confuses the two uses of "signify" and "intentional existence": (1) 'Chair' *signifies* that which is expressed in the *ratio* of 'chairness' and that which is thus expressed may be said to have 'intentional existence' in the mind. (2) 'Chair' may be used in conjunction with sense experience to *signify* or refer to a particular chair and the chair thus signified may be said to have 'intentional existence' in the mind. Because the *second* use of 'intentional existence' presupposes *reference to* an object distinct from the act of conceiving, Anselm assumes that the first usage must also presuppose a distinct object—an 'intentional being.' Such an epistemology reduces all significance to semantical or referential content whereas semantical or referential content presupposes syntactical significance. Aquinas' succinct rejection of the argument is therefore justified.

The second version of the ontological argument may be summarized as follows:

A. God is a being than which nothing greater can be conceived.

B. A being whose nonexistence can be conceived is not so great as a being whose nonexistence cannot be conceived.

C. God is, therefore, a being whose nonexistence cannot be conceived.

D. To say of a being whose nonexistence cannot be conceived that it does not exist is a self-contradiction.

E. "God does not exist" is therefore a self-contradiction.

F. God therefore exists and exists necessarily.

More than one interpretation of the second version of the ontological argument is possible; on any interpretation it is more profound than the first version. It does not, however, succeed.

The crucial step, of course, is the second one. The crucial question is whether or not it makes sense to refer to a being whose nonexistence cannot be conceived. Most contemporary philosophers would hold that the very notion of a being whose nonexistence cannot be conceived is a contradiction in terms.[96] The point can be made in several ways. (1) While it may be impossible to conceive *of* 'nothing,' since any instance of 'conceiving of' is an instance of conceiving of *something*, it is nevertheless true that we *have* the concept 'nothing.' 'Nothing' is a significant concept. The notion that all significant concepts must be concepts *of* something is a form of the Platonic notion that all significant concepts derive their meaning from a relationship to an 'entity.' We have already argued against that notion. 'Nothing' is a significant concept, not because it has *something* (namely nothing) as its content or object, but rather because it plays a significant role in our conceptual system. The notion that a concept has meaning because of its relation to 'objects' of one sort or another is criticized by Sellars in a rather brilliant paragraph:

Sentences of the form ' "Rot" means red' have had no less a hypnotic and disastrous effect on empiricists engaged in formulating theories of concept formation, than on the most naive mental oculists. Such sentences, which appear to present meaning as a tete-à-tete relation between a word and a universal, have been misinterpreted as entailing what might be called a 'matrimonial' theory of the meaning of primitive or undefined descriptive predicates according to which the fact that these terms have meaning is constituted by the fact that they are associated with (married to) classes of objects. Yet that these sentences *entail* no such consequences becomes obvious once we reflect that it is just as legitimate and, indeed, true to say 'The German word "*und*" means *and*' as it is to say 'The German word "*rot*" means *red*'; where it is clear that 'und' gains its meaning not by a process of association with Conjunction or a class of conjoined objects, but rather by coming to be used with other symbols in accordance with familiar syntactical rules.[97]

[96] A splendid example is J. N. Findlay, "Can God's Existence be Disproved?" in *New Essays in Philosophical Theology* (eds. A. Flew and A. MacIntyre, The Macmillan Company, New York, 1955).

[97] *Science, Perception and Reality*, p. 314.

So also we may say, "The German word *'nichts'* means *nothing*" without assuming that it gains its meaning (its *conceptual* meaning) by a process of association with Nothingness or with nonexistent states of affairs! Since 'nothing' is a significant concept, it is logically possible to conceive of 'the nonexistence of everything.' That is not to conceive of (or imagine) a state of affairs in which nothing exists, but rather to know the significance of "Nothing exists." If we can conceive of the nonexistence of everything, if we know what it would mean to claim that it is conceivable that there might not have been anything, then it cannot be the case that there is something whose nonexistence cannot be conceived. Without knowing what God is or what he is like, I already know that I can conceive of his nonexistence, since I can conceive 'nothing.'

A second approach might be: (2) To conceive of the existence of anything whatever is by definition to conceive of something the nonexistence of which is possible and therefore conceivable. To say of something that it exists is precisely to convey information of a contingent nature about the 'way things happen to be.' It is not to predicate something of that which is said to exist (unless it is said *still* to exist) but to predicate something of the world. To say that x exists is to say that x is part of the contents of the world or 'reality.' Anything that we can conceive of as existing is such that we could conceive of a state of reality in which that of which we conceived of as existing would *not* exist. Such is the logic of the word "exists" in our conceptual system. While the concept 'being' may be most radically a dispositional sense of 'reality,' we can only significantly *use* the word "exists" in conjunction with elements of our conceptual system which play such a syntactical role that their assertion ('___') is possible. Of any such element, it is logically possible that it *not* be asserted. That the concept 'being' is radically analogical—that it may have other modes of signification—does not mean that *we* can use it according to some other mode of signification in which it would not theoretically be syntactically restricted to such entities as those defined in terms of our conceptual system. Step (2) of Anselm's ontological argument assumes that '*contingent* existence' is for us a *specific* use of a more *general* term 'existence,' so that it is clear what 'noncontingent existence' means. 'Existence,' how-ever, is *not* a generic term: in our language it has *only* the meaning 'contingent existence.' To say of anything that it 'exists' in such a manner that its nonexistence could not in theory be conceived is to use the word "exists" in such a way that it has and could have no significance *within* the concep-tual system we in fact use.

In his defense of the second version of the ontological argu-ment, Norman Malcolm attempts to give meaning to the ex-pression "whose nonexistence cannot be conceived" in terms of *unlimited* existence.[98] It is clear that we have a concept of limited existence—we can conceive of things whose existence *depends upon* or *results from* other things or states of affairs. Concerning such things we may say that they *happen* to exist, or that they might not have existed. Malcolm thinks that a degree of 'existential independence' is clearly a matter of superiority. Thus, a set of dishes which are fragile and thus dependent upon gentle handling "are *inferior* to those of an-other set like them in all respects except that they are *not* fragile."[99] To say of God that he is (by definition) something than which nothing greater can be conceived is to say that he cannot be lacking in any degree of superiority—he must there-fore have the supreme degree of 'existential independence.' *Nothing* could be responsible for his existence and *nothing* could keep him from existing. God is an "absolutely unlimited being": "But it would be contrary to the concept of God as an unlimited being to suppose that anything other than God Him-self could prevent Him from existing, and it would be self-contradictory to suppose that He Himself could do it."[100] Since nothing could bring God into existence or keep him from existing, his existence is either impossible or necessary: "It can be the former only if the concept of such a being is self-contra-dictory or in some way logically absurd. Assuming that this is not so, it follows that He necessarily exists."[101] It would be a logical contradiction to assert that a being which necessarily exists does not exist. Thus any attempt to deny the existence

[98] N. Malcolm, "Anselm's Ontological Arguments," in *The Existence of God* (ed. J. Hick, The Macmillan Company, New York, 1964).
[99] *Ibid.*, p. 54.   [100] *Ibid.*   [101] *Ibid.*, p. 56.

of God or to conceive of his nonexistence is a logical contradiction.

Malcolm will not grant, as Kant asserted, that the ontological argument proves only that *if* God exists he exists necessarily.[102] Malcolm points out that 'if' language is incompatible
with the language of necessity. "If God exists" sounds in order
until we realize that "God" is to be defined as "that which
necessarily exists." By substitution we can then derive "If that
which necessarily exists exists" as a correct interpretation of
"If God exists." Since "If x exists" implies that x might *not*
exist, the expression, "If that which necessarily exists exists" is
a logical contradiction in terms.[103] I shall argue, however, that
the proposition "God is to be defined as that which necessarily
exists" is itself a contradiction in terms.[104]

The clue to Malcolm's mistake is the very fact that he sub-
stitutes the definiens of "God" for "God" in the expression "If
God exists." When a proposition is such that, "when defined
terms are replaced by their definientia, it becomes a substitution instance of a truth of logic," that proposition is logically
true or analytic. Any definition which is logically or analytically true is an instance of *explicit* definition. Thus, "A bachelor is an unmarried male" is analytically true if viewed as an
explicit definition. By replacing "bachelor" with its definiens,
we derive "An unmarried male is an unmarried male"—a substitution instance of a truth of logic. The only difficulty is that
the very logic of *explicit* definition is such it has no existential
import. In order to *give* it existential import, we must interpret
it in terms of contingent existence. Thus, to say that 'x means
(by explicit definition) y' is to *mean* "If anything is an x it is
also a y." To say " 'Bachelor' means 'unmarried male,' " or "All
bachelors are unmarried males," is to mean "If anyone is a
bachelor, he is an unmarried male." Thus, in order to *define*
"God" as "a being whose nonexistence cannot be conceived,"
one *must* admit the licit use of the proposition, "*If* anything

[102] *Ibid.*, pp. 57f.   [103] *Ibid.*, p. 63.

[104] It is a contradiction, that is, if asserted as a truth of *our* language.
It may be possible to assert that a statement with an analogous form
could intelligibly occur in *another* language based on another conceptual
system.

is God, it is a being whose nonexistence cannot be conceived." This is, as Malcolm maintains, a self-contradiction. It follows that it is a self-contradiction explicitly to define "God" as "a being whose nonexistence cannot be conceived."

In order to avoid that difficulty, God would have to be defined as existent by means of an *implicit* definition. An implicit definition states that a proposition is unconditionally assertable by the rules of the language. Unfortunately, it is also the case that such a proposition must itself be contingent. Thus, "God necessarily exists" would not seem to be a candidate for such status. We might say, however, that "necessarily" means only that "God exists" is unconditionally assertable within the language in which it occurs. "God exists" would then be a truth of the system—it would have to be asserted by anyone adopting the language system in which it occurs. By what means, however, might we argue that such a language *ought* to be adopted? Surely, any attempt to do so would be an instance of a cosmological proof—it certainly would not be an instance of the *ontological* proof.

Malcolm might reply that he is *not* explicitly defining "God" as "a being whose nonexistence cannot be conceived," but rather arguing that such a definition follows from the use of "God" to mean "that than which nothing greater can be conceived." One cannot use the term to mean "that than which nothing greater can be conceived" and refuse to predicate of "God" any possible perfection or quality that would indicate superiority over other sorts of things. Since he has shown that "necessary existence" is a perfection or sign of superiority, it must be predicated of God. To that move, we may reply that the definition " 'God' means 'that than which nothing greater can be conceived' " itself implies "*If* anything is God, it is that than which nothing greater can be conceived." That which Malcolm must grant as a licit inference from step one of the argument can hardly be the contradictory of any other licit inference from the same premise.

We may, however, ignore that for the moment. There is still some question as to whether or not Malcolm has succeeded in defining what he means by "necessary existence." His procedure seems to be to rely upon the meaningfulness of a straightforward and common understanding of what it means to say of anything contingent that it exists, in order to suggest that by mere negation we can define another sense of 'existence.' Because we all understand what it means to say that something has '*limited* existence,' Malcolm simply assumes that we also understand what it would mean to say that something has '*un*limited existence.' Once again, this seems to imply that 'existence' is a generic concept of which 'limited existence' is a specification. Surely, however, 'limited existence' is merely a redundant expression for 'existence.'

Malcolm might reply that he is *not* relying upon a generic sense of "existence," but is defining "unlimited existence" in quite meaningful terms. His argument might run as follows:

1. We may define "limited existence" as: The kind of existence such that anything which has it could be conceived as *not* existing.

2. Since every element in that definition is meaningful, we may define "unlimited existence" by means of a negation of part of the definition of "limited existence": The kind of existence such that anything which has it could *not* be conceived as *not* existing.

Unfortunately, those definitions are both incomplete. A complete version of the first definition would have to read, "There is a sense of 'existence' such that *if* anything thus exists it could be conceived as not existing." By parity, then, the second would have to read, "There is a sense of 'existence' such that *if* anything thus exists it could *not* be conceived as not existing." If Malcolm's argument were in order, that is all that it would prove. Malcolm himself admits, however, that the second proposition is self-contradictory. A self-contradiction cannot be validly inferred from any premises which are logically in order. The ontological argument is, therefore, out of order.

4. *Conclusions.* Aquinas' rejection of the Anselmian version of the ontological argument is not an isolated *argumentum ad hoc* in his writings. The article in which his rejection appears is entitled "Whether the existence of God is *per se nota*." As we have seen, *per se nota* is opposed to *per aliud nota*, and translates not simply as "logically self-evident," but also and

more radically as "known through itself." The existence of God could be said to be *per se nota* if (1) it were directly intuited or known on the basis of experience informed by the intelligible rules of our conceptual system; (2) it could be inferred by means of *per se* judgments from *per se nota* truths, whether based upon the contents of experience or upon the formal structure of the conceptual system itself;[105] or (3) it were known by an innate and significant idea or intelligible form of our intentional being.

In a sense all of the instances of *per se nota* truth may be summarized as "those truths which are known purely on the basis of the application of the norms of our conceptual system to the contents of experience or to intelligible truths of our language." To have such a direct sensible or intellectual intuition of the very nature of God is declared by Aquinas to be a logical impossibility. The intelligible forms of our conceptual system are able to render intelligible only the formal structures of the material objects of sense experience and to render partially intelligible that which created immaterial forms or entities have in common with the material objects of sense experience. God is in neither class. God does not follow by *per se* argumentation from any concept, entity, or proposition intelligibly definable in terms of our conceptual system. That judgment operates to the exclusion of the Augustinian and Bonaventurian forms of the ontological argument, as well as of certain misleading forms of the cosmological argument—such as the five ways quoted by Aquinas.

---

[105] It must be recalled that certain existential judgments are, for Aquinas, *per se nota*. When the 'cause' of an event referred to in a *per se nota* existential judgment is inferred by means of *per se* causal statements, that 'cause' is itself *per se nota*. Thus, an intelligible argument for the existence of God based on causal inferences justified by the syntax of our conceptual system is ruled out by the judgment that the existence of God is not *per se nota*.

CHAPTER THREE

THE QUINQUE VIAE AND SCIENTIA DIVINA

INTRODUCTION **M**OST analyses of the natural theology reflected in the *Summa Theologiae* depend rather heavily upon the form and vocabulary of the "five ways"—the brief 'demonstrations' of the existence of God found in Question Two of the *Pars Prima*. It is assumed without question that Aquinas is committed to each of the 'ways' as expressive of his own philosophical understanding of the nature of God. It is ironic—and tragic—that of a work so extensive as the *Summa*, a single page has so often been allowed to dictate the primary categories in terms of which to understand the whole. The proofs, on the contrary, are tangential to Aquinas' doctrine, and even dangerous. Four at least of the proofs purport to argue on the basis of a clear and indisputable empirical premise.[1] From such premises, the existence of God seems to emerge—by means of *per se* argumentation—as an intelligible answer to a conceptually clear question. For that reason, Aquinas' 'arguments' are often labeled "cosmological," a term that suggests that 'God' is needed in order to complete our picture—of even a *scientific* picture—of the 'cosmos.' The very term 'cosmos' is sufficient to set some theological teeth on edge: it seemingly suggests that there is an objectively given order *within which* God fulfills a rationally definable function. Ronald Hepburn, in his excellent critique of twentieth-century theology, *Christianity and Paradox*, not only rejects the logic of the cosmological arguments for the existence of a first cause, but he goes on to question what they would in fact prove if valid: "The God at whom we would arrive by tracing back the causal regress would be a God far too closely tied to his creation to satisfy Christian demands for his 'otherness' or transcendence. Whatever inaugurated the causal sequence would be part and parcel of the natural world in which it is causally

[1] The fourth way *may* be an exception.

QUINQUE VIAE AND SCIENTIA DIVINA

operative."[2] I believe that Hepburn is in essence correct: most formulations and interpretations of Aquinas' intent in quoting the five ways have by implication built God into a conceptual box from which no imaginative and mystical protestations of his paradoxical transcendence can extricate him. One of the theses of this chapter will be, however, that Aquinas intended to do the very opposite—he intended to posit in existence an unknown entity whose very relationship to the world is equally unknown. Before presenting that thesis, I shall argue at some length that the proofs as they stand in the *Summa Theologiae* are logically incompatible with Aquinas' own teaching on the nature of God and our 'cognitions' of him—that Aquinas' intention in quoting the proofs can be understood only in terms of a radical re-reading in the light of the immediately succeeding questions in which the intelligibility of God is defined in negative terms.

FALSE STARTS AND CORRECTIONS

The major problem confronting anyone who wishes to view the 'five ways' as *Aquinas*' arguments for the existence of God is their incompatibility with his own thought and vocabulary on the nature of God.

1. The first way, as it stands, is difficult to interpret. On no *interpretation* (as opposed to a total reconstruction) can it be viewed as a valid demonstration of God's existence in Aquinas' own terms. The most obvious interpretation (the one most often criticized by contemporary philosophers) would seem to imply that *motion* in the present cannot be explained by reference to an infinite regress of movers in the past, simply because such a regress is in theory impossible. Whatever kind of motion the first way may be discussing, it is not true that Aquinas denies the *possibility* of an infinite series of moved and moving events in the past. In Question 46 of the *Pars Prima* of the *Summa Theologiae*, Aquinas denies that it is possible to prove that the world had a beginning in time (that motion in the world began to be). Neither by an examination

2 R. Hepburn, *Christianity and Paradox* (C. A. Watts and Co., London, 1958), p. 166.

of the natures of things existing here and now, nor by an explication of the 'causal' relationship between God and the world, can it be shown that the world is not infinite in past duration. That the world came into being (that it 'began to be moved') is an article of faith.

The usual countermove to such an observation is to claim that Aquinas is speaking in the first way of "essentially subordinated movers" and not of "accidentally subordinated movers." By the latter is meant a series of causes which precede their effects in time and 'happen' to be the cause of motion in the effect, although some other similar cause might very well have caused the identical motion. Such 'movers' might conceivably cause motion in another and themselves cease to exist before the motion that they caused is completed or dissipated. By "essentially subordinated movers" on the other hand is meant a series of subordinated efficient causes which operate co-temporaneously with their effects—their present and actual causal operation is essential to the present and actual motion to be explained. Thus, the infinite regress generated by the first way is an infinite regress *in the present* of currently operative subordinated causes of motion. The 'first mover' must *now* be 'pushing' the second mover, in order that it may *now* be 'pushing' the next mover, in order that the 'push' may be communicated finally to the *here and now* object whose motion initiated our regressive analysis. Aquinas' analogy of the staff which "moves only because it is put in motion by the hand"[3] seems to suggest the accuracy of the analysis.

One of the chief supporters of that view is Father Garrigou-Lagrange. His means of distinguishing between accidental and essential subordination has become classic: it is the distinction between the motion of billiard balls and that of a grandfather's clock.[4] There are, he would say, two kinds of causal explanations that we might give of local motion. The question, "Why is Billiard Ball A in motion?" is usually taken to be fully answered by reference to the *previous* motion of Bil-

[3] S. T., I, 2, 3.
[4] P. Garrigou-Lagrange, *God: His Existence and His Nature* (B. Herder Book Co., St. Louis, 1934), Vol. I, Chap. 3.

liard Ball *B*, which would in turn be fully explained by reference to the still previous motion of Billiard Ball *C*, and so on. Assuming hypothetically a lack of resistance, the whole thing could go on to infinity. If one were to accept such an explanatory model and then go on to say, "You have satisfactorily and completely explained the motion of billiard balls *A, B, C . . . N*, but you have not explained the motion of *all* of them put together," or, "I thought for a moment that you had explained the motion of Billiard Ball *A* by pointing to that of Billiard Ball *B*, but I see now that the motion of *B* cannot *really* explain that of *A*, since it must *itself* be explained by reference to the motion of *C*," (both moves are fairly common amongst popularizing Thomist apologists) he would rightly be cut off with an exasperated "Nonsense!" You cannot accept the model and refuse to accept its explanatory power. Suppose, however, we were to reject that model as irrelevant to the kind of motion in which we are interested—the most basic or problematic kind of motion. For our model of such 'basic' motion, we might choose the grandfather's clock. If we ask, "Why is Cog *A* in motion?" it is not necessary to refer to a *previous* motion in order to answer the question. The present motion of Cog *A* is explained by reference to the *present* motion of Cog *B*, which is in turn explained by the present motion of Cog *C*, and so on. In this case, however, it would indeed make sense to say, "I see what's moving Cog *A*, and what's moving Cog *B*, and so on, but that does not explain the motion of all of the cogs put together. Unless there is something rather like a spring in that system, *nothing* ought to move." I should be most exasperated if the person explaining the motion of the cogs were to wave aside the question "What is *now* making all of those cogs go round?" with a shrugging, "I don't know. Maybe nothing—maybe there's an infinity of cogs." Not even an infinity of cogs would 'go round' unless something were making them. Surely Aquinas is suggesting that when something *is being moved* it is being moved by another—that *being moved* is being passive before the moving power of another. Somewhere, then, there must be that which is *not* passive before the moving power of another, but which is active and responsible for the motion of the *whole chain* of moved objects *totum simul.* Not even an infinity of *passive* objects will move without some agent.

There are a number of problems in Garrigou-Lagrange's analysis of motion. In terms of common sense, it seems rather strange to look at the world as a purely passive series of moved-movers, exhibiting the dynamism of a 'first mover' but no dynamism of its own. The kind of motion which we *see* when we look at the world does not seem to be the kind of motion which depends at each instant on "being pushed"—the world appears to possess its own dynamism. The world is not, really, very much like a clock, any more than it is very much like a bunch of billiard balls. If we single out the ways in which the world can be viewed as something like a clock, the analogy loses much of its force. Many things in the world are right now being moved by other things. Some of them are rather like the cogs of a clock. At this moment, for example, it is likely that somewhere in the world a mother is pushing a baby carriage. Like a cog in a clock, the carriage is moving because it *is being moved.* If the mother stops pushing, the carriage will stop— but not right away. As in the billiard ball model, so also in this case, if we abstract from such decelerating forces as friction, then even if the mother should cease to exist, the poor baby would go on and on in aeternam. Garrigou-Lagrange's argument from the grandfather's clock derived its apparent force from its illicit use of a familiar analogy drawn from ordinary experience. Of course we know that a *grandfather's clock* will not 'go' without a spring. We know that a *finite* series of *passive* objects will not move without an extrinsic mover. The question is, however, whether or not *the world* is such a finite series of passive movers—are we *sure,* for example, that an *infinite* series of cogs would need a spring? In our common sense analysis of motion, the exclusive choice between the billiard ball model and the grandfather's clock model is not so clear as in Garrigou-Lagrange's private metaphysical world.

The real question, of course, is whether *Aquinas* lived in the same private world. The answer is that he did not. For Aquinas, the motion of the world cannot be understood in terms of pure passivity. The moving forces of the world possess *real* agency, although it is a *communicated* or *created*

QUINQUE VIAE AND SCIENTIA DIVINA

agency. Objects within the created world possess a dynamism that they have received and which has been communicated to them *in and through time.* The reception of the power to move cannot, therefore, be understood in terms of a nontemporal subordination in the present instant, but must be viewed as a temporal process of being moved in such a way as to be able to move. The point can be made through a discussion of Aquinas' mistaken view of how a projectile (such as a stone) is moved through the air.[5] Starting with the principle that when a thing *is being moved,* it is being moved at that precise instant by a proximate mover, the following question may be raised: When the stone has left the hand of the thrower and is moving through the air, what is then causing its motion? Aquinas, in this context, rejects the 'impetus theory,' which would postulate a communication *to the stone* of the power to move itself. On the other hand, he does not adopt the simplistic notion of a cog-like system of passively 'pushed' mobiles. He does not argue, that is, that the stone is being moved by the air around it, which is in turn being moved by the air around *it,* and so on to 'God.' He argues rather that:

> . . . the first mover, that is, the thrower, gives to the second mover, that is, air or water or any such body which can naturally move a thrown body, the power to move and to be moved. . . . [For] as soon as the first mover, that is, the thrower, ceases to move, the air *ceases to be moved,* but it is *still a mover.*

> [. . . primum movens, scilicet proiiciens, det secundo moventi, scilicet aeri vel aquae vel cuicumque tali corpori quod est natum movere corpus proiectum, ut possit movere et ut possit moveri . . . statim cum primum movens, idest proiiciens, cessaverit movere, et aer cessat moveri, sed adhuc movet.][6]

In an analysis of natural motion, each proximate mover is able to move its object because it has itself been moved *in the past* from a merely dispositional possession of the power to move (*potentia passiva*) to the actual possession of that power. Garrigou-Lagrange's analysis would evacuate the reality of sec-

[5] *In Phys.,* VIII, 22.   [6] *Ibid.*

ondary causality, the integrity and independence of which Aquinas never challenges. Many things in the world do in fact move under their own power—there are 'self-movers' or 'natural-movers' in the world. In order to be able to move naturally by means of an intrinsic dynamism, it is merely necessary for a thing to come into the actual possession of that dynamism. If a thing is 'at rest' it will remain 'at rest' until it is moved by another in such a way that its potentiality for possessing the power to move itself or to move by nature is actualized by the communication of agency. Once it has been so moved, however, it possesses the power to move another. Each subordinated mover is *first passive* and *then active*. It is the temporal nature of such a communication of agency that underlies Aquinas' agreement with Aristotle that:

> The efficient cause, which acts by motion, of necessity *precedes its effect in time.*

> [Causa efficiens, quae agit per motum, de necessitate praecedit tempore.][7]

Aquinas' model of motion (be it local motion or any other reduction of a thing from potency to act) is that of the billiard balls without the second law of thermodynamics. The clock model holds only while a particular mover is being moved from potency to act. The first member (the relative first mover) of a series need not be existing at the present time in order for the secondary movers to operate—they have already received the power to move and can exercise that power independently of that to which they were at one time essentially subordinated, or *per se* moved. The stone will continue to be moved even if the man who threw it dies instantaneously of a massive coronary. It would appear, then, that God's *present* actuality can never be proved by an appeal to the present possession of the power to move by things that have been moved in the past. The first way generates a temporal regress.

Garrigou-Lagrange attempts to escape that consequence by calling the argument "metaphysical" rather than "physical,"[8]

[7] S. T., i, 46, 2, ad 1.
[8] *God: His Existence and His Nature*, p. 268.

in spite of the fact that Aquinas quotes most often, in the expanded version of the proof in the *Summa contra Gentiles*, from the *Physics* of Aristotle. The problem, Garrigou-Lagrange insists, is not that the communication of agency from one object to another stands in need of a transcendental explanation, but that the present possession here and now by anything of its internal 'principle of motion' stands in need of such an explanation. Such a claim would seem to be meaningless. What is it that the first way purports to explain? Surely, it is the fact that "some things are being moved." The question is, "What is causing the motion of this empirically observable entity?" Just as clearly, the first way begins by allowing as a possible reply, "The motion of some *other* empirically observable entity." If the observable motion of B is legitimately cited as the cause of the motion of A, then the motion of A has been *explained*, and our only problem is the motion of B. Such would seem to be the logic of the first way. Not, however, for Garrigou-Lagrange. He admits that the motion of B explains the *fact* that A is moving; he denies, however, that it explains the *motion* of A. He maintains that the motion of B (or of *any* mover other than God) "which was itself set in motion by something else, truly accounts for the *presence* of this movement, but it does not explain *the movement in itself*."[9] The "presence of movement" in an object is different from the "movement in itself" of that object! The "movement in itself" of A is something over and above the fact that A is moving! I can explain the fact that A is moving without explaining the "movement in itself" of A. This is unmitigated metaphysical nonsense of the most obfuscating variety. One thing, however, is clear: in the new 'metaphysical' sense of "movement," the "movement of A" is no longer an empirically observable fact which, in the language of the first way, "is certain and evident to our senses."

Garrigou-Lagrange might reply that "the movement in itself" of any object is not only *that* object's motion, but the "principle of motion" exhibited by the *whole series* of observable movers. What, however, is that "principle of motion"? It might be interpreted as "motion itself." Thus, the problem

9 *Ibid.*

raised by the first way would not really be the motion of any *particular* thing, but motion in general, as a universal phenomenon in the world. The explanatory regress generated by the first way is irrelevant and misleading. Aquinas *ought* to have written, "it is certain and evident to our senses that some things are in motion. What, however, is the cause of motion?" If that *were* the problem, I fail to see how it is solved by the postulation of a 'first *mover*.'

Or, it might be said, the "principle" of any motion is the source of the power to move which is manifested by the moving object. Thus, when *B* moves *A*, the question is not "What has in turn moved *B*?," but rather, "From where is *B* currently deriving its power to move *A*?" That question simply returns us, however, to the original misunderstanding—that a subordinated mover must be deriving its power to move another from something other than itself at the very time that it is moving another. According to Aquinas, who is closer on this point to contemporary analyses of motion, a subordinated mover has *already* derived, and thus *possesses*, its power to move at the time that it begins to move another. That is why the regress in the first way is relevant to the argument and must be seen as a temporal regress.

Since the temporal element is essential to the first way, it is difficult to see how it might operate in anything other than Aristotelian terms. The opening steps of the Aristotelian argument (which Aquinas seemingly accepts in his commentary on the *Physics*) are formally as follows:

1. Things are being moved.

2. Nothing can be moved unless it is moved by another.

3. Any efficient cause of motion must precede its effect in time and be contiguous in space.

4. If motion had a beginning, it must have had an efficient cause, since nothing can come from nothing.

5. The efficient cause of the beginning of motion must have preceded its effect in time and must have been contiguous in space.

6. Time and motion are mutually definitive—to precede in time is to be in motion.

7. The efficient cause of the beginning of motion must have been itself in motion, which is a contradiction.

8. Therefore motion did not have a beginning.

9. Motion is eternal.

If proposition (3) of the series is taken seriously (Aquinas himself repeats the first half of it), it automatically excludes the introduction of a nontemporal, nonspatial first mover who moves by means of immediate efficient causality. If the efficient mover is that which communicates to another the power to move (reduces it from passive to active potency), then the world must logically be said to *eternally* possess the power to move, without reference to a nontemporal God or mover—or alternatively it must be admitted that something can come from nothing. Aristotle apparently missed the point himself in the concluding passages of the *Physics*. The concluding steps of his argument are:

10. Eternal motion must be continuous and thus circular.

11. No finite mover can cause motion of infinite duration.

12. There must therefore be an infinite efficient cause of the eternal motion of the world.

13. That cause must itself be unmoved and thus nontemporal, immaterial, indivisible, et cetera.

14. In order to exert efficient causality, it must exist at the very circumference of the world.

Aquinas, in his Commentary, fails to note the contradictory opposition of (13) and (14), as well as that of (3) and (13). He also fails to note that (12) is only necessary if it be granted that the motion of the world is necessarily *eternal* in duration. He blithely concludes of the problematic immaterial being who exists *outside* of the world: "He is above all things, God, blessed for ever. Amen." Amen, indeed!

There is an important aspect of Aristotle's first mover, as

described in the *Physics,* which has often been overlooked: he cannot be said to *initiate* motion, but only to *cause* motion that was at no time *initiated.* The concept of a nontemporal efficient mover directly causing the *first* temporal instance of motion in the world is radically incompatible with Aristotle's basic categories. Even his first efficient and nontemporal first mover causes motion by some kind of contiguity (problematically described in the *Physics*) and by some kind of direct or physically immediate *push.* While Aristotle may fall into contradiction in the *Physics,* he does not entirely equivocate on the meaning of "move." His prime mover moves like any other mover, with the single exception of being exempt from the implications of proposition (3)—he does not pre-exist his effects *in time.*

Thus, Aquinas' failure to note the contradiction between (13) and (3) is not the most serious aspect of his 'use' or 'misuse' of Aristotle. Both Aquinas and Aristotle exempt their efficient first movers from the general rule that all efficient causes which act through motion necessarily precede their effects in time; but Aquinas exempts his first mover from the very meaning of the word "move." In order to clarify that claim, it is necessary to look again at the argument mounted by Aristotle. In the *Physics,* he maintains that to *move* something is to exert some immediate force upon it. Thus, if there was a first instance of something being moved, something *else* must have *begun* to exert immediate force upon it. Nothing, however, can *begin* to do something unless it is in time. Since there *are* particular motions which are initiated in time, the chain of temporally regressive finite movers must be infinite in past duration. Aristotle's next step seems to be a confusion deriving from his principle that any limited or finite communication of motion from one object to another will in time be dissipated to nothing. In addition to the infinite regressive series of *finite* movements in the world, he postulates a mover in the world (the outer sphere of the stars) which is itself eternally in motion. In a further *embarras de richesse* he posits a nontemporal cause of the eternal motion of the outer sphere, which in turn guarantees the eternity of the regressive series of finite instances of beginning to move and beginning to be moved that we observe in the world. The lack of logical validity in Aristotle's argument need not concern us.[10] The point is that unless one is willing to say that the regressive series of finite motions (which begin to move and begin to be moved) is of necessity infinite in past duration, there is *no possible way* of postulating a nontemporal efficient cause of the motion of the world. In order to move that which *begins* to move, an efficient cause of motion would have to *begin* to exert that force. In order to have a nontemporal first mover who really *moves* the world (in the sense of "move" defined by Aristotle and presupposed by the premises of the first way) all of the steps of the Aristotelian argument (including the eternal motion of the world) must necessarily be true.

Aquinas, however, could never grant the philosophical necessity of propositions (8), (9), and (10). For him, the temporal regress generated by the Aristotelian analysis of motion in the world *may*, so far as reason can discern, be either infinite or finite in past duration. (Aquinas believes on the basis of revelation that it is in fact finite.) Since Aquinas agrees with Aristotle that no motion can be initiated except by the agency of an efficient cause, Aquinas must postulate a nontemporal efficient cause which is able to initiate motion in time without itself beginning to move. In terms of the meaning of "move" as defined by Aristotle and as used in the opening sections of the first way, that is impossible. If Aristotle is correct that efficient or moving causality implies the immediate exertion of physical force upon an object (and what other sort of "motion" could we call "certain and evident to the senses"?) then the first mover cannot move the first mobile into a state of actual possession of the power to move another without beginning to 'push' or exert force. The first mover cannot be eternally in act and yet initiate motion in that which was not previously moved. Aquinas is equivocating on the word "move." There is no sense of the word "move" which can be used *both* to describe the way in which (a) an object in the world is moved by another object in the world, and (b) the postulated first mobile might be moved by a nontemporal first mover.

[10] It concerned Aristotle at a later date.

It might be thought that at least one characteristic remains in common between the 'motion' of the first mover as Aquinas conceives it and the motion of ordinary empirical movers: each is an instance of the communication of agency to a particular being capable—upon receipt of the agency—of operating in actual independence of its moving cause. If the problem of the first way *really is* the motion of empirical objects from potentiality to actuality—from not actually being in motion to being in motion—and if Aquinas *really means* that the motion of one empirical object can be explained by the previous motion of another empirical object (if, that is, the regress of movers in the argument is relevant to the problem) then the only 'problem' remaining for him is the reduction of the *first* subordinated mover from potentiality to actuality. From that temporal point on, the intrinsic dynamism communicated by the first mover to the first mobile will be sufficient to generate the series of movements culminating in the movement of that which currently appears to our senses. Aquinas, however, can admit no such 'communication of agency' in the case of God. That which escapes from the direct application of God's power to the world cannot be. Aquinas concludes—in the first way itself—that there is a first mover who directly and immediately moves all the movers in the series:

> for the secondary movers do not move except insofar as *they* are moved by the first mover, just as the staff does not move except insofar as it is moved by the hand.

> [quia moventia secunda non movent nisi per hoc quod sunt mota a primo movente, sicut baculus non movet nisi per hoc quod est motus a manu.][11]

God is related not only to the *first* of the secondary movers, but to the secondary *movers* as the hand is related to the staff. If, however, the empirically evident motion of A has already been explained by reference to the empirically evident motion of B, then the 'motion' exerted by the first mover on all members of the series cannot be of the same order or kind as that motion which initiated the regress and originally defined the problem. Once again, "move" is being used equivocally. The terms of the

[11] S. T., I, 2, 3.

first way can never generate a first mover who is "present to all things" as is the 'first mover' of Aquinas.[12]

It might be pointed out that even in the *Physics* of Aristotle, the prime mover does more than simply move a first temporal mover and then 'back off'—he continuously and eternally moves the eternally moved world order. The reason for the continuous and eternal agency of *Aristotle's* prime mover, however, is the conviction that the motion of the world is *necessarily* infinite in past duration, and the principle that any particular and limited communication of motion is necessarily dissipated over a finite period of time. Because the universe would have 'run down' by now if its source of dynamism were a finite entity, Aristotle must postulate (in the *Physics* at any rate) an infinite source of moving power which continuously keeps the finite amount of moving power possessed by the world from dissipating into impotency. Since Aquinas has admitted the logical possibility of the *finitude* of motion in the past, he cannot argue in the same way for the continued agency of his first mover. Furthermore, the agency of Aristotle's first mover—while infinite or eternal in action—is limited in its communication of agency to the first subordinated mover, the outer sphere of the stars. It would seem that no analysis of the motion of the world in terms of a temporal communication of the power to move can ever lead to the postulation of Aquinas' first mover.

As Aristotle came to see, it cannot even lead to the postulation of the efficient first mover of the *Physics*. The first subordinated mover of the Aristotelian universe (the outer sphere of the stars) is itself a self-mover—it eternally possesses the active potency by which it moves the universe. There is no question of its having been moved in the past from passive to active potency—there was in it no 'beginning of being moved.' True, it is 'accidentally' moved (in the sense in which the mind is 'moved' when the body moves), but it moves *per se* of its own nature. Since it was never in passive potency, or at rest, it seems gratuitous to postulate an efficient or moving cause of is actual motion, especially when the postulation of such an efficient cause results in the contradiction of a nontemporal moving cause at the circumference of the world. In the *Meta-*

[12] Cf., *S. T.*, I, 8, 3.

physics Aristotle is able to postulate an eternal first mover only by deserting the area of efficient or moving causality and restricting his attention to the equally problematic area of finality or purpose. The self-moving mover of the outer sphere is not, it would seem, entirely self-determining; while possessing the power to move, it needs a *reason* to actualize that power. As such, it is subordinated to the eternal prime mover as to its final end or motivating power. Such a further limitation on the agency of the prime mover is in keeping with the Aristotelian notion of movement as the application of immediate force on an object and with his principle that all efficient causes precede their effects in time; but it is hardly compatible with Aquinas' first mover, or with what Aquinas apparently believes to be the intention of Aristotle's own argument. It would appear, at least, that Aquinas is completely oblivious of the crucial discrepancy between the terms of the Aristotelian argument that he quotes and his own conclusions from that argument; it would also appear that he fails to note any fundamental difference between the first mover of the *Physics* and that of the *Metaphysics*.

There are, I believe, a number of reasons for Aquinas' use of an argument—such as the first way—which is basically incompatible with or irrelevant to the conclusion he wishes to draw from it. One reason is that Aquinas is a naïve philosophical critic. He misses the intention of a philosophical argument almost as often as he gets it. (It might be better to say that he often *reads in* an intention that is not and could not be there.) So long as the propositional form of the philosophical conclusion is one to which he can give a properly theological interpretation, he takes it for granted that the argument from which it derives is an argument for *his* interpretation of the conclusion. Since he believes (I think wrongly) that Aristotle's formulation of the argument from motion validly concludes to a first efficient mover, he adopts its language and formulates a conclusion which could never follow from it: there is a first mover who 'moves' every agent in the universe as a hand moves a stick and who initiates motion in time without himself beginning to move.

More specifically, however, Aquinas and Aristotle disagree

most profoundly about the true nature of motion. Aristotle argues that locomotion is the primary form of motion.[13] Generation presupposes locomotion, not in the sense that generation can be *reduced to* a complex form of locomotion, but in the sense that generation can never be the first word (temporally speaking) in any account of the motion of the universe. The notion of an efficient cause causing generation without first causing (or utilizing) a local motion of some *already existent entity* is, for Aristotle, unthinkable.[14] Generation is never *ex nihilo*, since efficient or moving causality is a mode of *extrinsic* agency—the action of one thing *on* another. For Aquinas, however, the most profound instance of 'motion' is the 'motion' of something from *complete* potentiality in all respects—from *nothing*—to first actuality or existence. This is clearly an equivocation on the word "move." Whatever Aquinas' first mover is doing (whatever 'power' or 'agency' he is communicating to objects in the world) it has nothing to do with motion as it "is certain and evident to our senses." Aquinas is reading Aristotle's argument, but he is hearing or intending the Doctrine of Creation. There is, of course, only one instance of such 'motion'—only one 'mover' who can 'move' from nonbeing to existence—and that is the action of God in bringing all things into being. It is clear that, in such a sense of the word, the 'mover' must immediately 'move' each and every agent "as the hand moves the staff"—there can be no communication of the power to create *ex nihilo*. It is equally clear, however, that such 'motion' has nothing whatever to do with the regress of movers defined in the first way.

The only link between the motion of things in the world and the 'motion' of God in bringing them out of complete potentiality into existence is the relationship that holds for Aquinas between the operation of any entity and its *natura* or essence. What a thing does (or can do) by nature is determined by what it is. *Natura* is the essence of a thing considered as the source of its operation.[15] The first way seems to imply that, while objects in the world are moved from passive potency to

---

[13] *In Meta.*, x. [14] *Ibid.*

[15] On the relationship between *essentia*, *natura*, and *ens*, see *De ente et essentia*.

active potency by the operations of other things in the world, the fact that there *are* such things as are capable of operating at all is not touched upon by an analysis of the efficiency of secondary causality. Given the fact of existence, of course, it follows that anything that exists must be of *some* determinate nature—agency or the power of operation is then no problem. It is Aquinas' misfortune, philosophically speaking, not to see in the essence or nature of things any intelligible ground for saying, "I see how it is that things with determinate powers of movement or operation manage to exist." That, presumably, is what Aquinas took Aristotle to be investigating—the fact of the existence of things. Thus, he can argue in his *Commentary on the Metaphysics* that Aristotle, in proving that there must be a first cause of the motion of the world, has simultaneously proved that there must be a first cause of the *esse* of things.

2. The irrelevance of the second way to Aquinas' doctrine of God can be deduced in large part from what has already been said of efficiency in the preceding section. It might be helpful, however, to repeat the kernel of the argument in terms of a technical definition of "efficient cause." It should first be pointed out, however, that Aquinas, like Aristotle, recognizes no essential difference between an efficient cause and a 'mover'; both terms are used interchangeably, and in many places Aquinas defines "efficient cause" simply as "a cause of motion or rest." In order to make a distinction in thought, however, we may quote the following as a proper definition of "efficient cause": "anything that makes anything *to be* in any manner whatsoever."[16]

It might appear that, on the basis of such a definition, it would be simple to arrive at the notion of a first efficient cause which "makes everything come to be." In fact, however, the second way will never generate a notion of "coming to be" sufficient to define the first efficient cause Aquinas has in mind; indeed, as was the case with the first way, if we take seriously the regressive aspect of the second way, Aquinas' God is rigorously and logically excluded from the picture.

We begin by asking simply, "What is causing *this particular*

[16] For a discussion of Aquinas' various uses of "cause," see Deferrari, *A Lexicon of St. Thomas Aquinas*, entry under *causa*.

thing to be?" If the answer is, "Some other thing or system of things *within* the world," then either we shall never arrive at God, or we shall arrive at a 'god' who is causing, by his immediate efficacy, the being or existence of the remote efficient causes of "this particular thing," but not the being or existence of "this particular thing" itself. If, on the other hand, we say that God *alone* is causing "this particular thing" to be, then God is the *only* efficient cause, the regressive feature of the second way is irrelevant, and we have no empirical premise with which to begin the argument—we have no basis upon which to say, with the second way, "We find among sensible things an *order of efficient causes*."[17] If, finally, we say that God *and* other things in the world are making "this particular thing" to be, then we must ask in what sense of the word God and other things are *both* "making" it to be. If in the *same* sense, then either God or the other "causes" will be gratuitous and unneeded. If they are "making to be" in *different* senses, we have equivocated on the expression, and the regress of empirically evident ordered causes is irrelevant to the definition of the manner in which God "makes to be." Furthermore, it must then be shown that there is in "this particular thing" some mode or aspect of its 'being' that is left unexplained by reference to those other things in the world that are in some sense "making it to be." To that mode or aspect of 'being' the secondary causes will be irrelevant, and the fact that they too are having their 'being' caused by another will be irrelevant to the way in which God is causing "this particular thing" to be. If we accept the terms of the second way, together with the regress they generate, then the only first efficient cause possible or definable is a 'god' who causes "this particular thing" to be by causing something else to be, in the same sense as that something else causes "this particular thing" to be. Without equivocation, Aquinas' God is impossible.

Aquinas recognizes that fact when he says of God that he is not in any genus, including the genus of 'cause.' Once again, we must say that Aquinas, in reading and reproducing an Aristotelian argument, is intending something quite different. When Aristotle uses the expression "makes something

---

[17] S. *T*., I, 2, 3.

to be," he has something quite different in mind from what Aquinas intends by that expression. Aristotle means only "make something to be what it is, where it is or when it is," whereas Aquinas means "make something to be *simpliciter*." In the latter sense (if it makes sense) nothing *but* God "makes to be." Once again, Aquinas has in mind the Creation (if it is possible to have the Creation *in mind*). But the terms of the second way, and the regress they generate, are irrelevant to the notion of 'creation *ex nihilo*.'

3. The third way is considered by most commentators on Aquinas (including Gilson, Garrigou-Lagrange, and Copleston) to be the most explicitly 'Thomistic' of the five. In spite of the fact that a variant of the fourth way appears more often in the works of Aquinas, the commentators are in a sense correct. Of all the categories introduced in the five ways, that of 'contingency and necessity' is least removed from the creational notion that Aquinas apparently has in mind throughout. Nevertheless, as the proof now stands, it does not intend the kind of 'contingency' that is implicit in the relationship between creator and creature. It operates rather in terms of the 'contingency' of an entity with relation to its immediately observable empirical context.

Once again, the terminology of the argument goes back to Aristotle: ". . . Necessity is that because of which a thing cannot be otherwise; and the same is true of the concomitant conditions of living and of the good. For when in the one case good and in the other life or existence is impossible without certain conditions, these conditions are necessary, and the cause is a kind of necessity."[18] Two uses of "necessary" can be derived from the quotation: (1) things and situations have necessary characteristics; and (2) the causes of the necessary characteristics of an actual situation are necessary. Both forms of necessity can be analyzed in terms of hypothetical conditionals: (1) If something is a man, it *must* be rational; and (2) If a man is to live, then the conditions of life, such as air, *must* exist. Within our conceptual scheme, both of these statements are true by implicit definition—the former deriving from the manner in which we intend the intelligible forms

[18] *In Meta.*, x.

of things, and the second deriving from our *per se* causal statements. Neither usage reflects the kind of necessity presupposed by the definition of God as "necessary existence."

The problematic notion of 'necessary existence' could be based upon a misreading of the following passage of the *Metaphysics*: ". . . Insofar as the heaven is moved, in this respect at least it is possible for it to be otherwise. . . . But *since there is* something which moves while being itself unmoved, *being actually existent*, it cannot be otherwise than it is in any respect. For the root of all change is locomotion and of locomotion, circular locomotion. And this is the motion which that being induces. Thus, it is necessarily existent and as necessary it is good. . . ."[19] It might be thought that Aristotle is here arguing that, once we have shown that a prime mover must exist, we are then able to prove that it could not conceivably not have existed. The phrase "it is necessarily existent," however, implies no such logical necessity. There are, I would maintain, two possible ways of analyzing the phrase: (1) Because the prime mover has been shown to be a necessary presupposition of the *actually observable* motion of the world, it follows necessarily that it exists; and (2) Since the prime mover actually exists and cannot be subject to change, it is impossible that it might cease to exist. The logic underlying these conclusions is faulty, but neither leads to the postulation of a being whose existence is absolutely necessary under *all* conditions. Aristotle can conceive of a world (motionless) which would not demand a first mover. Since the world in fact moves, it is necessary that the first mover exist. Aristotle never raised the question of why the world *exists* or with what kind of existence. It would have been foolish in his terms to ask if there might be something that could not under *any* circumstances not exist. To say that something "necessarily exists" is, for Aristotle, to say that it is the necessary presupposition of what is in fact the case. The prime mover is that sort of "necessary being," and it happens to be the kind of being that, if actual, is not subject to going out of existence —but one can conceive of circumstances in which it might not have been.

[19] *Ibid.*

Clearly, the argument from necessity has gone through some rather radical alterations before being used by Aquinas. The application of 'necessity' to the notion of "existence" is found in the Islamic commentators on Aristotle, from whom Aquinas undoubtedly takes its terminology. It has not been altered enough, however, to be of assistance in generating the *ens realissimum* of Aquinas. Clearly, the logic is: if it could be shown that there were *always* such things as now are generated and corrupted (possible beings), it would not then be necessary to postulate any *other* kind of being; since, however, if there were no other kind of being there would have been a time when no possible being existed, we must *therefore* postulate a being who could not not exist. The argument is comparable to the following Aristotelian argument: If it could be shown that a finite being could move another being or series of beings through an infinite period of time, then there would be no need of postulating an infinite mover. Since, however, communicated motion tends to dissipate in time, we must posit an infinite mover.

That such a being is not the God of Aquinas may be seen from an examination of the status of its 'necessity.' It is the necessity that must be granted to the immediate cause of an actually existent entity. It is therefore the second mode of necessity derived from the passage quoted above from the *Metaphysics*: *If* something exists, its necessary causes necessarily exist. *If* there are entities subject to generation and corruption, there necessarily exists an entity or entities *not* subject to generation and corruption. (That step of the argument is clearly based upon the dynamics of the Aristotelian argument from the dissipation of motion.) *If* such a being exists (and it does), *then* it is not *in fact* (contingently) possible that it not exist, since it cannot change. It is, however, *conceivable* that it might *not* have existed—i.e., if the order of contingent things did not exist. Furthermore, its causal efficacy, like that of the first mover and first efficient cause, is not defined as different in kind from that of the intermediate causes. It is part of a chain in which the existence of the lower entities might be entirely explained by the operation of the intermediate or secondary causes.[20] The first necessary being must exist in order to keep the chain of contingent beings from falling into nonbeing over an infinite period of time. There is *no* indication of the radical contingency presupposed by Aquinas' theology, such that contingent beings could not for one *second* maintain themselves in being without the *direct and continuous* creative act of God. As Aquinas puts it, in something of an understatement, no pagan philosopher was aware of the distinction between essence and existence. No philosopher *could* be, since it is a theological notion.

There is an interesting reading of the third way which would (against the evidence of the text) place God in a completely transcendent position with regard to all other beings. It may be called the 'flip of the coin' interpretation. A version of it is found in "De tertia via Sanctae Thomasi," by A. Dondeyne:

> That which has the possibility of either being or not being is of itself equally disposed to both possibilities, that is, of being or of not being. If it in fact exists, it does not do so of itself . . . but was determined to being by some cause other than itself.

> [Id quod possibile est esse et non esse, de se aequaliter se habet ad duo, scilicet esse et non esse. Si vero existit, hoc de se non habet . . . sed ab aliqua causa quae ipsum ad esse determinat.][21]

Far from saying that any series of possibles *could not exist*, unless there were something not subject to generation and corruption, Father Dondeyne would have it that the 'odds are fifty/fifty.' Since two alternatives are equipossible and one alternative is in fact instantiated, it follows that the 'determination' of the outcome must be attributed to some interfering power. Obviously, the 'odds' on the existence of the *determiner*

[20] "There must exist something the existence of which is necessary. But every necessary thing either has its necessity caused by another or not. Now it is impossible to go on to infinity. . . ." The intermediate 'necessaries' might account for the observable 'possibles.'

[21] In *Collationes Brugenses*, Vol. xxx, 1930, 107.

of the outcome must be one hundred percent in favor of existence. Thus, we get our 'necessary being' in the full sense of
the word.

In addition to the fact that it is in disagreement with the
text of the *Summa,* there are a number of things wrong with
such a reading. We may illustrate them by comparison with a
case in which the language of 'odds' is quite appropriate—
the flipping of a coin. Before the coin drops, it is quite true
that it is not determined which way it will fall. At least, however, there *is* a coin to fall one way or the other. What does
Dondeyne mean by saying that a *thing* which has the possibility of existing or not existing is equally disposed to either
alternative? The thing is not disposed at all! Nothing is 'disposed' *until it already exists,* and by then the bets are off.
Furthermore, in a forced option situation, when the odds are
'fifty/fifty' (when something *is* equally disposed to two alternatives) no one should be surprised that one alternative rather
than the other actually 'comes up.' If one of the two *must*
occur, and neither is more likely than the other, then the
whole point of 'even odds' is to say that no further explanation
is needed. Surely it is necessary that there either be something or nothing. The category of chance was invented for
just such situations—it renders them entirely intelligible. If
you introduce an interfering mechanism, you change the odds.
It would seem that the probability of 'things existing' is a flat
+1, now that the coin has dropped.

This digression may help us to make a further point: from
the concept of 'possibility-impossibility' you can never get the
language of 'probability-improbability.' To say that things
could *possibly* not exist means either that it is conceivable
that things *might not* have existed, or that what exists might
at some time *cease* to exist. In order to get a 'necessary inter-
ferer' out of such a judgment of possibility, something further
must be added in argument—that, for example, it is *im-
probable* that such things as chairs and people would exist
without something like God. In order for the third way to
have even the *appearance* of a valid argument, it must be
arguing, with Aristotle, that any series of things capable of

generation and corruption would "run down" over an infinite period of time. In other words, the third way must be simply a restatement of the first two ways, both of which are incompatible with Aquinas' theological use of "God."

4. The fourth way is the most ambiguous of the proofs. It depends ultimately on a traditional confusion of Aristotelian and Platonic categories. The confusion was not Aquinas' own, but that of the Islamic philosophers who received the Neo-Platonic work of Proclus under the spurious title of "The Theology of Aristotle," and speculated accordingly. The form quoted by Aquinas is close to that of Maimonides, the Jewish philosopher who derived it from the Islamic tradition. Oddly enough, Aquinas was the first scholar in the medieval period to reject the Aristotelian authorship of the "Theology"; in spite of which he is willing to quote an argument based on the same sort of confusion.

According to Plato, the principle of heat in anything is the 'form' of heat, which he calls both "heat itself" and "supremely hot." Similarly, the principles of the goodness, truth, or nobility of anything are the 'forms' of those 'generic' characteristics, and are themselves "supremely good, true, and noble." When Aristotle shifted his emphasis from formal to efficient causality, the Platonic forms reverted to their original status as the immanent or intrinsic principles of general characteristics—the real bases of the predication of universals.[22] A thing was then said to be *made* hot, not by 'heat itself,' but by a hot *thing* or *substance*, which operated in a way determined by its own possession of the form of heat. Aristotle would wrongly agree that all of the heat in the world derives from the 'element" of fire, which *naturally* possesses the form of heat in the highest degree. The notion, however, that all efficient causes are *substances* operating on the basis of their natural and accidental forms is incompatible with the notion that the transcendentals are themselves 'forms' or generic terms. Aquinas normally follows Aristotle, associating 'goodness,' 'truth,' 'nobility,' and the like with the transcendental 'being,' and denies that they

[22] This is all that the 'forms' originally were in Plato's own thought, as in the *Euthyphro*.

are *general terms*.[23] The fourth way, however, moves back and forth between Plato and Aristotle.

In the first instance, it seems to imply, through its parallel between heat and goodness, that the transcendental perfections are instances of generic characteristics. Indeed, it is difficult to see how the argument could operate if 'being,' 'truth,' 'goodness,' and the like were *not* viewed as univocal logical genera. The argument might be stated as follows:

1. In any general class of objects, there is in each object something which makes it a member of the class.

2. That which makes an object a member of a general class is the same thing that makes any *other* object a member of the same general class.

3. The cause of the presence in any object of such a general characteristic is that which possesses the same characteristic to the highest degree.

4. Existence, goodness, and truth are general characteristics.

5. Anything which exists, is good, or is true must possess that characteristic through the agency of something which possesses existence, goodness, and truth in the highest degree. That we call "God."

Putting aside for a moment the question of how there can be 'degrees' of existence and truth, the argument is still not quite clear. The parallel with fire would seem to imply that God possesses existence, goodness, and the like in the *same sense* as any other member of the class, just as fire is hot in the same sense of "hot" as is molten lead. In a purely Platonic version of the argument, it would be maintained that fire is hot *by participation in the 'form' of heat*, just as is any other univocally hot object. All would be hot, not by the agency of some other hot *thing*, but by the agency of 'heat itself'—the idea or 'form' of heat. It would still be maintained that 'heat itself' is *most hot*, but it is not essential to a Platonic analysis of heat that 'heat itself' be hot in the same *generic* sense as are hot things which are hot by participation. This is true what-

[23] 'Nobility' is here used as a transcendental.

ever Plato himself might have written in the *Parmenides*. By parallel, then, if God were 'good to the highest degree' in the way that fire is 'hot to the highest degree,' then he too would be good *by participation in the 'form' of goodness*, just as are the 'good things' of the world. It is clear, therefore, that the fourth way is not arguing in ideal or logical language. It is not looking for the basis of logical predication, which interested Plato, but rather for the *efficient cause* of the possession by a thing of such 'general characteristics' as 'being,' 'goodness,' and the like. It implies, therefore, that God *makes* things exist and be good in the same sense as fire might make something hot—by efficient causality. We are back to Aristotle. In this sense, however, it would *not* be true to say that a thing is made hot through 'heat itself,' but rather through that which possesses a high degree of heat, namely fire; so also, it would not be true to say that things exist or are good through the agency of 'existence' or 'goodness itself,' but rather through the agency of that which possesses those 'perfections' to the highest degree, namely God. God would be highest in the *general class* of existent and good things, just as fire is highest in the general class of hot things. But God, for Aquinas, is not in any general class.

In the Aristotelian understanding of causality, the substantial efficient cause of the generation of a formal characteristic in another being may be the *highest* in the genus, but it is univocally *in* the genus. If Aquinas accepted all of the terms of the fourth way, he would have to assert that God is supreme *in* the 'genera' of existence, goodness, truth, and nobility. Even if God possessed those 'forms' *naturally* (as fire possesses heat) and not *accidentally* (as water possesses heat), he would nevertheless possess them in univocally the same *sense* as his creatures. God would be 'better' and 'truer' (and 'more existent'?) than his creatures, just as fire is 'hotter' than heated water; but his possession of those characteristics would be through the possession of a univocal generic form.

Aquinas, of course, could not agree with the implications of either a Platonic or Aristotelian reading of the fourth way. He specifically denies that God possesses qualities by the "relation of many things to one" (e.g., many substances to one form). And in the *De Potentia*, he says that God is not related to the perfections of his creatures as "more perfect"—in the way that fire is "hotter" than heated water—but as the extrinsic and nonunivocal principle or cause of their perfections—as 'heat itself' is the principle of heat.[24] The fourth way depends on an equivocal confusion of Plato and Aristotle, and is compatible neither with Aquinas' own doctrine nor with the necessary premises of the first three ways.

5. The fifth way is certainly incompatible with the Aristotelian notion of causality presupposed by the first three ways. Aristotle would not know what to make of the postulation of an intelligent, efficient cause of the intrinsic formal teleology of the world. The immanent forms of things are sufficient reason for the regularity of operation manifested by most substances. At most, Aristotle allows for a *final* cause of the regularity of motion of the *outermost* sphere of the stars. There is no 'universal providence' possible in Aristotelian terms. The fifth way, however, assumes that the regularity of operation found in nonintelligent beings must result from the efficacious purpose or intentions of an intelligent being—"as the arrow is directed to the target by the archer."

While incompatible with the Aristotelian presuppositions of the first three ways, however, the fifth way may not be *finally* incompatible with Aquinas' doctrine of God. That the world is ordered providentially by God is distinctly a part of his teaching. He maintains, however, that God's "providence over all . . . cannot be proved."[25] In the *Summa contra Gentiles*, moreover, he denies that we can know the natures of things, and thus he denies that we can *in this life* know *how* God has ordered things to one another and to himself.[26] A discussion of how the fifth way might be reconciled with Aquinas' own thought on the subject will form a part of our discussion of Aquinas' understanding of the ordering of the intellect to God as 'first truth.'

Before moving on to a reconstruction of Aquinas' interpretation of the proofs, it might be helpful to indicate why the five ways *as they stand* cannot be reconciled with Aquinas'

[24] *De Pot.*, 7, 7, ad 2.   [25] *De Ver.*, 9, ad 8.
[26] *C. G.*, ɪᴠ, 1.

own doctrine. Unless we introduce an element of equivocation into the arguments of the five ways—an element that
would render them *immediately* invalid—we cannot derive
from them any 'first cause' or 'God' who is not univocally tied
into the causal chain or system of perfections of which he is
supposedly the intelligible explanation. Aquinas, I shall argue, has seen the logical point that Hepburn and others have
so clearly seen: if God can be made to function as an *intelligible* link—even the *first* link—in a conceptual progress or
causal chain, then of necessity any defect or problem associated with 'contingent reality' will be built into the concept
of God. To postulate a final context in which the world would
be intelligible, one must, ironically, postulate that which remains most opaque and unintelligible from the context of the
world itself.

AQUINAS' THEORY OF
NATURAL THEOLOGY

According to the constant teaching of St. Thomas, it is impossible to know of God "what he is."[27] It would therefore
seem paradoxical to attempt to prove that he exists. Aquinas
explicitly recognizes the problem in his *Exposition of the De
Trinitate of Boethius*:

> It is to be noted, however, that we cannot know of anything
> whether it exists unless it be known in some fashion what
> it is, whether it be known by a perfect cognition or a con-
> fused cognition. . . . And so we are not able to know whether
> God and other immaterial substances exist unless we know
> in some fashion what they are, even if in a confused manner.

> [Est tamen sciendum, quod de nulla re postest sciri an est,
> nisi quoquo modo de ea sciatur quid est, vel cognitione per-
> fecta, vel cognitione confusa. . . . Sic ergo de Deo et de aliis
> substantiis immaterialibus non possemus sciri an est, nisi
> sciremus quodammodo de eis quid est sub quadam con-
> fusione.][28]

It would be exceedingly odd to say, "I know that God exists,

---

[27] E.g., S. T., I, Introduction to Question 3.
[28] De Trin., VI, 3.

but I have *no idea whatever* of the meaning of the word
'God.'" Aquinas' claim is that it is possible to know what a
word *signifies* without knowing what the object *is* to which
the word refers. He depends for this claim upon the distinction between a real definition, based on knowledge of the
nature of a thing, and a nominal definition, based upon the
significant use of a word:

> In proving something to exist, it is necessary to take for the
> medium of demonstration *that which the name signifies*, but
> *not that which the thing is*: for the question 'What is it?'
> follows upon the question 'Is it?' Now the names of God are
> imposed from his effects . . . wherefore, in demonstrating
> from his effects that God is, we can take as a medium of
> demonstration that which the word 'God' signifies.

> [Quia ad probandum aliquid esse, necesse est accipere pro
> media quid significet nomen, non autem quod quid est:
> quia quaestio *quid est* sequitur ad quaestionem *an est*. No-
> mina autem Dei imponuntur ab effectibus . . . unde, demon-
> strando Deum esse per effectum, accipere possumus pro
> medio quid significet hoc nomen Deus.][29]

All that is required in order to claim a "confused cognition" of
what God is is a knowledge of what people intend to do when
they use the term "God."[30] The ordinary use of the term
"God," however, is such that no information is conveyed about
the nature of the intended referent, but only about the world.
In a nominal definition of "God," a reference to God is intended on the basis of a claim concerning something other
than God—his effects.

Aquinas maintains that the middle term of the proofs, which
would ordinarily be a formal definition of the subject of the
proof, is constituted by the 'signification' of the word "God"—
or, as he sometimes states it, the effects of God are used in
place of a definition of *what God is*. Thus, in a nominal definition of "God," formulated in preparation for raising the ques-

[29] S. T., i, 2, ad 2.
[30] Cf., T. McDermott, O.P., "The Meaning of the Word 'God,'" in
Summa Theologiae, Vol. ii, *The Existence and Nature of God* (Blackfriars, London, 1964), Appendix 4.

tions "Does it exist?" and "What is it?," a significant *use* is given to the word without introducing an intelligible notion of the nature of the referent.

One mode of explicating the status of a nominal definition is in terms of the conceptual basis of intentionality. Language is intentional—it is *about* things—because it is the expression of 'inner events' which are themselves, in some sense, intentional or *about* things.[31] The way in which a word refers to its object (its *modus significandi*) depends upon the intention that a person has of the object. An intention may be defined as a conception of the intellect by means of which an object (in the broadest sense) is known or thought:

> The intellect, informed by the species of a thing, forms within itself, by an act of understanding, a certain intention of the thing that is understood, which is the very notion that the definition signifies.

> [Intellectus, per speciem rei formatus, intelligendo format in seipso quandam intentionem rei intellectae, quae est ratio ipsius quam significat definitio.][32]

When the intention that one has of an object is a *ratio* or notion of what the object itself is *like* (its *quid est*), then the definition which expresses that notion is called a *real* definition. The intentional basis for using the word to signify the object is the nature of the object as conceived by the intellect. The intention of the object is judged to be formally identical (that is, isomorphic) with the nature of the object itself—the *ratio* or defining characteristic of the object as intended or conceived. That which makes the intention the "intention of the signified object" is that which makes the object *what it is*.[33]

[31] Cf., W. Sellars, *Science, Perception and Reality*, Chap. 5, "Empiricism and the Philosophy of Mind." See also, R. Chisholm, "Sentences about Believing," and W. Sellars and R. Chisholm, "Correspondence," in *Minn. Studies . . .* , Vol. II (1958).

[32] *C. G.*, I, 53.

[33] To say that there is something which makes an object *what it is* is not to commit oneself to a doctrine of radical realism. Granted that there are a potentially infinite number of ways of categorizing reality—of slicing up the world into kinds of things—it is nevertheless true that once a categorial system has been adopted, there is in each individual defined

In Aquinas' terminology, the *id a quo imponitur nomen ad significandum* is the formal nature of the *id ad quod significandum nomen imponitur*: "that on the basis of which the name is used to signify" is an intelligible notion of "that which the name is used to signify."[34] Since Aquinas makes no consistent distinction between signification and reference, it might be helpful to reword the definition in the following way: when a person uses a referential term of which he knows a real definition, the term *signifies* the very nature of that to which it refers. The *id a quo* of the term is, then, its subjective significance for its user (its intelligible content), while the *id ad quod* of a term is the nature of the intended object. In a real definition, the two coincide.

In the case of a *nominal* definition, the intention that one has of the object is not a *ratio* or notion of *what it is*, but only a *ratio* of the syntactical role of the word. The subjective significance of the term for its user is not an intelligible notion of the nature of the intended referent. There are many kinds of nominal definitions, based on different sorts of syntactical relations, but in each case the *id a quo* differs formally from the *id ad quod*—the intention which allows the term to be used to refer to an object is not the *ratio* of the object itself. A nondefinitional instance of such a formal disparity may be found when a particular object is referred to on the basis of something that *happens to it*. Thus, "whatever it was that I hit with my car" can be used to refer successfully to an unknown object. "Being hit by my car" is the *ratio* or intelligible notion on the basis of which the expression "whatever it was that I hit with my car" is used to signify, not the hitting itself, but *what* was hit. It is clear that what is 'in the mind' is not a notion or an intention of what the object really *is*: the *id a quo* differs formally from the *id ad quod*. Nevertheless, what is in the mind may be called an intention of the object—since it is used to signify the object—but under the formal aspect or *ratio* of something that *happened to* the object. Thus it is

by that system a real basis for saying that it is an *x* and not a *y*. A real definition expresses a notion of that which is capable of constituting one of a kind in terms of the categorial system or conceptual framework expressed by the language itself.

[34] These terms will hereafter be abbreviated to *id a quo* and *id ad quod*.

QUINQUE VIAE AND SCIENTIA DIVINA

possible to know what a word or expression signifies and how it intends a reference without knowing what the designated object *is*—without having an intelligible notion of what the object is.

Aquinas has two favorite categories of nominal definitions: those which signify on the basis of an accident, and those which signify on the basis of a relation. (He also refers to those which signify on the basis of etymology; but such examples are irrelevant to this study.) Thus, it is possible to give a nominal definition of "woman" as "one of those people who keep their hair long." Such a definition, based on an 'accident,' works well enough in the contemporary world (although, alas, less well every day), but it does not express the very thing that distinguishes a woman from the more general class of "human beings." The 'very thing' which distinguishes any class from a more general class is called by Aquinas the "specific difference" (*differentia speciei*)—the real basis upon which we collect individuals into a special class. It is not our *intention* to collect human individuals into special classes on the basis of the length of their hair.[35] The length of a woman's hair is a nonessential difference (*differentia accidentalis*) and not an essential one (*differentia substantialis seu essentialis*). The essential difference constitutes the class—it makes the members what they are precisely as members of the class (*differentia constitutiva*). When we use a nonessential difference in order to signify a member of a special class, we do not intend to signify that member precisely under the aspect of the nonessential difference, but rather we intend to signify it as essentially constituted in its class. Thus, when we define "woman" as a "long-haired person," we do not intend to specify a member of a class whose essential constitutive element is "being long-haired"; we intend rather to specify a member of that class which is distinguished from its generic class by a constitutive sexual difference. We do not intend our definition to be a *real* definition, but a *nominal* or working definition.

A great deal more information about the object signified is

[35] Needless to say we *could* collect human individuals in that fashion if we so wished. Most of our 'constitutive differences' are determined by socially defined pragmatic needs.

· 139 ·

both presupposed and conveyed by a nominal definition based on accidents than by the opaque reference "whatever I hit with my car." At the very least, it places an object in an intelligible general class and indicates some ground for distinguishing it from the other kinds of things in the same general class. Something is known and signified of the nature of the object. If all that a person knew, however, was the nominal definition of such an object he would not know its *precise* nature. For Aquinas, most of our names for nonspiritual substances signify on the basis of what we take to be their most important or proper accidents. We know *something* of the nature of most things, but we do not know *precisely* what their natures are. That is only to say that those accidents that we *use* to collect individuals into special classes may not in fact be the best indications of the most basic functions or operations of the realities in question. (What is meant, for Aquinas, by *natura* is that which determines what a thing *does* or how it operates.) If God could be signified through accidents, we could claim to have *some* knowledge of his true nature, however imprecise.

Since God *has* no accidents, however, it is impossible to formulate a nominal definition of "God" on such a basis. All nominal definitions of "God" fall into the second category of nominal definitions, those based on relation:

> In place of accidents, we have in the case of immaterial substances their *relations* to sensible substances, either by a comparison of cause to effect or by a comparison of excess.
>
> [Loco etiam accidentium habemus in predictis substantiis habitudines earum ad substantias sensibiles, vel secumdum comparationem causae ad effectum vel secundum comparationem excessus.][36]

Nominal definitions of objects based upon relations may presuppose and convey a great deal of information about the nature of a thing, or no information at all. All nominal definitions based on relations are subject to some degree of referential opacity.[37]

[36] *De Trin.*, VI, 3.
[37] On referential opacity, see, W. Quine, *Word and Object* (The Tech-

In its clearest form, referential opacity is a characteristic of statements in which an expression that *could* be used to refer is used in such a way that it fails to make a reference. Thus, in the statement, (1) " 'Cleopatra was killed by an asp' was written in the book," the word "Cleopatra" does not refer to the famous individual by that name. To ascertain the truth of that claim, it is necessary only to substitute a synonymous referring expression for "Cleopatra": (2) " 'The Egyptian queen beloved of Antony was killed by an asp' was written in the book." While (1) is true, (2) may be false: it is not the same proposition. Since "Cleopatra" fails to make a reference, we may say of the context in which it occurs ('Cleopatra was killed by an asp') that it is referentially opaque with regard to the individual normally referred to by "Cleopatra." On the other hand, " 'Cleopatra was killed by an asp' " is the name of "Cleopatra was killed by an asp," which *does* refer to Cleopatra.

Since we are interested in the 'subjective' aspect of referential expressions (the *id a quo*), we may raise the question of what the person who utters (1) understands by the words that he uses. Does he understand " 'Cleopatra was killed by an asp' " to be the name of a statement that *does* refer to the Egyptian queen beloved of Antony, or does he merely take it to be the name of a statement that seems to refer to 'someone' who was killed by an asp? If the latter, then "Cleopatra" is being used in such a way that it is, for the speaker, *notionally opaque* with regard to the uniquely defining *ratio* by means of which its normal referent is designated; the speaker does not have a proper notion of Cleopatra.

In most interesting instances of referential opacity, however, the lack of transparency is not so unequivocally evident, and a judgment must be made on contextual grounds. Willard Quine, in his discussion of opacity, points out instances in which a construction may be considered as either opaque or transparent, depending on the interpretation given to the propositional attitude expressed.[38] Thus, in the statement, (3)

---

nology Press of The Massachusetts Institute of Technology and John Wiley & Sons, Inc., New York, 1960), Chaps. 4 and 5.

[38] *Ibid.*, pp. 145ff.

"He believes that Cleopatra was killed by an asp," the word "Cleopatra" can be viewed either as making or as *not* making a transparent reference to Cleopatra. Proposition (3) could be construed as parallel to, (3a) "He believes that 'Cleopatra was killed by an asp' is true," in which case it is clear that we are faced with a referentially opaque construction. Given *that* construction of (3), it would be wrong to conclude, (4) "He believes that the Egyptian queen beloved of Antony was killed by an asp." He might be completely unaware of Cleopatra's Antonian exploits, or he might mistakenly believe that the Cleopatra who negotiated with Caesar and was killed by an asp is not the same person as 'that Egyptian queen beloved of Antony.' In neither case would he believe that "The Egyptian queen beloved of Antony was killed by an asp" is true. On the other hand, (3) might be construed as parallel to, (3b) "As for Cleopatra [who was *in fact* the Egyptian queen beloved of Antony], he believes that she was killed by an asp." On such an interpretation, "Cleopatra" in (3) makes a transparent reference, and it is entirely in order to conclude that (4) is also true.

To place emphasis on the possible nontransparency of belief-statements is to call attention to the possible importance in certain contexts of the *id a quo* of a referential term—the importance, that is, of the subjective *ratio* or notion on the basis of which a real reference is intended. The person who utters (3) and who intends by "Cleopatra" *only* 'the Egyptian Queen who negotiated with Caesar,' makes a reference which is *notionally opaque* with regard to the *ratio* of the co-designative expression 'the Egyptian Queen beloved of Antony.' In such a case we would simply deny the truth of proposition (4), if the context in which the question of its truth value was raised was such as to suggest the primary importance of what the person who uttered (3) 'had in mind,' as opposed to what *we* know to be true of the intended referent—as opposed that is to a more complete definition of the *id ad quod* of "Cleopatra." The *modus significandi* of a referential term may in certain contexts be more relevant to the determination of the truth of a belief-statement than the actual nature of the *res significata*.

As trivial as the point may seem in its current context, failure to note its rationale might lead one to raise unnecessary or ambiguous questions as to whether or not a nominal definition of "God" succeeds in signifying the "God of Abraham, Isaac, and Jacob"; or, as it is sometimes put, whether or not the 'entity' signified in the proofs is really what "all men mean by God." If we assume for the moment that it is indeed possible to mount a convincing philosophical argument for the existence of God, we might be quite willing to say, "Philosopher Brown believes that God exists," even though the term "God" might have for Brown no other *id a quo* than 'A being capable of rendering our experience of reality transparently intelligible.' Should a Barthian theologian indignantly ask, "Does Philosopher Brown then believe that the Father of our Lord Jesus Christ exists?," we should not know immediately how to reply. Our indecision, however, would not stem from any doubt as to the essential truth of our initial claim, but would stem rather from the ambiguity of the question itself. We might reply (in terms of referential transparency), "Yes! As for that being capable of rendering our experience of reality transparently intelligible [whom we know *in fact* to be the Father of our Lord Jesus Christ], Brown believes that he exists." In most properly *theological* contexts, however, the *modus significandi* of "God" is of such overriding importance, that it would be much less misleading to reply (in terms of referential opacity), "No! Brown believes that 'A being capable of rendering our experience of reality transparently intelligible exists' is true: but he does not believe that 'The Father of our Lord Jesus Christ exists' is true."[39]

Indeed, the problem is even more complex in the writings of Aquinas. Since Aquinas grants that Aristotle proved the existence of God, it would seem to follow that Aquinas ought to grant that Aristotle believed that God exists. In certain contexts, he does just that, while in other contexts he denies that *any* pagan can be said to believe that God exists. It would be

---

[39] Brown's disbelief in the truth of the latter proposition might be either active or passive: he might vehemently deny that Christ has anything to do with the final source of intelligibility, or it might simply never occur to him to suppose so.

tempting to interpret such strange linguistic behavior purely in terms of our Cleopatra example: "He might know that Cleopatra negotiated with Caesar, but if he doesn't know that she had an amorous affair with Antony, he just doesn't know *Cleopatra!*" Thus, "Aristotle might have known that God is the ultimate source of the dynamism of the world, but if he didn't know that God is the one who revealed himself in Christ, he just didn't know *God!*" The parallel is, however, misleading. I may believe, rightly or wrongly, that one can only understand the character of Cleopatra if he knows that she had an amorous affair with Antony; it nevertheless remains true that the very same individual is equally satisfactorily, equally intelligibly, and equally historically *signified* by 'the Egyptian queen who negotiated with Caesar.' Either *id a quo* successfully locates "Cleopatra" within the same logical space of 'historical personages'; each provides *different information* of the *same logical order*. When we say, however, "God is the ultimate source of the dynamism of the world" and "God is the one who revealed himself in Christ," we are not providing *different information* of the *same logical order*. The *id a quo* of "God" as that term is used in natural theology has such a radically different *modus significandi* from the *id a quo* of "God" as that term is used in dogmatic theology, that the two could not be explicated in terms of the same conceptual framework or logical space. Aquinas' use of "God" is primarily theological: the very meaning of "God" as used in the *Summa Theologiae* is so dependent upon *rationes* supplied by revelation and supernatural faith that its use in natural theology is already *equivocal*, unless understood in terms of a transparent construction of natural belief-statements. Thus, when Aquinas admits that Aristotle proved the existence of God, we ought to read, "Aristotle proved the existence of an ultimate source of the dynamism of the world, and *we* know that the ultimate source of the dynamism of the world is in fact the *God* referred to by the revealed articles of faith." To the question "Did Aristotle believe that God exists?" we may then answer in the terms that are most appropriate to the situation. We may say, "Yes! As for that being that is the ultimate source of the dynamism of the world [and that *we* know to be the God referred to by the revealed articles of faith], Aristotle believed that it exists." In order to emphasize, however, the controlling role of revealed *rationes* in the properly *theological* use of "God," we ought rather to reply in terms of referential opacity: "No! Aristotle believed that 'An ultimate source of the dynamism of the world exists' is true: but he did not believe that 'The God referred to by the revealed articles of faith exists' is true."

While the term "God" *need* not be entirely appropriated to its properly theological use, the justification for such an appropriation is not hard to see. In the case of "Cleopatra," either *id a quo* ('An Egyptian queen who negotiated with Caesar' or 'An Egyptian queen beloved of Antony') provides intelligible information about the *nature* of the celebrated Cleopatra who was killed by an asp. A nominal definition of "Cleopatra" based on her relation to Caesar or Antony would, at the very least, locate Cleopatra in a general class of individuals and add a uniquely signifying basis for distinguishing her from the other members of the class. Something of Cleopatra's nature would be either communicated or presupposed. A nominal definition of "God," however, neither presupposes nor communicates any intelligible information about the God referred to by the revealed articles of faith. In order to function as a satisfactory nominal definition of "God," 'A being who is the ultimate source of the dynamism of the world' must be construed in such a way that it places its referent in no general class whatsoever! How can a nominal definition *signify* an object without providing intelligible information about that object?

We may utilize Cleopatra's death in order to indicate how tenuous a nominal definition based on relation can become. A schoolboy might say, for example, (5) "I believe that an asp killed Cleopatra." If he believes in the historicity of Cleopatra, he has already committed himself to, (6) "There has been at least one asp." Without further investigation, a nominal definition might be constructed of "asp": "something of the same sort as that which killed Cleopatra." Only further questioning, however, will reveal what the boy himself *intends* by the word "asp." Construing belief-statements opaquely, it might be quite

QUINQUE VIAE AND SCIENTIA DIVINA

false to say of the boy, (7) "He believes that a viper killed Cleopatra." The boy might not believe that 'A viper killed Cleopatra' is true. Indeed, he may not know whether "asp" is the name of a germ, a man, an animal, a thunderbolt, or something quite different from all of these. In such a case, the word "asp" in (5) is subject to radical notional opacity.

Two interpretations could be given of what the boy intended by (5). He may only have meant, (5a) "I believe that *something* killed Cleopatra." Since by postulation we cannot exclude any sort of thing from the possible range of "asp," including old-age or Cleopatra herself,[40] the statement is either making the trite observation, "Cleopatra is dead so something killed her," or it is calling attention to the death of Cleopatra and disclaiming knowledge of the cause. In neither case is anything but the death of Cleopatra intelligibly represented. A more probable interpretation of (5) would be: (5b) "I believe that whatever killed Cleopatra is correctly called an 'asp.'" In this proposition, the word "asp" is not *used*, but *mentioned*—"'asp'" is the name of "asp." It is mentioned in order to have its use equated with that of the phrase "whatever killed Cleopatra." As we have seen, that phrase is equivalent to "something." Thus, as used by the boy, the word "asp" has no more predicative, restrictive, or referential value than "something." Under those (admittedly extreme) circumstances, proposition (6) reduces to the ultratrite claim: (6a) "There has been something." Such is the extreme to which the notionally opaque character of nominal definitions may be carried.

It is clear that a nominal definition of "God" cannot follow such a pattern. Extreme statements of the negativity of our knowledge of God, while perhaps correct in intention, may verge on assimilating "God" language to pure "something" language—with trite or worse results. Thus, the following nominal definition of "God" may be constructed: "God" signifies "the sufficient reason for the existence of the world." Parallel to (5) and (6), we could then derive: (8) "I believe that God is the sufficient reason for the existence of the world," and, (9) "There is a God." If *all* that is intended by "God"

[40] Compare the statement, "I believe that a viper killed Hitler."

(its *only ratio*) is 'whatever is the significant reason for the existence of the world,' then we must allow complete indeterminacy with regard to the referential range of "whatever." Clearly, *with no further presuppositions*, it is compatible with this definition that the world might be its *own* sufficient reason for existing, as might 'nature,' 'space,' or 'gravity.' Following our pattern of reduction (8) becomes either: (8a) "The world exists, so something is the sufficient reason for the existence of the world," or, (8b) "Whatever is the sufficient reason for the existence of the world is correctly called 'God.'" Proposition (9) once again turns into the super-trite claim, "There is something." Thus, in terms of such a definition, "God" would have no more predicative, restrictive, or referential value than "something"—or, for that matter, than "asp" as used by a schoolboy.

Neither can it be said that such a definition is sufficient until it be proved in the arguments themselves that the world is *not* its own sufficient ground for existing. If that were the case, the proofs would be presupposing, according to their own definitions of "God," that God exists; and they would serve only to prove that God is not the world. The stated intention of the proofs, as they occur in Aquinas, however, is to conclude that what is *already signified* by "God" in fact *exists*. A related maneuver would be to say that the proofs presuppose only that there is *some* sufficient reason for the existence of the world, and that they go on to prove that that sufficient reason is in fact *God*. Clearly, however, in order to prove that the sufficient reason for the existence of the world is in fact *God*, and not something else, the proofs must utilize some definition of "God" other than "The sufficient reason for the existence of the world." It is for that reason that Aquinas invariably subordinates the notion of God as the "sufficient reason for the existence of the world" to a prior definitional move which distinguishes God from the realm of finite or worldly reality. An extension of our example will clarify the logic of a nontrite nominal definition based on relation.

It may not be the case that the boy in our example intends only "whatever killed Cleopatra" when he uses "asp." He may have grounds for believing that "whatever killed Cleopatra" does not refer either to Cleopatra herself or to any other normal cause of 'natural death.' When he says that an *asp* killed Cleopatra, he means to imply that something external to her produced a violent or sudden death: "No, Cleopatra did not directly kill herself, nor did she *just die*; an asp killed her, what ever that is." The boy could then add a number of significant negations to his original statement: (5c) "I believe that an asp killed Cleopatra, and an asp is not an 'x' or a 'y' or. . . ." Proposition (6) would then read: (6b) "There has been something other than 'x's, 'y's, and. . . ." If we further suppose that the boy has grounds to believe that, whatever an asp is, it is nothing of which he has had direct experience or of which he possesses a specific concept, then "asp" begins to take on a distinctive *ratio*. (5) could now be rewritten: (5d) "I believe that something of which I have had no experience and of which I have no specific concept killed Cleopatra; and whatever it was, it is called an 'asp.'" While the word "asp" does not refer in (5d), it is at least made clear in what way the boy *could* use it to refer with only partial indeterminacy. A nominal definition of "asp" would now read: "A sort of thing of which I have had no experience and of which I have no specific concept, one of which killed Cleopatra." Proposition (6) becomes something more than a claim that "something exists": (6c) "There has been something unlike the sorts of things of which I have had experience or of which I have a specific concept."

If, in order to distinguish our example from nominal definitions of "God," we restrict the intended referential range of (5d) and (6c) to "objects existing in the world," then it is clear that the negative element that we have added to the causal relationship is quite significant. While the negations add nothing to the positive knowledge that the boy has of *what an asp is,* they restrict the referential and significational range of "asp" sufficiently to allow for a partially determinate reference and for a nontrite nominal definition. Even *one* significant negation would have been enough to solve the difficulty involved in (5a), (5b), and (6a), but the more negations, the more determinate does the *ratio* become on the basis of which the boy intends a reference to an asp—and

this is true even though the boy does not have a precise accounting of the sorts of things included in the class of "things
unlike the sorts of things of which I have had experience or
of which I have a specific concept." The phrase "things existing in the world" has enough notional content to form a univocal basis for the nominal definition. In Aquinas' terms, the
class of "objects existing in the world" forms the *remote
logical genus* restricted or specified by the further elements of
the definition. The *proximate logical genus* (a subset of the
remote logical genus) is determined by the negations ("unlike
the sorts of things of which I have had experience or of which
I have a specific concept"); and, in place of a specific constitutive difference (which would define a determinate logical
species), the intended class of objects is signified by way of
relation ("the sort of thing that killed Cleopatra"). Thus,
negations take the place of positive knowledge of generic distinctions, and a relation takes the place of a knowledge of
accidents, on the basis of which we normally assign specific
predicates.

The pattern is generally similar to that followed by Aquinas
in constructing a nominal definition of "God":

> In the place of a cognition of the genus, we have, in the
> instance of immaterial substances, a cognition by negation.
> . . . And the more negations we know of them, the less con-
> fused is our cognition of them; for through subsequent nega-
> tions, the first is contracted and determined, like a remote
> genus through differences. . . . And in place of accidents,
> we have in the instance of those substances their relations
> to sensible substances. . . .

> [Sed loco cognitionis generis habemus in istis substantiis
> cognitionem per negationem. . . . Et quanto plures nega-
> tiones de ipsis cognoscimus, tanto minus est confusa earum
> cognitio in nobis; eo quod per negationes sequentes prior
> negatio contrahitur et determinatur, sicut genus remotum
> per differentias. . . . Loco autem accidentium habemus in
> praedictis substantiis habitudines earum ad substantias sen-
> sibiles. . . .][41]

[41] *De Trin.*, VI, 3.

The major difference between the two cases is the nature of the remote logical genus contracted by the negations. In our example, that genus was constituted by the notion of "things existing in the world." In the text quoted from Aquinas, however, the remote logical genus would seem to be itself a negation: "In place of a cognition of the genus, we have . . . a cognition by negation." A negation, however, does not define a meaningful general class unless it is used to restrict an already meaningful and more general class. Mere negations are incapable of making *another negation* "less confused."

In practice, however, Aquinas supplies a unique and problematic substitute for a univocal logical genus in his nominal definitions of "God": "This name 'God' is imposed to signify *something existing* above all things." (Impositum est enim nomen hoc ad aliquid significandum supra omnia existens.)[42] "Existence," however, is not itself a genus—it does not define a univocal general class—while "existence in the world" is, for Aquinas, both a natural genus and a univocal general class.[43] It is not at all clear that "existing" conveys a single coherent notion unless it is restricted to referents other than God. We know the meaning of the word "exists" when it is applied to objects in the world, to ideas, or even to characters in novels— we know in each case the kind of claim being made by "*x* exists"—but it is not at all clear that we know what "exists" means *in vacuo*—what it means in abstraction from the various conceptual frameworks generated by our conceptual system. Aquinas insists that insofar as we *do* understand a mode of signification of the word "existence" we must *deny* it of God—we do not know "how" God exists.[44] It would appear that the prima facie meaning of "something existing" is destroyed by the further specification "above all things." If the expression is not to be taken as an outright contradiction (how can there be some*thing* above all *things*?) it must be interpreted to mean "above anything that we experience or of which we can conceive." Aquinas' qualification of God's 'existence' as "removed from all things" (remotum ab omnibus)[45] generates the logic of *remotion*, by means of which every uni-

---

[42] S. T., I, 13, 8, ad 2.
[44] *Comm. in Sent.*, I, 7, 1, 1.
[43] S. T., I, 88, 2, ad 4.
[45] S. T., I, 13, 8, ad 2.

vocally meaningful *ratio* or intelligible notion is denied of God. Of such an entity, as Aquinas himself so clearly stated, we could not know "how it exists" but only "how it doesn't exist." Without a generically meaningful notion of "existence in general," how can we then define God as existing?

Far from *depending*, however, upon a generically meaningful use of the term "existence," Aquinas cannot admit such a notion in the case of God. He depends rather on an essentially analogous use of "existence." An essentially analogous term is such that its various uses (in different conceptual frameworks) cannot be derived from one another or defined in terms of any other conceptual framework than the one in which it occurs. The various analogous uses of an essentially analogous term bear a purely formal syntactical resemblance that can be intelligibly specified only in a common meta-language. There is no intelligible *content* that is common to all of the analogous uses. To say that a word is "essentially analogous" is therefore to say that there is a word with a syntactically isomorphic role in another conceptual framework. We have seen that "exist," as it occurs in *our* conceptual system, could in theory have an analogue in *another* conceptual system—used to inform another mode of experience—which would differently specify the radical dispositional concept of 'being' by allowing references to be made to radically different sorts of entities, which would, by consequence, "exist" rather differently. (To say that such an entity would "exist" rather differently is merely to say that rather different sorts of things could be inferred from the claim that something of that sort existed.) To ask if '*x*' exists is to ask if some kind of reference to '*x*' is possible. It is to ask if there is some logical space within which '*x*' could be located, and which could be used to inform experience.

The question of the existence of God, therefore, is a radical one: it asks whether it is possible to make a unique *kind* of reference to a being definable in a unique *kind* of logical space, of which we cannot intelligibly conceive. It does not ask if there is a certain entity which can be located within a kind of logical space which we have already defined; it asks rather if there may be a kind of logical space which we have *not* defined. Aquinas feels that we cannot prejudge such a question. There is no way of being a priori certain that we have already determined the only possible sorts of references that might in theory be made—that we have already defined all of the logical spaces that might control an analogical use of "exists." Thus, far from *having* to specify how the word "existing" is being used in the nominal definition of "God," Aquinas may not do so. A nominal definition is constructed in order to *raise* a question—not to convey information about reality. To ask if God exists is to ask if a new kind of reference is possible —if there is a use of "exist" other than that defined by the sorts of references we find ourselves making to things of which we can naturally conceive.

It is not, however, to ask if we can make a peculiar kind of reference in total abstraction from the meaningful sorts of references we already make. To *invent* a logical space in terms of which to refer to something named "God" would give us a framework in which to say that he exists, but it would not give us a religiously relevant use of "existence." God's 'existence' would—like that of numbers—be true by definition, but it would float in logical space completely unanchored to our only existential reality principle—the world of sense experience. That is precisely what is wrong with the ontological argument.

One does not want to say that God exists *as* tables and chairs exist, but one does want to say that God's existence is in some fashion related to that of tables and chairs, independent of our thoughts about him. Although we cannot fit "God" *into* the logical space defined by our intended references to objects *in* the world, we want to define a kind of logical space (however unique or peculiar) which can be intended on the basis of our references *to* the world. Thus, Aquinas defines "God" not merely as "above all things and removed from all things," but also as the "cause of all things."

It is clear that Aquinas is using the word "cause" rather oddly. He *cannot* mean that God is to be defined in terms of the causal relations of which we can conceive, for, as we conceive it, the causal relation is such that we could, by implicit definition, place the intelligible definition of the cause in the definition of the effect—and vice versa—thus establishing a synthetic a priori relationship of entailment enabling us to move by *per se* judgments from the assertion of one to the assertion of the other. If that were possible, God would no longer be "removed from all things." The intelligible form of 'God' would of necessity occur within a conceptual system (ours) in terms of which significant references can only be made to contingent beings—to beings whose *ratio* is syntactically related to the *rationes* of sensibly experienced realities.[46] Aquinas cannot place God in *any* general class, including that of "causes." How then is he using the word "cause" in the nominal definition?

I would suggest that it is possible to give to the word "cause" an essentially analogous status similar to that of "exist." To say that "cause" is essentially analogous is to say that a word or expression with a syntactically isomorphic role might occur in a conceptual system radically unlike ours, in terms of which it would be possible to *think* and *understand* the statement "God exists and is the cause of the world," or its equivalent in that language. Oddly enough, we do not have to possess, conceive, or examine such a conceptual system in order to claim that, if it existed, it must contain a term with a syntactic role isomorphic with "cause" in our language. That follows from the very meaning in this context of "conceptual system": "A conceptual system is an intelligibly interrelated set of intentions capable of being used to introspect experience, refer to and render intelligible 'that which is.' " In *any* such conceptual system, the so-called transcendental terms would occur analogically, for all such terms express the fact that the system as a whole is being used to inform experience and to render intelligible the objects of experience. All transcendentals, that is, occur *within* a conceptual system as reflexive or meta-linguistic expressions of the *role* of the system as a whole—which is why they ought never to be assimilated to generic expressions, which have a use only in expressing that which is true *within* the system.

My suggestion, therefore, is that "cause" has or can be given precisely such a role—and that Aquinas has done so. The

46 S. *T.*, I, 84, 7.

word "cause" functions in Aquinas as a transcendental term (as well as an intrasystematic or generic term). If we grant that the essential role of a conceptual system (in the context of the intentional relation of an 'intellect' to reality) is to provide a syntactical or inferential basis for understanding reality, we must say that *any* conceptual system must provide "sufficient reason" for the elements of reality it renders intelligible. To provide "sufficient reason" for an element of experience or a known reality is to provide a set of intentional statements from which the existential assertion of the experienced or known reality can be inferred by *per se* judgments— by the syntactical rules of the game. That to which the "sufficient reason" refers, or that which it expresses, may be called the "cause" of the explicandum. Therefore, *any* conceptual system semantically related to reality *must* contain an analogous expression for "cause." It follows that Aquinas is justified in using the word "cause" in his nominal definition of "God."

Since God is said to be "removed from all things," we may reformulate the question posed by means of the nominal definition in the following way: "Is there an 'entity' (as defined intelligibly in *another* conceptual system) such that (in *that* conceptual system) it would be referred to or expressed by an intelligible form or set of intentions such that the existential assertion of that form would immediately justify (by the intelligible rules of *that* conceptual system) the existential assertion of all things that exist (as that word is used in *our* conceptual system)?"[47] The 'logical space' on the basis of which *we* might—however oddly—refer to God is to be based upon a formal description in *our* conceptual system of *another* conceptual system (which we do not understand) in which an analogue of "God" might intelligibly occur. Such a formal description will utilize the meta-linguistic vocabulary of our conceptual system.

---

[47] The implication that the existence of the world would be seen to follow immediately from the existence of God does not commit us to a belief in the necessity of creation. The logic of "cause" as it occurs in the 'language of God' would be such that the justified move from assertion of 'God' to assertion of 'world' would take into consideration that which we name 'will' and 'freedom' in God. The world would follow from 'God' in his *actual* and *free* determination.

It may now be somewhat clearer why I rejected the traditional form of the five ways as Aquinas quoted them in the *Summa*. All five (including, I believe, the fifth) attempted to tie God into the world by extrapolating a notion of causality or perfection from our conceptual system such that what God is or what God does (as the intelligible context of the world) can be expressed—or partially expressed—in terms of concepts which play an *intra*-systematic role in our language—in terms, that is, of generically meaningful terms. If the causal regression of the first two ways is to be relevant to the proofs, God must "move" or "cause" in a manner generically univocal with the manner in which things in our language are said to move or to cause other things. If God, in the third way, is to be 'necessary,' his necessity must be transitive—communicable by 'chain reaction' to beings (such as angels) of which we *can* to some degree conceive. In the fourth way, God appears explicitly as the highest in a general class defined within our conceptual system. Even in the fifth way, the proof is meant to be intelligible precisely because we understand what it means to be an intelligent being with purposes expressed in a material mode. If the fifth way implies—as I think it does— that we are able to apprehend the purposes of God as they are expressed in the regular order of the world, and are therefore able to know how the 'will' of God *explains* those purposes, then it also reduces God to an instance of an intelligible relation specifiable within our conceptual system. Aquinas must rather argue that God 'explains' such things as the order of the universe—such as it *really* is and not such as we conceive it—in terms of God's *own* conceptual framework or intentional being. As we shall see, "intelligent" and "volitional" are themselves essentially analogous terms in Aquinas' theology.

God, for Aquinas, is "outside of the general category of intelligible things" because his 'intelligibility' cannot be defined in terms of *our* conceptual system—it does not appear in the 'light of reason.'[48] "Intelligibility" is clearly an essentially analogous term, implying only that an entity can be implicitly defined within *some* conceptual system. The intelligibility of God could be seen or apprehended only in another kind of in-

[48] *De Trin.*, I, 3, ad 4.

tentional or conceptual light—which Aquinas names the "light of Glory"[49]—enabling one to comprehend the intentional form of God himself (the inner "Word" of God). While Aquinas' views on the intelligibility of God can be justified on philosophical grounds—while, that is, it can be shown that 'God' is *not* intelligible in *our* conceptual system and that there is in theory no way of excluding the possibility of there being a system in which it *would* be intelligible—it is nevertheless quite clear that his chief motivation for removing God from the range of our conceptual powers is a *theological* concern that we not be able to conform our minds to God by our own natural powers ("natural," that is, in the order of sin and grace). God is not "at the disposal" of man until, in his freedom, he chooses to place himself at man's disposal under the formality of grace or 'gift.' Even that gift, however, becomes man's possession—at his disposal—only in the "light of Glory" when reality is seen in terms of God's intentions. In this life "God" remains a word in *another* language—a word *mentioned but not used in our language.*

The problem of 'natural theology,' therefore, is what, in our effort to inform our experience in terms of *our* conceptual system—might conceivably lead us to assert that there *is* an intentional framework in terms of which an 'entity' (definable in *its* terms) would play the role of the "sufficient reason" for the existence of everything to which we significantly refer in *our* terms. At this point I should make it clear that I do not accept the validity of Aquinas' form of argument. Nevertheless, it is an interestingly wrong position and helps to clarify the logic of "God." Aquinas' claim that we have grounds for asserting the reality of God's intentional being is based upon his understanding of the 'first principles' of reason—and particularly upon his understanding of the "principle of the intelligibility of being."

Aquinas' position is deceptively simple. His most profound 'reasons' for asserting the existence of God are 'throw aways'—laconic claims made in contexts other than the five ways. Basically, they reduce to the optimistic claim that no natural inclination of the human mind or the human will can be *inane.*

[49] S. T., I, 12, 5.

There must *be* in reality something that is able to give rest to the frustrated love and intellectual appetite of man.[50] When we find ourselves naturally disposed to seek the intelligible ground of some frustrating circumstance or content of experience, that ground *must* exist. Since nothing of which we can conceive possesses the fecundity and intelligible transparency sufficient to guarantee the final complacency of the human will and intellectual appetite, there must be that of which we *cannot* conceive, whose 'goodness' and 'intelligibility' would provide the inexhaustible source of the fulfillment of our natural cravings. There must *be* that which is capable of giving rest to the restless seeking of the mind of man for total intelligibility.

The often overly sophisticated "principle of the intelligibility of being" can be fairly simply stated: "That is intelligible which can be measured or judged in terms of the intentionally created forms which result from the agency of 'intellect'; everything that exists can be so measured or judged, and thus understood." Truth, for Aquinas, is the *aedequatio intellectus et rei*—the analogical isomorphism that allows us to know reality in the immanent conceptions of our own intentional being.[51] Truth is *per se* intelligible—it follows the rules of the conceptual game—but it has, in human experience, several modes or facets. There is an adequation between 'mind and thing' which results from the passivity of the human subject to the causal influence on him of external reality. The *truth* of an existential judgment—that there really *is* an *x* over there—is not dependent upon the conceptual powers of the mind, but upon the ability of the subject correctly to state the existential implications of that which he has passively and nonintentionally experienced or undergone. Truth in its semantic mode or aspect is a function of what happens to the knowing subject. That passive and material moment in the act of knowing, however, is not the source of the formal *intelligibility* of our knowledge. While the mind of man is 'measured' by reality in that semantic truth depends upon sensation, the mind of man also 'measures' reality, in that it conceives the forms in which external reality is known and understood. Reality does not *dictate* the forms of our knowing, but is rather *known*

---

[50] S. *T.*, I, 12, 1; 75, 6.　　[51] S. *T.*, I, 16, 2.

in them. For Aquinas, this means that the intelligible is not the simply 'given' to which the mind *merely* bows, but the *created* to which reality corresponds. The *nonintelligible*, for Aquinas, is the 'given'—that which measures the mind and to which the mind must *merely* bow. To the nonintelligible, the mind must be blindly conformed without the immanent possession of a form which declares that reality in its formal structure is measured or measurable by 'intelligence.' That blind conformity is not an act of intelligence but an experience of frustration. That which is nonintelligible to the mind of man is that which he cannot freely *conceive* in the fecundity of his intentional being.

Aquinas believes that we are naturally inclined (as a part of the very disposition defining our radical sense or concept of 'being') to *try* to conceive the whole of reality in the light of reason—on the basis of the syntactical rules that define for us that which is and that which is intelligible. We intend the world as intelligible, but the world ultimately shatters our intention. Lying at the root of all our experience—the final context in which our intelligible judgments take place—there is a radical absurdity, a *merely* "given" which remains as a surd when all possible intelligible judgments have been made, and which thus frustrates the 'intellect' in its search for total intelligibility.

There is an immediate problem in making such a claim: if that of which we can be aware—that which we are able to notice *within* our experience—is already *informed by* our conceptual system, it would seem that we are not and cannot be aware of a *totally* nonintelligible aspect of our experience, to which we judge that there is an existential correlate. Natural theology could never, it seems, be based on a positive and intelligible insight into a problem inherent *in* our experience. We may be aware of 'problems' in our experience, but we could never be aware of a total and theoretically irresolvable *absurdity* in our experience.

Indeed, the 'radically unintelligible' problem that Aquinas locates at the very heart of human experience is *not* the kind of thing that we can be aware of as an absurd element *in* our experience: it is *esse* or the very existence of things. Existence is not an abstractable *part* of the world. We cannot point to the 'existence' of an object and ask for an explanation. If we point to the *object itself* and ask for an explanation, the object can be explained without reference to entities, causes, or contexts beyond those specifiable in our conceptual language. Explanations in our language may be given (in theory) of anything that we are able to *notice* in terms of that language. We do not *notice* the 'existence' of an object in the way that we notice an intelligible *quality* of an object: "Look, that table over there is not only square, but it also exists!" We might, of course, notice the 'existence' of something in the predicative sense of "existence": "Look, that rock that we saw twenty years ago *still exists* over there!" The predicative sense of "exist," however, presupposes the nonpredicative sense, which is, for Aquinas, the 'problematic' sense. Aquinas is worried about getting cards *into* the catalogue, not about putting them into separate compartments once they are there.

If we ask what the 'existence' of an object *is*[52]—what it is about the world that puzzles Aquinas—we cannot give a definition by means of composition and division (although existence is presupposed by the composition of an existential judgment). The 'existence' of an object is not *what remains* when we abstract from all of the *other* qualities of the object.[53] If we abstract entirely from *what* the object is, we do not have a concept of the *existence* of the object—we have no concept at all. "Existence" is a transcendental term that can never be 'pried loose' from the particular contents of experience.

Such is the consequence of Aquinas' teaching on the real categorial distinction between *esse* and *essentia*. Since they are expressed in categorially different ways, we cannot arrive at a notion of one by abstraction from the other. The essence of an object is that which is analogically represented in the intelligible forms conceived immanently by the 'intellect.' Existence, on the other hand, is that which is expressed in the *act of judgment* or existential assertion. There is no intelligible

---

[52] How odd the very question sounds: What *is* existence? Are we to say that 'existence exists,' as the phenomenologist insists that 'das Nichts nichtet'?

[53] S. T., I, 5; I, 11, 1; and, I, 16, 3.

form of 'existence.' To judge *that* '*x* exists' is a syntactically significant *move* of our language, but the 'existence of *x*' is not a syntactically significant *concept* of our language. It follows that we cannot be aware of or notice 'existence' as a problematic *aspect* or *part* of our experience. In terms of our discussion of the formal and semantical aspect of our conceptual language, it may be said that, while we understand the syntactical status of the assertion '___', that move only derives its *existential force*—it only expresses the radical concept of 'existence'—when the system as a whole is used to refer. The radical concept of 'existence' is not a significant concept *in* our conceptual system. The force of "exists" is presupposed by our use of intelligible forms to refer—it is not itself an intelligible form.

To raise a question, therefore, about the 'existence' of the world, or to say that 'existence' is problematic, is not to raise a conceptually significant question about reality, but to raise a *transcendental* question about the very relationship of our conceptual system to 'that which is.' To say "Why is there something rather than nothing?" is to reflect upon the fact that we naturally *find* ourselves using the intelligible forms resulting from our informing of experience to *refer* to 'that which is,' without being able to think or conceive 'existence' or (better) 'reality.' There are no *per se* inferences justifiable on the basis of the syntactical rules of our conceptual system that would enable us to comprehend or understand the facticity or being-there of the world to which we find ourselves referring. We cannot *conceive* that which makes our experience transcendentally *real*. We do not *know*, in short, *what* we are expressing in the existential judgment. The natural dispositional *sense* of reality which is presupposed by our referential use of a conceptual system is not an *act* of intelligible knowing. While our minds can measure *what* things are—by the use of analogical concepts—it cannot measure the *esse* or being-there of reality. Our minds are ultimately measured by the "givenness" of things. The *only* intentional correlate of the 'existence' of things is the judgment. The existence of things is not known in an immanently created form. Unlike the intelligible essences of things, which are known in and through creations of our own intentional powers, the *esse* of the world is that to which the intellect bows without comprehension. Existence is the only preconceptual *given* in our awareness of things.

Such a judgment is, of course, highly reflective: it results not from concentration on the *objects* of knowledge, but from concentration on the *act* of knowing.[54] To know that 'existence' is a problem—a nonintelligible surd at the root of our experience—is not to know something about the *world*, but to know something about the status of human *knowledge*. To judge the world in terms of its intelligiblity is to confess the extent and limits of one's own conceptual powers. Human knowledge of *what is* (the *quiddities* of things) takes the form of a specification of the radical intentionality of the mind. All intelligible thought takes place in the context of a dispositional openness to or pre-cognition of a 'field' of existence or reality which is simply *given*—not as a *content* of experience, but as the transcendental *arena* of experience. Existence is the medium *in which* we think, it is not that *of* which we think—except by reflection on our act of thinking. Clearly, existence is not intelligible: no account or explanation of 'existence' could conceivably be given in terms of our conceptual system. That there is something rather than nothing is simply a fact—we cannot conceive of anything that might explain or account for that fact.

Why does Aquinas seem to think that the existence of things *needs* to be accounted for, if we cannot in theory know what it would be like to *give* such an account? Aquinas' interpretation of the 'principle of the intelligibility of being' seems to imply that we naturally *must* assume that reality (from *every* point of view) is susceptible of *per se* intellectual analysis— that all being is in some fashion 'necessary.' "That is intelligible which is necessary" and "Being is intelligible" are, for Aquinas, *per se nota* principles of intelligibility. Since we do not *see* the necessity for the *esse* of things, the intellect is frustrated in its search for total intelligibility and must postulate an intentional point of view in terms of which the neces-

[54] Aquinas himself stresses the role of reflection in our knowledge of existence. See *De Ver.*, 1, 9. See also P. Hoenen, *Reality and Judgement According to St. Thomas*, Chap. 5.

sity of the *esse* of the world *could* be seen—a conceptual framework, that is, in which the assertion of the *esse* of things would follow (by the rules of the conceptual game) from the assertion of some other (now unknown) intelligible reality. The existence of the world, that is, could be inferred from the formal nature of its postulated cause by means of inferential moves justified by the axioms and rules of the postulated conceptual framework. To see the *esse* of the world in terms of such a *per se* causal relationship would be to alter the conception of 'the world' by placing in it the definition of its proper cause—a formal statement of that in the cause which renders the existence of the world intelligible. Such a definition would express what the world *really is* from the viewpoint of the postulated and adequate conceptual framework.

Without *possessing* such a conceptual framework, we can nevertheless say something about "that in the cause which renders the existence of the world intelligible." Since, for Aquinas, that is finally intelligible which is measured by intellect, and not that which measures intellect, it is clear that the entire complex of 'world-and-cause' cannot itself be a *given* existential arena *within* which a hypothetical possessor of our postulated conceptual framework would *find* himself using the intelligible forms of his conceptual system to refer to 'that which is'—in this case 'world-*and*-cause.' The postulated relationship between the world and its 'sufficient reason' must *itself* be an instance of reality being measured by 'intellect.' The *esse* of the world must *follow from* the agency of an intentional being. The *esse* of the world must be the objective correlate of free conceptual agency, and not a given transcendental field of reference within which 'intellect' is free only to postulate objective isomorphic correlates of its own essentialistic intentions. The postulated intelligible reality from which the 'necessity' of the world may be inferred must itself be the *locus* of the postulated conceptual framework in terms of which the inference is intelligible. Only in such a fashion could 'existence' be said to be 'measured' by 'intellect'—only in such a fashion could reality *in its entirety* be rendered intelligible by the *agency* of intellect, with no admixture of passivity.

The *aedequatio intellectus et rei* which constitutes the truth
of our essentialistic judgments about reality (our judgments
concerning *what is*) results from our free 'intentional creation'
of intelligible forms. The *whatness* or *quiddity* of reality is
susceptible of expression in terms created by our own conceptual powers; it is measured by the categories of our minds.[55]
The essential intelligibility of the world is only *potential* until
we create immanently the forms of essential intelligibility.
These forms, in terms of which we judge objects really *to be*
of certain 'sorts' or 'kinds,' are intelligible precisely *because*
they are creations of intellect. The element of passivity in our
knowledge of the world, however, qualifies the intelligibility
that the world has for us. The isomorphism between external
states of affairs and the material states of our sensory systems
—an isomorphism presupposed by the very notion of perceptual knowledge—is independent of our conceptual activity,
and only contingently related to the formal structure of our
conceptual system. That the forms created by intellect can be
used to inform experience and thus to refer intelligibly to
external reality is a *contingent* fact. It is for that reason that
reality in its own intrinsic *esse*, although judged to be *isomorphic with* the forms of our conceptual system, may be only
imperfectly, inadequately or misleadingly represented by our
language *about* reality. For Aquinas, in order to be intelligible
in the strict and full sense of the word, reality must *exist* precisely *as conceived by intellect*. Reality must be entirely passive to the agency of some 'intellect.'[56] It would appear that
'God,' as the intelligible ground of the *esse* of the world and
the locus of the intentional principles of intelligibility in terms
of which the final intelligibility of all reality might be seen, is
implicit in the natural first principles of human understanding! Philosophical reflection simply makes clear the manner in
which the intellect has *always* been ordered to a mode of in-

[55] Aquinas never *says* that the mind 'measures' the essential structures
of things in its judgments of what 'sorts' of things there are, although it
is implicit in his understanding of the conception by the agent intellect
of the intelligible form. He emphasizes what I have called 'semantic
truth,' and thus emphasizes the *passive* nature of an existential judgment of contingent fact.

[56] On the intellect of God as the 'measure' of reality, see S. *T.*, I, 14.

telligibility that it could never supply or comprehend on the basis of its own conceptual powers.

While we are not primarily interested in the validity or invalidity of Aquinas' argument on the basis of the natural ordering of the human mind, it must nevertheless be clear that, from one point of view, the argument is circular when seen in the light of Aquinas' 'principle of the intelligibility of being.' If Aquinas took the propositions—"Being is intelligible," "That is intelligible which is necessary," and "That is necessary which is measured by intellect"—as *premises* of an argument, the circularity of the procedure would be evident. Aquinas attributes to such propositions, however, the status of 'first principles'—they are not *premises of an argument* but *rules of argumentation*. Our reconstruction of a truly Thomistic 'argument' for the existence of God cannot be viewed as a knockdown logical argument constructed according to the criteria of validity dictated by the first principles of the intellect, but rather as an argumentative interpretation of the implications of our constant *use* of such principles. From Aquinas' scattered statements on the kind of intelligibility naturally demanded by the human intellect, we have constructed, as it were, an *Ur*-argument for the existence of God. Aquinas evidently believes that the natural desire of the intellect for complete intelligibility cannot be satisfied by anything other than God. That is the probable root cause of his willingness to accept *any* historical argument for the existence of God based on contingent or empirical matters of fact—they manifest the created tendency of the intellect to seek after God. Thus Aquinas reads all arguments for God from the viewpoint of creation. The human mind is ordered to God the *Creator* as to One Unknown. The intellect implicitly demands that the 'existence' of the world be measured and made necessary by a *free intentional or conceptual act*. It does not know, however, in what way that is possible.

Our chief concern is not the success or failure of Aquinas' argument, but the kind of reference to God that results from the assumption that it is valid. It is not a reference to an entity intelligibly defined in terms of our conceptual system. It ought not to be called a significant reference, since we are not in possession of the syntactical rules by means of which significant things could be predicated of the referent. It may be called a "meta-empirical reference." To say that God *exists* is to take advantage of the essentially analogous status of our sense of 'existence' and to postulate the possibility of an intentional point of view from which "God" (or its analogical correlate) *would be* an intelligible 'form.' To possess such a point of view would be to have a radically different sort of experience from our current sense experiences, and to introspect that experience in terms of a different conceptual light (the 'light of Glory'). The manner in which meaningful characteristics could be predicated of God would be determined by the rules of *that* conceptual system. All that we can predicate of God are those essentially analogous characteristics that must inhere *by definition* in any actual being who declares the intelligibility of reality in terms of meaningful concepts or intentions.[57] All of the attributes of God that are 'known' on the basis of natural theology follow analytically and vacuously from the analogical proposition that there *exists* an unknown and incomprehensible intentional context in terms of which the intelligibility of all reality *could* be seen if one could share that radically different conceptual point of view. The 'modus significandi' of such attributes—the syntactical meaning that they would have *in God*—remains unknown.[58]

Since "goodness," "unity," "truth," and the like are 'convertible' with "being,"[59] it follows immediately that those terms can be predicated of God. They are transcendental terms which *must* apply to the intentional locus of *any* significant conceptual system on the basis of which references can be made to 'that which is.' We do *not*, however, know what the "goodness," "unity," or "truth" of God are *like*. We assert only that, in any adequate description of the intentional being of God, there would occur intelligible terms or statements which would play a role that is syntactically isomorphic with the role played by such terms in *our* conceptual system. In order *to be* the intelligible context in terms of which the *esse* of the world would be comprehensible, God must be "a *good* what-

---

[57] *C. G.*, I, 3.   [58] *S. T.*, I, 13, 2.
[59] *S. T.*, I, 5, 1; 11, 1; and 16, 3.

ever he is," that is, there must be no existential defect in him
that would demand a *further* "accounting for."[60] God must
also have that mode of 'unity' that is appropriate to the locus
of a syntactical system in terms of which both itself and all
other things are intelligible *per se*. The form of 'God' must be
an *intelligible* and *adequate* representation of the being of
God, and that which is not formally unified is not intelligible.
But the mode of God's 'unity' is a mode appropriate to the
conceptual system in which the intelligible form 'God' occurs—
it is *not* that mode of unity defined by the rules of our conceptual system.[61] If the intentional being of God is to be seen
as the "sufficient reason" for the *esse* of reality—if the world
(both *ens* and *essentia*) is to be measured by the conceptions
or intentional forms present in God—then there must be an
aedequatio intellectus et rei between God and the world.[62]
Since, however, that adequation must result from the conceptual agency of God, and not from his passive submission to the
given fact of existence, the world must result from *his* conceiving.[63] Thus, "truth" in God is a mode of truth appropriate
to *his* intentional being, not to ours.

"Intellect" and "volition" follow by definition from the non-
significant predications already made. Any being which 'conceives' immanently the intelligible forms of reality may be
called an 'intellect,' whether or not we know what it would be
like for such a mode of conception to exist.[64] When a state of
affairs follows from the intentional state of any 'intellect,' we
may speak of the 'volition' of that being, even if we fail to see
how such 'volition' efficaciously achieves its 'intentions.'[65] Even
"love" and "mercy" can be *vacuously* predicated of God. To
intend toward that which is 'good' or 'willed' in terms of one's
own conceptual system is to 'love' that toward which you intend.[66] Since 'mercy' may be defined as the granting of that
which is not demanded by a justice *imposed from without*,

60 S. T., I, 6, 3.   61 S. T., I, 11, 3 and 4.
62 S. T., I, 16, 5.   63 S. T., I, 14, 8.
64 S. T., I, 14, 1, ad 3: "Knowledge is not in God after the mode of
created knowledge."
65 Aquinas simply assumes that 'volition' is part of the meaning of 'intellect': S. T., I, 19, 1.
66 S. T., I, 20, 1.

God can be said to be 'merciful'—the *esse* of the world results from the free intention of God and not from any demands imposed on God *ab extra*.[67] In a *vacuous* sense, even 'providence' and 'omnipotence' can be predicated of God, since he is by definition (although not by *intelligible* definition) the "source" of all the *esse* and agency that there is; and he may therefore be said to express 'purposes' (definable in *his* conceptual system) by means of 'external operation' in the world.[68]

Thus, there is a mode of affirmative predication involved in Aquinas' natural theology. The transcendentals—and terms which may be given transcendental or meta-linguistic force— are used to name or signify something which is actually true of God in his own being.[69] Since, however, the terms *as they really apply to God* have intelligible meaning only as analogues in a postulated and unknown conceptual system, and not in *our* conceptual system, we must simultaneously deny that we use them to intend the specific and intelligible intensional content that they possess for us.[70] All predications proper to God are either essentially analogous uses of transcendental terms or negations of conceptually significant terms or a combination of the two.

The key to understanding analogical predication in the writings of Aquinas is, therefore, the essentially analogical status of 'existence' as it plays a role in our use of a conceptual system to inform experience. Once we have admitted that reality may be *inadequately* expressed in *our* created intelligible forms, and that there may in theory be *another* conceptual framework in terms of which 'that which is' could be *adequately* represented, we open the possibility of a meta-

[67] S. T., I, 21, 4: "Nothing is due to creatures, except for something preexisting in them, or foreknown. If this in turn is due to a creature, it must be due on account of what precedes. Since we cannot go on to infinity, we must come to something that depends on the goodness of the divine will alone. . . . So, in every work of God, mercy appears at the primary source." In Sacred Theology, this principle applies far beyond the mere bestowal of natural existence.

[68] Cf. C. G., II, where the entire creation is defined as God's 'external operation.'

[69] S. T., I, 13, 2 and 12.

[70] S. T., I, 13, 5: "When we apply 'wise' to God, it leaves the thing signified as incomprehended, as exceeding the signification of the name. . . . The same rule applies to the other terms."

linguistic description in analogical terms of that which must be formally true of any such conceptual system. If we take the proofs of the existence of God to be convincing forms of argumentation, we may claim to *know* that the natures of things, as they *really are* in their own *esse*, derive from 'forms' inherent in the 'intellect' of an 'intentional being.' From the viewpoint of that 'being,' the *esse* of the world would express the intentional state of that 'being' by the analogy of *intrinsic attribution*: from God's point of view the world *really* expresses what he 'has in mind'; it really *is* as he thinks it.[71] From *our* point of view, however, the world as *we* think it can only be said to express the 'intentions' of God by the analogy of *extrinsic* attribution: the intelligible forms by which *we* know reality are not capable of expressing 'what God has in mind.'[72]

---

[71] God's knowledge of the world is not analogical in the sense that it represents the world by means of an isomorphism merely contingently related to the forms that things have *in se*.

[72] Analogy of any kind is, as we have noted, a meta-linguistic matter: to say that a word is analogical is to point out that it plays a particular kind of role within a language. In the case of the *analogy of proper proportionality*, it is claimed that a word in *one* conceptual framework plays a role that is syntactically isomorphic with the role played by an analogous word in *another* conceptual framework. Thus we might say that various uses of 'exist' are analogous by the analogy of proper proportionality, since the concrete or specific implications of its use are radically different according to the kind of conceptual framework in which it occurs. That which can be inferred from the claim 'John exists,' when that claim occurs in the context of existential or real description, is entirely different from that which can be inferred from the same statement form when it occurs in the context of fiction or literary analysis. Nonetheless, the role played by 'exists' in each case ties its subject into its relevant logical space in a formally similar manner. So also, 'Some men exist' and 'Some numbers exist' make specifically different sorts of claims, while nonetheless relating their subjects to their proper linguistic contexts in a fashion that can be described in a common meta-language as formally similar. In the case of those transcendental terms that can be applied to God, the level of comparison is of a higher order, since the transcendentals themselves play meta-linguistic roles. In effect we are saying that, in a meta-linguistic account of God's language, there would occur expressions playing syntactical roles isomorphic with the roles played by certain expressions in a meta-linguistic account of *our* language. In the theological use of the analogy of proper proportionality, we do not possess a common meta-language in terms of which to show precisely *how* the expressions play roles that are syntactically isomorphic —we merely claim that they do. In the case of the *analogy of attribution*, it is claimed that a word or expression in a particular conceptual frame-

As a result, we must deny the intelligible content of such forms (the meaning that they have for us) in applying them to God. We must, that is, use a form of the analogy of proper proportionality in our language about God.

Aquinas' own habit of moving almost chaotically from one form of analogy to another has created much confusion in the literature of analogy. A contextual examination of Aquinas'

---

work is implicitly defined (by the syntactical rules of that conceptual framework) in terms of another word or expression in the same conceptual framework. The definition of one word is placed in the definition of another word on the basis of a syntactically justified inference such as that which is made in a *per se* causal judgment. The relationship signified by 'analogy of attribution' is therefore an intrasystematic or intralinguistic relationship. When we speak of the analogy of *intrinsic* attribution, we imply that the relationship signified by 'analogy of attribution' holds between two words or expressions of that language whose metalanguage we are using to make the claim. ('Urine is defined as "healthy" on the basis of a *per se* causal relation to the "health" of a person.') In the language of God, for example, things in the world would be defined as 'good' on the basis of a *per se* causal relation to the 'goodness' of God. The perfections of the world *really are* as God intends them, and thus the formal notion of God's creative intentions may be placed in the formal notion of the perfections of the world. This may be implicitly and intelligibly done only in the context of *God's* language—not in the context of *our* language. When we speak of the analogy of *extrinsic* attribution, the situation is somewhat more complex. To say that two words or expressions in *one* conceptual framework are related by the analogy of *extrinsic* attribution is to claim that their analogues in *another* conceptual framework are related by the analogy of *intrinsic* attribution. A nontheological example may be found in ordinary-language descriptions of scientific theory; such descriptions are always analogical interpretations. Thus we might say, 'In physics, "mass" and "energy" are implicitly co-defined.' What we *mean*, however, is that the theoretical counterparts of 'mass' and 'energy'—as they occur in the language proper to physics—are syntactically related in such a fashion that one is implicitly defined in terms of the other. It is not true, however, that 'mass' and 'energy' are implicitly co-defined by the syntactical rules of the *English language*. So, when we say that in *our* language the 'goodness' of the world is related to the 'goodness' of God by the analogy of *extrinsic* attribution, we are claiming that there occur in *God's* language proper and adequate expressions of the perfections of the world, and that those expressions are implicitly defined in terms of *God's* perfection. (That implicit definition would, of course, be based on an intelligibly expressed relation of *per se* or proper causality.) We deny, however, that *our* notions of the perfections of the world can be implicitly defined by the syntactical rules of our language in terms of *our* notions of the perfection of God. It can be seen readily that the analogy of extrinsic attribution combines the analogies of proper proportionality and attribution.

use of analogy will reveal that whenever he uses terminology similar to that of *intrinsic attribution* he is speaking hypothetically from God's point of view.[73] At those moments he is being most radically a theologian. When, on the other hand, he uses language which seems to imply that there is a relationship of *extrinsic attribution* between God and the world, he is speaking of our knowledge of reality.[74] He is denying that we can see things precisely as willed by God. Finally, when he speaks in terms of proper proportionality, he is emphasizing the fact that we do not have access to the language of God.[75] The traditional tendency to unite all of Aquinas' analogical terminology into a single unity or "doctrine" (generally a kind of proper proportionality) results apparently from Cajetan's initial judgment that the language of 'proper proportionality' reflected in *De Veritate*, II, 11, is identical in intention with the language of 'intrinsic attribution' in the *Commentary on the Sentences*, I, 19, 5, 2.[76] Man's point of view is confused with God's point of view. As a result, many Thomists have failed to see that the 'doctrine of analogy' is not a means of knowing God, but a meta-linguistic analysis of the state of certain words and propositions used to *name* God.[77] From God's point of view there is undoubtedly an 'analogy of being'; from our point of view, however, there is only an 'analogy of "being."' The proofs for the existence of God are our way of confessing our ignorance of the 'analogy of being.' We do not know the principle which might unify all aspects of our awareness of 'that which is.'[78]

[73] As in S. T., I, 13, 6. The word 'good' applies primarily to God, since the goodness of the world flows from God's goodness.

[74] As in S. T., I, 7, 4. From *our* point of view, however, things cannot be called 'good' through the 'goodness' of God.

[75] *De Ver.*, II, 11.

[76] Cf., B. Mondin, S.X., *The Principle of Analogy in Protestant and Catholic Theology* (Martinus Nijhoff, The Hague, 1963), pp. 40f. Mondin points out that, in the Sentences example, Aquinas is speaking of the analogy of 'one to another,' which involves the relationship of a derivative analogate to a prime analogate. The logic is subject to that of 'intrinsic attribution' as I have construed it.

[77] It is significant that S. T., I, 12 discusses our *knowledge* of God (reserved for the eschaton), whereas I, 13, which discusses *analogy* is simply entitled 'On *Naming* God.'

[78] My discussion of analogy is in general dependent not only on Mon-

THE LANGUAGE OF NATURAL THEOLOGY

Once we grant to Aquinas the presuppositions of his argument, it follows analytically that the answer to the question posed by the nominal definition of "God"—"Is there a being which is above all things, that is, removed from all things and the source of all things?"—must be "Yes." Aquinas certainly is correct in maintaining that the *esse* of the world is a *given* context in which all of our thinking and argumentation takes place, and for which we cannot in theory conceive of an intelligible explanation. The demand, "Give me an explanation of the existence of everything," is a pseudo-demand, since we cannot conceive of anything which could be such an explanation except in terms of *our* use of "exists"—which is the use needing, for Aquinas, further justification. If we grant to Aquinas that existence *must* be 'intelligible' and that "intelligibility" means "necessity," and if we further grant to him that "necessity" in this instance means "measured by the free intentional activity of some 'intelligent' agent," then it follows analytically that there must exist some 'intelligent' entity from whose intentional point of view the *esse* of the world is seen to be intelligible *because* it follows from his own immanent powers of 'conceiving' reality.

Or course, we need not grant the presuppositions. Aquinas may be correct in saying that men naturally *do* expect their experience to be intelligible in all particulars. He may also be correct in his judgment that a thing is only intelligible if we can see its "sufficient reason" or cause. It does not follow, however, that our desire to "see the necessity" for the existence of things is more than a psychological ideal doomed to frustration by "the way things are." Indeed, some philosophers might consider it a mental disease requiring philosophical therapy. On the other hand, it *might* be argued that we *ought* to take our natural intellectual expectations as evidence for 'the way things really are': even if we assume hypothetically that the

---

din's work, but also on R. McInerny, *The Logic of Analogy* (Martinus Nijhoff, The Hague, 1961), which contains an excellent analysis of analogy as a meta-linguistic device, and to a ground breaker in the field, H. Lyttkens, *The Analogy Between God and the World* (Almquist & Wiksells, Uppsala, 1952).

world *is* related in some nonconceivable fashion to some non-conceivable entity from which it derives its existence, we still could not expect to find evidence *within* the world of that relationship. We could never know what *counted* as evidence for the reality of a nonconceivable relationship to a nonconceivable entity: we only know what counts as evidence for those things of which we can conceive. Given the theoretical impossibility of there being conclusive evidence for or against the hypothesis, it might not be irrational to *take* the natural tendencies of our own minds as somehow indicative of the nature of things. Our minds are, after all, products of nature—what they 'look for' in reality might well reflect the nature of reality. The point is, however, that such a 'taking' is not forced on us; it would be a *decision*. We are free to argue that our natural desire to see the necessity for the existence of things is *somehow* indicative of how things are, but the presupposition that *no* natural desire is in vain is not self-evidently true. To elevate such a hypothesis to the level of a synthetic a priori of our conceptual scheme seems a bit rash. Why, then, has Aquinas done so? I would argue that his prime motivation is not philosophical but theological. He 'knows' on the basis of
✓ revelation that the mind of man is ordered to God as to One Unknown, and he accepts as revealed truth the statement that man is able, on the basis of reason alone, to reflect on that ordering. He then offers as external and probable evidence of the truth of revelation a philosophical account of the 'first principles' of reason which manifests that ordination of the mind to the First Truth. Whatever other interpretation of the status of the 'first principles' might be possible, Aquinas 'knows' that *his* interpretation is correct.

The more important question for our purposes is what Aquinas thinks he has proved. What does he take to be the status of the language in terms of which he affirms the existence of God and predicates of him certain 'necessary' transcendental characteristics? Aquinas admits that all of our language about God is a 'kind of equivocation.'[79] It is not, however, a *pure* equivocation.[80] While we do not know *how* our language about God is true of him, we know that it must succeed in

---

[79] S. T., I, 13, 5, *sed contra*.   [80] S. T., I, 13, 5, *respondeo*.

naming something real in him. Thus, to say that God 'exists' is
to say that there is another conceptual system (an ideal language) in terms of which a syntactical move isomorphic in
usage with our syntactically significant existential assertion
('___') could be used in conjunction with an entity radically
unlike the entities which are existentially assertable in our
language. That which could be inferred (by the rules of *that*
conceptual system) from the assertion that something 'existed'
(or its analogical counterpart in *that* language) would differ
significantly from that which can be inferred from an existential assertion in our language. In order for God to be intelligible *in se* (in terms of *his* conceptual system) the assertion
of 'God' must be immediately justified (by the rules of the
game) on the basis of the syntactical role of 'God' in that system. 'God exists' is an unconditionally assertable sentence of
the language; or, in more traditional terminology, God's existence is, *quoad se*, self-evident—in God there is no distinction
between essence and existence. Unfortunately, we do not
know what kind of intelligible form would adequately express
his 'essence' or what syntactical rules govern 'existence' as
predicated of him! We affirm the *id ad quod* of the terms (that
which they are used to name or signify), but we deny the
id a quo of the terms (the subjective significance that they
have for us).[81] The term 'existence' applies affirmatively, substantially, and properly to God with regard to that which it
names or signifies in *his language*, but it does not apply to
him *at all* with regard to what it names or signifies in *our*
language. In Aquinas' terms, it applies with regard to the *res
significata* (the reality signified), but it does not apply with
regard to the *modus significandi* (the way that it signifies for
us).[82] If our analysis of the essentially analogous status of
"exists" was correct, however, we know that the word could
in theory have uses other than those which are significant in
terms of our conceptual system. To say that God 'exists' in some
unknown sense of the word is not necessarily irrational.

That is why, for Aquinas as for pseudo-Dionysius, any term
that may be affirmed of God may also be denied of him.[83]
Indeed, all terms *must* be denied of him in the sense in which

[81] S. T., I, 13, 3.   [82] Ibid.   [83] Comm. in Sent., I, VII, 1, 1.

QUINQUE VIAE AND SCIENTIA DIVINA

they are affirmed (in our language) of things *other* than God. While to say that God 'exists' is to say that there *is* a conceptual framework in terms of which the proposition "God exists" would be intelligible, it is nevertheless true that the proposition is *not* intelligible in terms of *our* conceptual framework, and thus, insofar as the word "exists" plays an intrasystematic role in our language, it must be *denied* of God.[84] To say that God 'exists' and that God does not exist is a paradox, but it is not the *kind* of paradox that it seems to be—it is not a self-contradiction. We are familiar with the sort of paradox that results from using the same word in two senses: "Well, I suppose that John is 'good,' but he certainly is not GOOD!" If an analyst were to accuse the speaker of falling into self-contradiction, he need only reply, "Oh, but I meant that John is good in the sense of conforming to the traditional rules and demands of society, but he is not good in the sense of being the kind of person I admire." When the statement has the form of a self-contradiction, it is merely a *paradox* if the same word occurs within it in two different senses. If both senses of the word can be defined in terms of our conceptual system (if I can exhibit the meaning of the word in both its occurrences in the statement), we may speak of a 'soft' paradox. Aquinas' statements about God, however, are such that only *one* of the uses of a word can be shown to be significant *within* our language; the other use is metasystematic. I can tell you in what sense I am *denying* a word of God, but I cannot tell you in what sense I am *affirming* it. I can only tell you the *reason* that I affirm it, and why the affirmation is not irrational. Thus, we may call the paradoxes of theology 'hard' paradoxes.

The reason that Aquinas applies the term 'existence' to God (or claims that God 'exists') is that the existence of the world would remain radically unintelligible if there did not 'exist' something from which the existence of the world derived its hypothetical necessity. "God" is defined nominally *in terms* of a relationship. The proposition "God exists," however, does not *mean* that God is the source of the hypothetical necessity of the existence of the world. While the attribution of 'existence' to God is based on a postulated relation between the

---

[84] *Comm. in Sent.*, ad 4.

world and its 'intelligible context,' the term 'existence' does not *signify* that relationship—it signifies God himself.[85] The *way* that it signifies God, however, is unknown to us since we do not know the true nature of the postulated relationship on the basis of which we use the word to refer to God. Unlike a reference to 'that which I hit with my car,' the references of natural theology are subject to complete notional opacity. The intentional basis upon which we use "existence" to refer to God is notionally opaque to the intentional basis upon which the analogous counterpart of 'existence' in the language of God would be significantly used of him.

The notion that there are two sorts of natural theology— affirmative and negative—is radically misleading if it is thought that the affirmations of natural theology are not themselves subject to a kind of remotion (or removal from them of significant content). It is true that some terms are denied of God *simpliciter*. Such terms are those which are constitutionally unable to play anything but an intrasystematic role in our language. "Hard" simply cannot be given a transcendental use such that it would appear in the *meta-language* of any intelligible conceptual system (needless to say, there would be an analogical counterpart of the word *in* God's language). "Hard," that is, cannot be shown to be implicit in the very notions of 'existence' and 'intelligible.' It is simply denied of God. Other terms, such as 'good' or 'intention,' may be given a transcendental use, such that they *must* appear in the meta-language of any conceptual system in terms of which reality is rendered intelligible. Nonetheless, when they are hypothetically and analogically applied to *other* conceptual systems, the meaning that they have in *our* conceptual system (where they *also* play an intrasystematic role) must be denied. Thus, while Aquinas denies in article two of question thirteen of the first part of the *Summa* that all of our statements about God are purely negative or used to signify the relation between God and the world, he nevertheless claims that all of our *affirmations* have the effect of signifying *to us* how God is *not*.[86] The two claims are not incompatible. While we affirm that there *is* something in God which is analogous with something in our

---

[85] S. T., I, 13, 2, ad 2.   [86] S. T., I, introduction to 3.

language, we deny that we know *what it is in God*. To argue
that there *is* another conceptual system in terms of which
reality is rendered intelligible is not to possess that system or
to know how it manifests those formal characteristics (such
as unity and syntactical order) that *any* such conceptual system must manifest.

As we have shown, any number of 'attributes' are immediately and vacuously derivable from the meta-empirical claim
that he 'exists' and is the 'intelligible context' of the world.
Since that which he is postulated to render intelligible is the
esse of the world, it may be said that things really are as he intends them to be. The real significance of any aspect of reality
can be known only when we know in what way it expresses an
'intention of God' or is intentionally 'measured' by God. If the
esse of the world is to be rendered intelligible by reference to
the 'intentions' of God, then those intentions must infallibly be
expressed in 'that which is.' Everything, then, expresses an
'intention' of God. That is to say that God exercises a 'universal
providence' over all things. Indeed, the 'providence' of God is
the foundation of one of Aquinas' favorite nominal definitions
of "God":

> This name of 'God' is imposed on the basis of a universal
> providence over all things; for everyone who speaks of 'God'
> intends to call that being 'God' which has a universal provi-
> dence over things.
>
> [Imponitur enim hoc nomen ab universali rerum providen-
> tia; omnes enim loquentes de Deo, hoc intendunt nominare
> Deum quod habet providentiam universalem de rebus.][87]

Yet Aquinas maintains, as we quoted him above, that such attributes as 'providence' cannot be known except by revelation.
What he means, I believe, is that the *significance* of saying
that all things express an 'intention of God' cannot be known
except in the 'light of faith.' It is only through revelation that
we have some notion of what can be inferred from the statement "God exercises providence over all things." That is what
is disturbing about the formulation of the fifth way. It seems
to imply that we already know what it is for a thing to mani-

[87] S. *T.*, I, 13, 8.

fest the intelligence and purposiveness of God: such things exhibit an 'orderliness' in their operations!

The fifth way could, however, be read in a rather different way. It might be saying only that the regularity that we discover in the operations of nature (as we syntactically conceive it) is taken to be a 'sign' of the kind of intelligibility that we naturally wish to impose on *all* reality in *all* of its aspects. Thus, the occurrence of *partial* intelligibility—the sort expressible in *per se* causal statements in our language—cannot be finally said to occur in the over-all context of a nonintelligible *given* such as the 'existence' of the natural order in which the partial intelligibility is judged to have an objective correlate. The regularity of operation discovered in nature is taken as the basis of a negative insight that existence does not itself possess for us the same kind of *per se* predictability or intelligibility possessed by events definable in terms of our conceptual system. On that basis we *may* be led to postulate a being for whom the *esse* of the world is *per se* intelligible. To know that things operate in a regular fashion is not to know *how* they express the 'providential intentions of God,' but it may be used as a basis for asserting that things *do* express such 'intentions'—in a way known only to God:

> Even if the natures of things were known to us, their order, according to which divine providence has disposed them toward each other and directed them to an end, could be noted by us only tenuously, since we do not succeed in knowing the plan of divine providence.

> [Sic, etsi ipsae naturae rerum essent nobis cognitae, ordo tamen earum, secundum quod a divina providentia et ad invicem disponuntur et diriguntur in finem tenuiter nobis notus esse posset, cum ad cognoscendum rationem diviniae providentiae non pertingamus.][88]

Judging that reality manifests regularity of operation might be the basis on which we assume that, *if* we knew the natures of things (which we do not), we would "tenuously note" that all things are ordered in some sense of the word by the Provi-

---

[88] *C. G.*, IV, 1.

dence of God. We are now able to note only that certain things regularly tend toward certain ends in the natural order *as we conceive it*. But the end to which *God* has ordered all things is *himself*, and that we cannot see.[89] We are ordered to God as to One Unknown.

[89] *S. T.*, i, 12, 13, ad 1.

CHAPTER FOUR

SCIENTIA DEI AND THE UNKNOWN GOD

INTRODUCTION **T**HE conclusions of natural theology form an ordered series of sententially vacuous statements which follow logically from the 'packed' presupposition that reality must in all its aspects be measured by intellect. They consist either of an admittedly hypothetical application of transcendental predicates to a nonconceivable meta-empirical entity, or of a denial to that entity of intrasystematically meaningful predicates, or a combination of the two. When judged from the viewpoint of an empirically circumscribed criterion of meaning, they are without intelligible content. In isolation from the propositions of Sacred Doctrine, they are soteriologically worthless and religiously uninteresting. Since they contain no empirically significant concepts or *rationes*, they fail to supply the intellect with intentions of reality capable of being used to make meaningful references to God. In place of intelligible notions they posit a negative judgment that the range of human intentional reference does not exhaust 'that which is.' In making that judgment, they already presuppose a meta-empirical or transsystematic usage of the transcendentals—they presuppose the primacy of the dispositional concept (or *Vorgriff*) of 'being' over all empirical specifications of that concept. Since conceptual judgments do not exhaust the demand of the intellect for intelligibility, the mind is able to recognize problematics or absurdities which cannot be expressed in intelligible terms. It is the program of natural theology to lead the intellect through a series of judgments which hopefully will result in a negative insight productive of the further judgment that the intellect has encountered a nonintelligible level of experience incapable of formulation in a conceptually meaningful question. The conclusion of natural theology is then the paradox that the human intellect is ordered to a reality that it cannot know and is seeking an intelligibility that it cannot understand. In judging the world to be radically unintelligible, we are implicitly seeking God, and in talking about 'God' we are judging the world. All the language of natural theology is language about that which is sought after but unknown. It is incapable, therefore, of conforming the mind to that which is sought. It conveys no *knowledge* of God —even of an imperfect sort—and it terminates in the judgment that there is that of which we have no knowledge.[1]

Aquinas, who lived before the great days of therapeutic linguistic clarification and compulsive univocity, was more generous with the term 'cognition' than any contemporary linguistic philosopher would dare to be. He spoke easily on certain occasions of "natural cognitions of God," while denying on alternative occasions that we have knowledge of God. Our natural 'cognitions' of God are radically negative specifications of what he is not and how he does not exist. It is uncharitable to convert Aquinas' linguistic generosity into a covert claim to possess a kind of knowledge of God (conceptually significant) that Aquinas himself disclaims. Because we in the modern world generally restrict the word "cognition" to empirically significant contexts, we tend to insist that Aquinas intend what we intend by the word; we thus insist that he fall into self-contradiction.

The same lack of linguistic generosity has exhibited itself in analyses of Aquinas' teaching on the nature of faith. Aquinas blithely states that a higher 'cognition' of God can be had through grace than through reason.[2] Not only do moderns translate *cognitio* by the unqualified term "knowledge," they also assume against the repeated protestations of the text that the "knowledge" of faith must be coherent from a conceptual point of view. They tend to water down Aquinas' claim that faith itself relates us to God as to One Unknown,[3] substituting for it the ambiguous claim that faith imparts *partial* knowledge

---

[1] Karl Rahner, who utilizes the methodology of contemporary phenomenology in his analyses of Aquinas, nonetheless comes to remarkably similar conclusions. For example, in *Hörer des Wortes* (Kösel-Verlag, Munich, 1963), he warns against the attempt to convert metaphysics into a kind of 'natural religion.' In metaphysics, God is 'cognized' as the Unknown: "Damit is aber gesagt: Die Metaphysik, die in sich schon Religionsphilosophie is, muß derart sein, daß sie Gott als den freien Unbekannten erkennt. . ." (pp. 28f.).

[2] S. T., I, 12, 13.   [3] *Ibid.*

of God. Like natural theology, it would seem, sacred doctrine tells us 'some things' about God—different things, to be sure, but 'things' in a straightforward sense. On the basis of reason, it would appear, we know that God is 'good'—on the basis of faith, however, we know also that he is 'Three in One.' Why the latter is a "saving truth" and the former is not is presumably a matter of the meritorious character of believing the unexpected.

Aquinas, to be sure, uses the expression "imperfect cognition" of the teachings of the faith. He does not mean, however, *incomplete* knowledge of a *conceptual* sort, but *imperfect* knowledge of its *own* sort. It is the peculiar *sort* of 'knowledge' produced by faith that is not yet perfect—faith is not merely a further extension of or addition to conceptual knowledge. For this reason, Aquinas can say that faith *perfects* reason. Faith is a perfection precisely because it is *not* merely an extension (and an incomplete extension at that) of the natural powers of the intellect. Faith perfects the language of natural reason by enabling it to do what it cannot do on its own—point toward the God of faith. That is the sum and perfection of what the language of reason can do—it can do no more. And that 'pointing toward' is not even in the light of faith an intelligible 'terminating in'—God is not rendered intelligible even by faith. Conceptual reason can be given no further actuality or noetic value than faith in fact gives it; from that point of view faith is a perfection. However, faith itself demands an actuality and noetic value that it cannot itself supply. It is that 'demand' or tendency of faith, coupled with hope, that constitutes the 'cognition' of faith. Faith, then, perfects the language of natural reason by giving to it a referential value that it cannot achieve on its own; like natural reason itself, however, the 'cognition' of faith is not a possession but a demand for that which is not possessed. In this life, a 'cognition' of God is always a matter of falling short. The cognitions of natural reason and the cognitions of faith are knowledge of what God is not—a tantalizing foretaste that whets the intellectual appetite without providing sufficient substantial food:

Felicity is the perfect operation of the human intellect. . . .
In the cognition of faith, however, is found a most imperfect
operation of the intellect . . . since the intellect does not grasp
that to which it assents in believing. . . . Furthermore,
through felicity, since it is a final end, natural desire comes
to rest. However, the cognition of faith does not give rest to
desire, but sets it on fire. . . . Therefore, man's ultimate felicity does not consist of the cognition of faith.[4]

Before explicating and defending these judgments, I shall
examine in nontheological terms the 'state of the question,' in
order to clarify the nature of the epistemological problem involved in the apparent claims of faith, and in order to eliminate the possibility of certain attempts to resolve the problem.

THE PARADOX OF FAITH

The problem of reference raised in the context of our discussion of natural theology cannot be resolved by a mere appeal to the will to believe. The popular notion that natural
reason can take us part of the way toward God and thus
supply us with a logical platform from which we can take a
'leap of faith' fails to discern the locus of the problem. If there
were any clear conceptual content to the natural 'notion' of
God—an intelligible way to bring 'God' into our conceptual
system—it might be possible to make a 'leap of faith.' If there
were a series of cognitively significant propositions about God,
it might be the case that the only question remaining is their
truth or falsity. A coherent list of criteria of evidence which
might in theory confirm the truth of such propositions could
be produced. In the absence of conclusive evidence one way
or the other, one might decide, rationally or not, to opt for the
truth of logically significant propositions about God. It could
then be known, at least, what it was that one was believing—
in what direction one was leaping. The propositions of natural
theology, however, postulate the 'reality' of a meta-empirical
being to which no significant and intelligible reference can be
made. To assent to the conclusions of natural theology is not,
therefore, to postulate the existence of a being about whom

[4] C. G., III, 40.

significant and intelligible propositions, subject to confirmation and disconfirmation, can be believed.

The problem of faith is not that reason can establish *certain* significant things about God, while evidence is lacking for *other* significant things that *may* be true of him; the problem is how we could ever see the significance of *any* proposition about God, revealed or not. It would be misleading to say that the problem is merely linguistic, but there is clearly a linguistic aspect to the problem. Human language is intentional—it is *about* things—because it is the expression of thoughts which are themselves intentional or about things. Successful reference depends upon a meaningful intentional or conceptual context.[5] "God," however, is a name which can never occur within a conceptual context which is meaningful to us. It is the name of that of which I can have no meaningful intention. There can be no meaningful act of the intellect without reference to the contents of sense experience (*conversio*).[6] As Aquinas concluded, concerning God it is *in no way* (*nullo modo*) possible to know anything affirmative according to a *ratio* or notion common to God and the natural objects of the human intellect—material things.[7] We cannot, then, have a meaningful affirmative notion of God. Not to know anything affirmative and meaningful is not to be able to affirm anything meaningfully. Much as we might desire to know the unknowable (blind desire that it is) we cannot know it—we cannot even think it. It follows that we cannot believe it, since believing is "thinking with assent."[8]

To put it most simply, all of our naturally meaningful language is language about the world or about that which is intelligibly related to the world. It is impossible to see how language about the world could be used to make significant statements about an entity whose very relation to the world is so problematic that it cannot be expressed in our language. A person might think that he is affirming something meaningful about God by mouthing the words "I believe" before a number

---

[5] The point of the argument is unchanged even if we specify (probably correctly) that we only come to have thoughts because we learn to use the given language of human community.

[6] *S. T.*, I, 84, 7.   [7] *S. T.*, I, 88, 2, ad 4.   [8] *S. T.*, II-II, 2, 1.

of strange propositions; but, if believing is "thinking with assent," he cannot be significantly affirming anything of God without having that which he believes significantly in mind. There is no natural human activity that might be called "having God in mind." What I have called a 'meta-empirical reference' is *not* a cognitively significant reference; the way in which it comes to be possible has been discussed at length. The desire to convert such a 'meta-empirical reference' into a cognitively significant reference is natural for those who admit the possibility of a 'meta-empirical reference'—the psychological ground of the will to believe, which is the ground of all natural religion, is quite clear; but its logical ground is nonexistent.

The clear conclusion from Aquinas' own epistemology is that no proposition can both convey significant notions and refer to God with the same significance. It might be suggested, however, that it is possible to *believe* the language of faith without understanding it; the medieval position seems generally to be that man believes *in order to* understand, not that he believes *because* he understands. Is it not possible to believe *that* the propositions of faith *do* refer to God, and *are* true to his nature, without claiming to know *in what way* they refer or *how* they are true? Such 'belief' would seem to parallel the claim of natural theology that the world *is* related to God, but in a way unknown to man. Is not 'belief' in the language of faith but another instance of a negative judgment supporting a nonintelligible meta-empirical reference? Aquinas himself defines faith as assent to truths which are not apparent,[9] an obvious parallel to believing propositions whose reference is not clear. Several distinctions, however, must be made.

1. The negative judgments and meta-empirical references of natural theology are not to be construed as significant acts conforming the mind to God. Their lack of soteriological value is not unrelated to their noetic status; it would therefore be difficult to justify soteriological claims for any beliefs exhibiting the same sentential vacuity.

2. The propositions of natural theology follow vacuously

9 *S. T.*, II-II, 4, 1.

from the postulation of a nonconceivable context of transcendental intelligibility. Once that postulation has been made, the propositions of natural theology can be 'believed' without reservation: they do not purport to convey further information of their subject. It cannot be shown, however, that the propositions of revealed theology follow analytically from those of natural theology. If the articles of faith are taken in their own terms, it would seem to be impossible to convert them into predications of transcendental perfections or negations of meaningful concepts—i.e., the terms used by the articles of faith do not seem to play a meta-linguistic role. Furthermore, the language of faith clearly posits another ground than natural reason for the acceptance of the articles of faith, which can be known only by 'revelation.'

3. It follows that the problem of the language of faith is not a trite problem, as was the 'problem' of the language of natural theology. The latter is problematic only if one assumes that it purports to make significant and conceptually meaningful references to God. It would appear that the language of faith purports to do just that.

4. One cannot believe—or disbelieve—a proposition as such without understanding it. To understand a significant referential proposition is to know how it intends its reference— how to use it in order to refer. Since the propositions of natural theology can be explicated in terms of *vacuous transcendentals*, they can be understood in those terms and thus believed. Since the propositions of faith seem to predicate specific qualities of God (how could 'trinity of persons' be interpreted as a negation or transcendental predication?), it is difficult to see how they might be understood. But to believe is to "think with assent."

5. To believe *that* a proposition refers is not necessarily to believe the proposition—indeed, to believe that a proposition is *true* is not necessarily to believe the proposition. If I believe that my friend has just uttered a proposition, the terms of which I did not hear, and if I take it that he was referring to something, then I may believe that the proposition he uttered made a successful reference and was a true statement—my friend is to be depended upon in such things. I

cannot be said, however, to believe the *proposition*, since I have no idea what the proposition stated.[10]

6. In order to believe that a proposition makes a successful reference without myself understanding it, I must assume that someone else understands it and thus knows how it refers. A proposition, formally considered, is not the kind of thing that simply appears 'out there' and refers. A proposition must be *used* to refer. The notion of propositions having an independence from human intentions and simply 'referring' on their own is as odd as that of evidence objectively appearing and simply evidencing. Reference and evidence are dependent upon the intentional structure of human conceptual frameworks. Thus, in order for a proposition to refer, there must be someone who knows the meaning of the proposition and is able to use it successfully to refer.

The attempted solution of the problem of reference, then, does not succeed: a) The propositions of faith cannot be assimilated to the propositions of natural theology—they are not intended as meta-empirical predications of transcendentals; b) They cannot be believed to refer without someone understanding them—which is exactly what was taken to be impossible. We are left, then, with the disturbing dilemma that *either* man is able to have a meaningful intention of God *or* the propositions of faith cannot be believed or believed to be true. Faith, it would appear, denies both alternatives.

The analysis would seem to be a contemporary one. It might be thought that Aquinas—or others in the medieval tradition —would find it irrelevant. Such, however, is not the case. Medieval logicians possessed equivalents of all of the terms used above.[11] The fundamental distinction is that between *vox* and *verbum*. A mere sound (*flatus vocis*) does not have meaning; nor do printed signs (*verba scripta*). A purely extensional description of a proposition will make reference only to sounds and marks. In order to refer or intend, therefore, the

---

[10] The confusion results from a failure to distinguish between the material and formal modes. To say (materially), "He believes that what John said is true," does not necessarily imply the more formal claim, "He believes 'that-p,' which John uttered, to be true."

[11] For Aquinas' statement of the moderate realist position, see, *In Libros Peri Hermeneias Expositio*, L. I and L. II.

sounds and marks must be used in the context of intentional or conceptual space. A word must be used to express an intention. An *intentio* is a *conceptio intellectus* on which is based a symbolic or mental *verbum*. The spoken *verbum* is a use of *vox* to express the intentional word and concept. Thus it can be concluded that a proposition can only refer if it expresses the intentional state of someone possessing meaningful concepts. To say that a proposition refers even if I do not know how it refers, is at least to claim that there *is* someone for whom the proposition is an expression of conceptually meaningful intentions.

Aquinas seems to be referring to such an insight when he rejects the notion of establishing faith upon the apologetic of fundamental theology.[12] "External inducements" to faith are never sufficient causes for belief: not even a miracle directly observed can produce assent to the articles of faith.[13] Nor can the persuasive powers of any man.[14] As *evidence* for that claim, he points out that several men may see the same miracle or hear the same persuasive words, while one believes and the other does not. It might be thought—and many Catholic interpreters seem to think—that Aquinas is merely saying that miracles and apologetic arguments do not constitute *compelling* ground for assenting to certain propositions, the meaning of which is nevertheless clear. In the next paragraph, however, Aquinas offers, not evidence, but the *reason* why man cannot believe on the basis of miracle or apologetics: "Man, by believing the articles of faith, is taken beyond his natural condition." The language of faith cannot be believed[15] in the light of man's natural conceptual powers—in order to believe the propositions of faith man needs a new, nonnatural mode of understanding, a *principio supernaturalis*.[16]

Since Aquinas identifies the supernatural principle of faith with God himself, it is tempting to offer a compromise solution to the problem of the language of faith. The 'solution'

[12] The discipline which attempts to establish the credibility of the faith.
[13] S. T., II-II, 6, 1.   [14] *Ibid.*
[15] Although one might be of the opinion *that* they are true (improper faith, or faith 'commonly so-called').
[16] S. T., II-II, 6, 1.

depends upon the distinction between assenting to a proposition that one understands, and assenting to a proposition which one believes *another* to understand. While I cannot (without proof) believe another *man* to understand the language of faith, I might believe *God* to understand it. Aquinas often speaks of assenting to the articles of faith on the authority of God who utters them. The propositions of the language of faith can be believed to refer to God because *God* can use them to refer to himself; God possesses the proper intentional state in terms of which to use the propositions in a meaningful way. Strictly speaking, to assent to the propositions of faith is not to assent to a set of intelligible truths, but to assent to the authority of the One who utters them.

Without denying the entire substance of such a claim, it can be shown that its implications are highly unsatisfactory. A parallel from ordinary experience might be instructive. The average man-in-the-street does not understand much about contemporary physics. Nevertheless he believes that the propositions of physics are true. If he were to look into a textbook on submolecular particles (one written in the proper theoretical language) he would not make the mistake of saying, "I know the meaning of most of the words, but not the meaning of the sentences." The opacity of scientific language to the average man does not result from the scientist's using ordinary words in an unfathomable way—although that may *also* occur. Rather, the scientist seems to be using new words or symbols in a new language. It is the *theoretical language* of science that the man-in-the-street fails to understand, and not merely an extended or odd use of old familiar terms. The scientist utters his propositions in a new formal language with a highly complex syntactical structure and a set of semantical rules unheard of in ordinary language. The distinctive and controlling concepts of the language are not special uses of ordinary concepts, but entirely new concepts whose intensions and extensions are determined by the syntactical structure and semantical use of the whole intentional framework of which they are a part. Suppose, however, that a scientist were to 'reveal' some of his truth by speaking to the man-in-the-street in words taken from ordinary language. He might say, for example, that "electrons" behave like both "waves" and "particles." The man would understand each of the words, for each of them has a significant syntactical role in ordinary language. (Even "electron" has such a role for the average man: "electron" is the name of a 'bitty-little thing' that scientists talk about.) The major difficulty is that the syntactical rules governing the use of "wave" and "particle" in our ordinary conceptual framework are such that the statement that something behaves like *both* of them seems not to be well ordered. The man-in-the-street might assume that the statement is significant and intelligible to the scientist; but he will not *see* its intelligibility. Nevertheless, he can hold the statement in mind and assert that he believes it to be true on the authority of the one who revealed it to him. He would be correct to do so. While the words "wave" and "particle" are such that they could not mean what they mean in ordinary language and still be used in a proposition such as "Electrons behave like both waves and particles," the occurrence of the word "electron" signals the fact that "wave" and "particle" are to be analyzed ultimately in terms of their mathematical correlates in the theoretical language, and those correlates are not used by the scientist in such a way as to break any of the syntactical rules which govern the language in which they occur.

Might we not say, then, that something parallel occurs in religious belief? If the average man could 'take a look at the eternal word of God'—open God's own textbook, as it were, in the language proper to God himself—he, like the nonscientific man-in-the-street, would not say, "Ah, I know the words but do not understand the sentences." We must assume that the inner language of God has its own proper syntax (mode of formal intelligibility). Suppose, however, that God were to reveal some of his truth by speaking to man in the ordinary object language. He might say, for example, "God is three persons in one substance." Once again, each of the words has a distinct syntactical status in our language. (Even "God" has such a role for the average man: "God" is the name of 'that being' the Bible mentions.) The major difficulty is that the syntactical rules governing the use of "person" and

"substance" in our conceptual system are such that the statement that something is *three* persons in *one* substance seems
not to be well ordered. We might assume that the statement
is significant and intelligible to God; but we do not *see* its
intelligibility. Nevertheless, we can hold the statement in mind
and assert that we believe it to be true on the authority of
the one who revealed it to us. Perhaps we would be correct
to do so. While the words "person" and "substance" are such
that they could not mean what they mean in our language and
still be used in a proposition such as "God is three persons in
one substance," the very occurrence of the word "God" signals
the fact that "person" and "substance'" are to be analyzed
ultimately in terms of their intentional correlates in *God's*
language, and those correlates are not used by God in such a
way as to break any of the syntactical rules which govern the
language in which they occur.

There are two disturbing points at which the analogy
breaks down. To start with, it is not an *electron* that reveals
to the man-in-the-street the proposition to which he gives
opaque assent. It is another man. It is not necessary to be
able meaningfully to refer to electrons in order to make sense
of the claim that the proposition which *mentions* electrons is
intelligible to the one who reveals it. There is no problem of
referring to scientists. On the other hand, it is *God* who is
said to reveal the theological proposition. It is not so clear
that we can make sense of the claim that the proposition
which mentions *God* is intelligible to *God*. There is a problem
of referring successfully and meaningfully to *him*. It is quite
clear what is meant by "accepting the truth of a scientific
proposition on the authority of a scientist," but it is *not* clear
what is meant by "accepting the truth of a theological proposition on the authority of *God*."

The second difficulty concerns the potential intelligibility
of the two 'theoretical' languages. The statements in the esoteric language of science have a syntactical significance that
could be taught to any nonretarded adult with a degree of
mathematical proficiency. They presuppose no conceptual
powers or modes of conceptualization beyond those normally
found in "thinking animals." Barring the infelicity of intract-

able stupidity, the ordinary man could be led from total ignorance of the meaning of scientific propositions to a high degree of familiarity without the introduction of *arcadian powers*. Indeed, the analogical interpretations in the object language would help. Furthermore, the manner in which the theoretical language of science makes intelligible judgments about reality can be communicated by means of interpretive correlations between statements in the theoretical language and referential statements in the public observation language.[17] Understanding the semantical use of scientific language does not presuppose any novel 'modes of apprehension or perception.'

It is again not so clear that the man of faith is equally blessed with regard to the language of God. It does not seem that any man could be taught the syntax of the Eternal Word of God (the rules of intelligibility governing the intentional being of God) without the introduction into his nature of new powers of conceptualization and indeed of new sorts of experiences. That is why Aquinas denies that God is in the *genus* of intelligible things.[18] He cannot be thought of in terms of a conceptual system significant to man in the light of natural reason. Nonetheless, Aquinas clearly asserts *both* that the articles of faith are believed on the authority of the one who reveals them, *and* that believing God entails believing *those things* that God teaches.[19] To believe, however, is to think with assent! How can we *think* the articles of faith when Aquinas himself admits (yea, insists) that no account of their meaning or intelligibility can be given in terms of the natural principles of our conceptual system. To natural reason, he says, it is not even clear that the articles of faith refer to real possibilities.[20]

The implications of what might be called *the* paradox of faith are rather more general than commonly thought. They cut across every attempt, however, indirect, to exhibit the meaning of religious language in empirically accessible terms. They negate every attempt to assimilate the 'truth claims' of

[17] So-called correlative definitions. Actually, they correlate more than they define.
[18] *De Trin.*, I, 2.   [19] S. T., II-II, 2, 2.   [20] C. G., I, 1.

SCIENTIA DEI AND THE UNKNOWN GOD

faith to any other conceivable kind of truth claim. They make
it logically impossible to prove that the propositions of faith
say anything at all or even that they conceivably *could* say
anything. The attempt of a group of contemporary theologians[21] to manifest the intelligibility of the language of faith
in terms dictated by an empirical principle of meaning, appears in the light of the paradox of faith a study in tragic irony.
Its grotesque futility is surpassed only in the perennial attempts to play new music to the "divine dance of the 'Cartesian
Dolls.' "[22]

The reason for the generality of the analysis is not hard to
find. Modes of intelligibility are discovered when the mind
informs experience. Modes of recognized intelligibility are
those ways in which man discovers that he understands that
which he apprehends. Intelligibility is the self-apparent result
of the conjunction of the contents of experience and the natural
operation of the mind on that content. Communication within
a universe of discourse presupposes *both* a common intellectual
nature (or conceptual system) *and* a common mode of experience. Communication is *of* intentions of a common nature *by
means of* reference to the common object of experience—the
world.[23] All real intentions have meaning in that they are
communicable in the public universe of human discourse, defined and restricted by the nature of human experience. The
only object naturally common to all men is the world. The
world defines the limits of the natural universe of human discourse. Any conceptually coherent criterion of meaning applies only and exhaustively to statements made about real
things which can be intended on the basis of reference to the
physical order. (This is not to say that they must be *direct*
references to the world.)

God, it seems, cannot be intended within the natural universe of discourse unless: a) he is commensurate with the

21 I have in mind the majority of those British philosophers of religion
who accept the limitations of Oxford analysis and attempt to explicate
religious language in its terms.
22 Kierkegaard characterizes the ontological argument as 'one of those
Cartesian dolls'—when you let go of it it stands on its head.
23 By 'the world' I mean only 'that which can be experienced through
the senses.' What the world is *like* is also a function of our conceptual
system.

world, and thus a limited being among others;[24] or, b) he is a part, an aspect, or the totality of the world;[25] or, c) he, like the world, is a primary and common object of human apprehension. The only theologically interesting alternative is (c); it was sufficiently familiar as an extension of Augustinian and Anselmian epistemology to be specifically denied by Aquinas. The entire 'ontological approach' to theology obviously implies that in some sense God can become the direct object of human experience in this life. The question would seem to be whether he becomes object in revelation and faith, or is already object in natural human cognition (perhaps merely *identified* as such in revelation). If the former alternative is the correct interpretation of the 'ontological school,' then the universe of discourse established by faith would not be *naturally* universal. Its radical intentions and principles of intelligibility would be those shared only by those for whom God was (in faith) a common prime object of apprehension. The intelligibility of God—even if directly apprehended by the faithful—could not be expressed in *natural* human language unless either (a) or (b) were also true. While Aquinas does not believe that God becomes a direct or prime object of the intellect in ordinary faith, he does admit that God might, in his absolute freedom, render himself immediately present to the mind of some living men—he calls that possible experience "Rapture." He maintains, however, that such an experience would do such violence to the normal mode of apprehension that the subject might be said to be taken for the time out of his life in this world. Furthermore, it would not be a *significant* noetic experience: nothing significant could be communicated concerning it to those who did not experience it (and even then, not in the language we use during our life *in* the world), nor could anything intelligible in human terms be retained by those who *have* experienced it. They might be aware of having had such an experience, and might bear memory traces of it; but they could never comprehend it in terms of natural language. Occasional mystical illumination would supply no intelligible concepts in terms of which the

---

[24] Denied by Aquinas in, e.g., S. T., I, 12, 2.
[25] Also denied by Aquinas. Cf. S. T., I, 8, 1.

SCIENTIA DEI AND THE UNKNOWN GOD

object of such experience might be described. As a radically private experience, it could neither be thought nor communicated. Even if it were granted, however, that God could become through faith the direct object of intellectual apprehension and *remain* such so long as live faith were present, it would not follow that intelligible statements could be made about him in the *natural* universe of human discourse. Men of faith would have no difficulty referring to him: he would be a prime and common object of their experience. It is difficult to imagine what kinds of *propositions* might be generated out of such experience, aside from mere mentions or bare references. No propositions about God as experienced would share the syntax of our language. Indeed, it is the propositional form of the language of faith that underlies in part Aquinas' conviction that God is *not* the direct and immediate object of the intellect in the act of faith.[26] If there were propositions about God derived from immediate apprehension, however, it is clear that they would not be significant from the standpoint of natural reason.

If, on the other hand, God were a prime and direct object of *every* human intellect, there would be no problem of reference or significance in religious language. We would all possess the significant concept of 'God.' The arguments of the Augustinians, who tried to make Augustine claim just that, are too familiar to require detailed exposition. Suffice it to say that they depend upon the doctrine of immediate illumination by the First Truth as presupposed by any knowledge of truth. Against this position, Aquinas' arguments are deceptively simple: "Since the human intellect, in this life, cannot think created immaterial substances, as shown above, much less can it think the essence of uncreated substance. Wherefore, it is simply to be said that God is not the first object which is cognized by us. . . . The first, however, which is thought by us according to the state of present life, is the what-ness of the material thing, which is the object of our intellect."[27] He appeals to the fact that we all know that we do *not* understand

---

[26] The proposition is a mode of composition and division, which would not be an appropriate form for statements about God as directly experienced.

[27] S. T., I, 88, 3.

"God"—that we *cannot think* him. God may be present to the intellect as the *source* of the light of intelligibility, but he is not the *object* of the mind. If God *were* a prime object of the intellect, then "our minds would think him instantly"—he would be *per se nota*. If someone mentioned God, I should have the same immediately intelligible experience that I have when someone uses a referential term to refer to a common object of our ordinary experience.[28] Men could refer to God in a straightforward manner without reference to any material object, and they would be universally understood by all who had learned to use the language common among all men. Such is *not* the case, for the reason that the only common object of human apprehension—and thus the only common basis of reference—is the material world.

The logical impossibility of exhibiting the intelligibility of faith in terms of concepts comprehended by all men has not been widely admitted by theologians since the sixteenth century. While few have taken the extreme stand that reason can prove even the central truths of revelation, there has been a tendency—particularly in the Catholic manualist tradition—to assimilate the act of faith to normal acts of human judgment. What in Aquinas would appear as congruent arguments *within* dogmatics for the rationality of accepting Christ as a divine spokesman, now appear as independent arguments for the *probability* of his divinity *apart* from the light of faith. While Aquinas maintained that such arguments "are not necessary, or even very probable, except to one who believes . . . ,"[29] the science called fundamental theology often purports to make the faith so probable in terms of ordinary reasoning that its rejection can scarcely be attributed to 'invincible ignorance.' Apologetics for Aquinas proceeds "by way of demonstration *ad hoc*";[30] in contemporary Catholic theology, it is often spoken of as demonstrably able to elicit that *free act* of will and intellect that is properly called *faith*. Faith, it would seem, is preceded by a rational judgment that Christ is *probably* telling

---

[28] In order for God to be an immediate object of the intellect, we would have to possess the concept 'God' and know how to use it to inform whatever sort of nonepistemic experience or perception the claim to know God might presuppose.

[29] *De Trin.*, 1, 4.   [30] *Ibid.*

the truth. All of the arguments of fundamental theology are based upon a positive reading of 'natural theology': since there is evidence of the existence and nature of God such that a significant concept of God is possible, there can be evidence of his 'traces' in history.[31]

The probable cause of the modern distortion of medieval theology is the impact of rationalistic humanism. In a period when natural reason is being exalted as supreme arbiter of all truth claims, it is natural to attempt to attract attention by making the claims of faith in terms of natural reason. Such was the case in seventeenth and eighteenth century Catholicism, and such is the case in twentieth century religion in general. The popularity of the most unconvincing accounts of faith is perhaps added evidence for the conclusion that God does not will to save the world through metaphysics. It is perhaps also evidence that man, on the contrary, would rather be saved in terms he thinks he understands than by a God whose actions appear, in the light of reason, 'awe-fully' gratuitous. The distinction between the gratuitous and the absurd, like every other distinction of faith, cannot be clearly made in the language of men. It will suffice for the present to indicate good grounds for judging that all attempts to convert the gratuitous into the humanly intelligible are themselves absurd.

Twentieth century apologetics have generally taken one of two forms: either an attempt is made to show that the paradigm cases of clear and distinct language—such as the language of science—are themselves as problematic as the language of faith, or the language of faith is itself commended as ordinary and nonproblematic. Either form is an attempt to assimilate the language of faith to ordinary or natural language—to prove that "there is no problem," or that at least "we have no more of a problem than you." Apologetics in this sense is a clearly defensive game. Indeed, the almost desperate attempt to exhibit the meaningfulness of theological language may signal some doubt on the part of theologians as to their

[31] My criticisms apply only to the more rationalistic forms of fundamental theology. A philosophical discussion of the negative possibility of revelation—of man as possessing the passive obediential power to respond to the word of God—is both possible and necessary. See K. Rahner, *Hörer des Wortes.*

own meaning and as to the self-authenticating sufficiency of faith. The modern theologian clearly feels put upon by the raucous acceptance of scientific paradigms of significance and apparently wishes to sell his product—like aspirin—in the white glare of clinical objectivity.

Perhaps the apologist has never gotten over the imperialistic attempts of positivism to eliminate all human discourse that does not accord with the canons of scientific clarity and meaning. The dethronement of positivism was taken to be a positive triumph of theological truth, as though the mere fact that the positivist was wrong about natural language conveyed upon faith a natural status. There is something odd in the apologetic celebration that often occurs when a philosopher informally concedes that the language of faith is not without meaning, but *merely* false. "Aha," says the apologist, "then it *could* be true." The apologist fails to see that if the language of faith is *meaningful* in the analytic philosopher's own terms, then it *cannot be true*. A God of whom I can think can be shown *not* to exist (contingently, of course) within the realm where conceptual thought is valid: the postulated existence of a thinkable God is a scientific question, susceptible of scientific disconfirmation. Nevertheless, the attempt to show how to think of God continues.

Apologists, and even systematic theologians, have striven to show that the language of faith is in many ways *similar to* other kinds of meaningful human language. Similarities, however, are meaningless in themselves; it must be further determined whether the similarities are relevant to the kind of truth claims the theologian is trying to make, or whether they are merely surface similarities masking crucial and radical differences which place his language on a basis wholly different from all other human speech.

It would be impossible to examine all attempts to assimilate the language of faith to ordinary forms of human speech. There are, however, three general types which enjoy considerable popularity: a) assimilation to natural noetic powers; b) assimilation to theoretical systems; and c) assimilation to intentional symbol making. In each case, the language of faith is purported to be a perfectly natural interpretation of empirically describable events or facts, not wholly discontinuous with the interpretations of a) common epistemic claims, b) scientific explanations and, c) poetic expressions. The conclusions of this chapter will be rather more general than the individual examples might indicate. It will argue that, whatever formal similarities an apologist might establish between natural and religious language, there is a radical disjunction between the two which makes of all such formal similarities a matter of minor importance. That disjunction will take the form of an answer to a simple question: "Can the language in question do what it intends to do—say what it is meant to say—if the world is the *only* natural and direct object of human experience; or does it contain a kind of intention that could not be had or communicated unless there were some *wholly other* object of apprehension besides the world, an object which manifests itself in a novel way and creates a new and noncommunicable mode of intelligibility shared only by those to whom it has manifested itself?" It will be concluded that *only* the language of faith demands such an object.

A. While Aquinas and others of the medieval tradition rejoiced in the discontinuity between man's understanding and God's intelligibility, finding in it a hope for something new and astounding, the man of today is so content with his present science that he feels he must prove that heaven will be only more of the same. John Hick, for example, in his now famous version of the 'eschatological verification' of religious language,[32] finds the distinctive difference between heaven and earth a difference in degrees of evidence for the existence and nature of God.[33] He truly desires to take account of the traditional Christian view that Beatitude is accompanied by a saturating noetic experience of God himself; but he will not commit himself to any account of that experience which would imply a mode of understanding radically discontinuous with empirical interpretations of reality. Beatitude is thus an intensification of the certitude already available to man in faith. Faith, moreover, is itself continuous with ordi-

[32] In, *Faith and Knowledge* (Cornell University Press, Ithaca, 1957), Chap. 7.
[33] *Ibid.*, pp. 155ff.

nary modes of human understanding. "Religious faith . . . shares a common epistemological structure with cognition in other fields."[34] The key to all cognition is, for Hick, an act of belief based upon interpretation.[35] There is no epistemic claim which is both informative and absolutely certain. The mind apprehends no absolutely 'given' and uninterpreted facts. Strictly speaking, then, there is no knowledge—there is only belief; or rather, to claim to know is to possess a belief based upon an interpretation of experience that is not called into question. Interpretations, however, are not, at the most basic level, conscious or reflective; they are dispositional reactions to what is 'taken to be' the significance of an apprehended object or situation—the interpretation *is* the 'taking to be' of the significance. Since no experience is uninterpreted, we cannot find a 'purely empirical' or 'given' anchor to stabilize a criterion of evidence.[36] To take an example from Hick, I see something white and oblong. I might take it to be a newspaper, a handkerchief, or any other of many 'objects'; what I do 'take it to be,' however, is normally not dependent upon a conscious process of reflection and decision. Most interpretations are spontaneous and automatic (although previously learned). Any interpretation might conceivably be wrong: I may say, "Ah, there's the newspaper," only to discover upon closer approach that I now 'take it to be' a handkerchief. Why say "now 'take it to be'" rather than "now *know* it to be"? Because *no* interpretation is in theory incorrigible: there may be hidden factors which would call the most 'certain' interpretation into question. I could be confronted with evidence on the basis of which I would have to retract my 'taking' of the object to be a handkerchief, and so on. When I *do* correct a 'taking,' I must do so by reference to *another* 'taking' which is not simultaneously called into question. The 'takings,' interpretations, or beliefs, which are not *now* called into question, and which are the bases of correcting other 'takings,' are expressible as epistemic claims beginning "I know that. . . ."

It seems a long way from "I know that that is a handker-

---

[34] *Ibid.*, p. 164. [35] *Ibid.*, Chaps. 1 and 2.

[36] See also, R. Chisholm, *Perceiving: A Philosophical Study* (Cornell University Press, Ithaca, 1957), Chap. 7.

chief," to "I know that my Redeemer liveth," but Hick provides a deceptively short route. His epistemological analysis introduces a strange entity—the 'object of direct acquaintance.'[37] He somehow manages to make a distinction between what I *see* and what I *believe*.[38] "When, for example, I look at the paper before me and see a white patch, I do not *believe* that I see a white patch; I *see* it. But I believe that the white patch is a piece of paper (rather than a handkerchief or a hallucinatory appearance)."[39] Under the guise of 'seeing,' Hick has reintroduced that marvelous entity, the 'sense datum' or 'uninterpreted appearance'—an *epistemic* or *intentional* "given." Beliefs, then, are interpretations of that which appears. (Incidentally, "That is a white patch" seems to be just as much of an interpretation as "That is a newspaper"—if one can be 'seen,' why cannot the other?) We can now introduce the possibility of solipsism. "Is this a dagger that I see before me . . . or art thou but a dagger of the mind?" Macbeth is faced with a choice of possible interpretations—but with interpretations of the same 'appearance' or 'object of direct acquaintance.' Thus, the *same* 'object of direct acquaintance' may be *either* an object in the 'real world' *or* an hallucination! True, Macbeth might resolve his uncertainty by appealing to something *else* that he 'takes to be' in the real world: "Milady, do you see it too?" But even if they *both* see it, and check the lighting and finally conclude that there *is* a dagger 'out there' in the real world, there still remains the possibility of error. 'Milady,' 'her agreement,' and 'the lighting' may *all* be hallucinations. Any appearance *may* be called into question and interpreted as a hallucination, and thus *all* might logically be so interpreted. Solipsism, it would appear, is possible. Of course, Hick *knows* that the world is really 'out there,' and he knows that *we* know it. How to account for our certainty when the alternative is possible? Hick postulates a strange and hidden judgment or assumption which, prior to all specific

[37] *Faith and Knowledge*, p. 24. The expression 'object of direct acquaintance' (together with his insistence that reality has significance *in se*) seems to contradict the notion that all knowledge is belief.
[38] Such a distinction can be maintained only so long as we regard 'seeing' as a purely physical process with no intentional significance.
[39] Hick, *Faith and Knowledge*, p. 24.

interpretation, "reveals to us the very existence of a material world. . . ." That "unevidenced and unevidenceable" judgment "carries us beyond the solipsist predicament."[40] That judgment of course cannot be submitted to the verifiability criterion of meaning.

At any rate, the road is now clear for the introduction of God. Because of our "unevidenceable" judgment, we can now interpret the objects of direct aquaintance—what we *see*—as expressions of real objects. All of our epistemic claims about the natural world are readings of ambiguous 'objects of direct acquaintance' (themselves neutral with regard to reality or hallucination) based upon a prior commitment to the reality of the world. We do not *know* that the world really exists; we believe it on the evidence of what we see, even though what we see is evidence only because we have already "judged" the world to exist. And so it is with God! Just as Macbeth takes 'what he sees' to be an expression of an object which he does not see but believes, so also we take 'what we see'—ultimately *all* that we see—to be an expression of an object that we do not see but believe. We must postulate another "unevidenced and unevidenceable" judgment which reveals to us the very existence of God. Such a judgment would establish the 'preconceptual' or given rules of inference or interpretation by means of which we 'take' events to be expressions of God.[41] Hick does not have to be concerned that "the theistic believer cannot explain *how* he knows the divine presence to be mediated through his human experience. He just finds himself interpreting his experience this way." The materialist is in the same epistemological boat with regard to the real world: "We cannot explain . . . how we are conscious of sensory phenomena as constituting an objective physical environment; we just find ourselves interpreting the data of our experience in this way." As realists, we are aware that we

[40] *Ibid.*, pp. 122ff.

[41] Hick denies that taking an appearance to be the 'expression' of a real world is a matter of inference on the basis of *evidence*. If it were not, however, I fail to see how we might ever be in the position of having to decide (and being able to decide) whether an object of 'direct acquaintance,' which itself could be either an expression of a real object or of a hallucination, is in fact one or the other.

live in a real world, though we cannot prove by any logical formula that it *is* a real world. The theist is no worse off: "He lives in the presence of God, though he is unable to prove by any dialectical process that God exists."[42]

The theist, however, *is* worse off, from the point of view of an empirically significant criterion of meaning: in order to 'take' apprehended events to be expressions of God, it is quite true—as Hick maintains—that I must already judge God to be, and already know what constitutes an expression of his presence; it is *not* true, however, that in order to avoid solipsism, I must already judge the material world to exist and already know that neutral 'sensory phenomena' may be taken as 'expressions' of a real world. There is no "problem of solipsism"; solipsism is logically impossible. We could only introduce its possibility by showing that there *are* "uninterpreted" objects of direct *epistemic* acquaintance, which must be "interpreted" as real objects.[43] Hick's attempt to do so—like every other attempt—is incoherent. There is nothing that we can describe as a 'sense datum' or sensory phenomenon that is not already interpreted. There are no objects of direct epistemic acquaintance which are 'seen' as opposed to 'believed' or 'interpreted.' *Seeing* a white patch involves interpretation as much as does *believing* that it is a newspaper, if we construe seeing as an epistemic or conscious process, which Hick must do. I *see* a paper as directly as I *see* a white patch. *Both* are instances of 'taking' or 'believing.' Conscious perceiving is itself an epistemic or intentional activity.[44] The very notion of a 'sense datum,' an 'appearance,' or an 'object of direct acquaintance' is itself an *abstraction from* interpreted experience, and is dependent for its meaning on the 'commonsense' language about real objects: "Sense-data terms can be

[42] *Ibid.*, p. 132.
[43] Hick's epistemology bears a surface similarity to my account of the dispositional concept of 'existence.' To say, however, that there are *nonintentional or material states of the sensory system* which must be taken or informed is *already* to posit the 'real world'—it is not to posit something that may be 'merely a hallucination.' Hick seems to think that 'sensory phenomena' are *both* conscious or 'in the mind' *and also* uninterpreted. That is impossible.
[44] Cf., R. Chisholm, *Perceiving: A Philosophical Study*, esp. Chaps. 8 and 10.

used and applied only as part of the vocabulary of common sense. In short, the 'language' of sense data is not an autonomous language. . . ."[45] No more is the language of 'objects of direct acquaintance' an autonomous language. What do we mean by, "I am seeing a white patch"? We mean, "Something is appearing to me in the way that white *things* of a certain shape appear under specifiable 'standard conditions.' "[46] We are not acquainted with, aware of, or *perceptually* related to anything that might coherently be described as an uninterpreted object. It is true that any interpretation in particular may be wrong—it does not follow that there *exists* an *uninterpreted* object or sense datum that we are misinterpreting (and thus of which we are aware). If we are wrong, we are taking one *thing* to be something that it is *not*. That 'one thing' that we are wrongly taking will turn out on closer analysis to be an *interpreted object*. It is true that any particular interpretation can be called into question. We do this, however, not by reference to sense data or 'objects of direct experience,' but by reference to other interpretations of experienced objects: "I would have sworn that that was Jones, but it could not have been, since I *saw* Jones being buried." Even in the case of hallucinations, there is no sense in referring to some *object* of sight or direct acquaintance which could be either real or a 'mere appearance.' True, if I 'seem' to be seeing a dagger, I can ask whether there really *is* a dagger 'out there,' or if I am only *imagining* that I am seeing a dagger. If I decide that it is 'all in my imagination,' then we can simply say that there *was* no object of sight or direct acquaintance. I was not 'seeing something' that *could* have been an expression of a real dagger; I was not seeing *anything* —I only imagined that I was. We can only decide what counts as a 'mere appearance' of a dagger, or a dagger-hallucination, in the context of some epistemic claim of relatively unquestioned evidence about that which is *not* a 'mere appearance.' I cannot simultaneously call *all* of my realistic interpretations into question and still give meaning to the claim that some-

[45] E. Nagel, *The Structure of Science* (Harcourt Brace, New York, 1961), p. 121.

[46] The color language presupposes the object language.

thing may be a *mere* appearance. The logic of *"mere* appearance" ("not *really* a dagger, but *only* a hallucination") presupposes the logic of that which is *not a mere appearance, but a real object. Some* experiences must be interpreted as experiences of *real* things, before we can interpret *any* experience as a 'mere appearance' or hallucination. To interpret some experiences as experiences of real things, however, and then to say that perhaps the world is not really 'out there' is not just a claim with no 'practical significance' (to use Hick's characterization); it is an outright contradiction. Solipsism is impossible. The world is the *only* object of *unquestionable* reference in our conceptual framework.

If someone says, "I believe in rats because I *saw* one," it makes no sense to ask, "What are the criteria of evidence which allow you to take *what you saw* as the expression of a real object?"; but if someone says, "I believe in God because I saw Christ and took him to be an expression of God," it *does* make sense to ask, "What are the criteria of evidence which allow you to interpret what you saw as an expression of an existing Being *whom you did not see?*" Once again, it is the world which is the primary and direct object of unquestionable reference. All other references must be justified on the basis of intelligible criteria which enable us to say that something in the world is evidence of that to which we are referring. If Hick desires a parallel with ordinary experience, he must allow for that which he so carefully denies—a direct perception of God himself. He denies it because he knows that such a claim would be totally unintelligible to one who has had no such experience—that it would introduce a mode of perception and intellectual judgment radically *dis*continuous with that of "cognition in other fields." Hick argues as though the formal similarities between religious cognition and natural cognition are radical and their differences superficial. The reverse would seem to be true.

Perhaps Hick is somehow aware of the problem. At least, he finds it convenient to put the judgment that God exists on a firmer basis than the judgment that the world exists, by submitting the former to the verification principle. If he could give meaning to "God exists" apart from the activity of taking things to be expressions of God, then his total account would be less problematic. In this too he fails. There is a clear alternative: either the experience of taking events to be expressions of God, *itself* gives meaning to the statement "God exists"—in which case we must possess criteria of evidence which exhibit that meaning—or it does not. I have argued that it does not. To postulate in the life-to-come a process of verification which itself involves taking situations or things which are *not themselves God* as expressions of God, merely reintroduces the problem into the verification situation, even if we claim, as does Hick, that the evidence in heaven will be clearer. What are the criteria of *clearer* evidence, or *more evident* expressiveness? Unless we already have criteria of evidence for judging something to be an expression of God, we cannot be said in heaven to have criteria of *clearer* evidence; but if we already have criteria of evidence, we do not need an 'eschatological' verification.[47]

To generalize, any interpretation of the language of faith which would reduce it to the status of an interpretation or an empirical description of observable events or facts taken to be evidential of the existence or nature of God, falls under the same condemnation as the attempts of some natural theologians to find evidence for the existence of God in general facts about the world. In order to explicate in intelligible fashion what is involved in taking x to be evidence of y, criteria of evidence must be established which already contain in intelligible form a description of the nature of y and general laws of a logical and empirical nature giving reasons for seeing x as evidence for y. In Aquinas' terms, a *quia* argument does not establish in intelligible form the existence or nature of the postulated cause, unless we could independently create a *propter quid* argument leading from the postulation of y to the affirmation of the existence and nature of the observed event x. Hick's reduction of dogma to "a descriptive and em-

[47] My criticisms of Hick's position might give the impression that I find his book of no value. On the contrary, it is an exceedingly suggestive and remarkably insightful analysis of the structure of religious certainty. My only serious criticism is the continuing attempt to prove that this certainty is subject to the same sorts of analyses and verification as is certainty in ordinary matters.

pirical process, the aim of which is to express the basic data apprehended by faith," and his characterization of that process as a "pointing to the area of primary religious experience," when those experiences are assimilated to ordinary occasions of taking x to be evidence of or an expression of y, reduce faith to a form of natural theology, even if the events in question are special or clear instances of God's evidential presence in the created order. Professor I. T. Ramsey, in disputing the view that the basic language of faith is merely "history plus interpretation," makes the same logical point. The facts interpreted cannot be ordinary historical facts, or the interpretation is gratuitous; if, on the other hand, the facts are *peculiar*, then the act of taking the facts to be what they are (acts of God) is itself discontinuous with ordinary empirical observation. His justified conclusion: "No attempt to make the language of the Bible conform to a precise straightforward public language—whether that language be scientific or historical—has ever succeeded."[48] The only facts which can be 'evidential of the existence and nature of God' are facts which are already *apprehended* as 'mighty acts of God.' How God can be included in the act of taking an observable event to be what it is, is not expressible in any ordinary or natural way, and would certainly not be continuous with cognition in other fields. Religious faith does not and cannot share a "common epistemological structure with cognition in other fields" unless God himself can be said to be an ordinary and nonproblematic object of human perception. That alternative fails to signify a real possibility to anyone for whom it is not already true. Only the world would seem to occupy such a privileged position.

B. The language of faith, therefore, can no more be explanatory or illuminative of natural events than can the language of natural theology. Any attempt to explicate the language of faith as a theoretical explanation of facts known or apprehended in an ordinary way will either result in a gratuitous and incomprehensible explanatory entity, or will introduce in a covert fashion 'facts' which already contain or presuppose

[48] I. T. Ramsey, *Religious Language* (SCM Press, London, 1957), p. 106.

an apprehension of God—unless, of course, we already possess a meaningful definition of God, capable of generating public criteria for taking events to be evidential of his existence and nature. I have argued that we have no such definition or criteria. In rejecting the attempt to assimilate the language of faith to natural noetic structures, we have already eliminated the possibility of a straightforward assimilation of that language to theoretical language structures such as the language of scientific theory. Any explanatory entity within a significant theoretical system must either itself be related by correlative definitions to the object language or be intelligibly and commensurably related to lower order concepts or entities of the system which are themselves correlated with the observation language.

A word must be said, however, about a possible apologetic move at this juncture, a move which contains enough truth to be seriously misleading. There is a popular misunderstanding of the relationship between the language of contemporary science and that of common experience. In the eyes of many people, science has destroyed the world that we *think* we see and has put in its place a mysterious world of imperceivable entities inaccessible to human experience. Man cannot sense 'what is really out there': what we take to be solid objects are 'really' made up of largely empty space occupied by a number of minute 'particles' as far apart in relative terms as the earth and the sun. Science and religion are allied against human experience, each positing as 'most real' that which man cannot see.

Such unfortunately paradoxical ways of explicating the theoretical language of science were popularized by the philosophically idealistic journalism of Eddington and Jeans, who, writing in 'simple terms' for the layman, delighted in shocking the audience (and perhaps themselves) by playing off ordinary and scientific language against one another, as though they were both parts of the same linguistic framework. They speak as though the theories of physics can be correctly understood in terms of the imperfect and highly misleading models of aspects of those theories that can be constructed in terms of ordinary language. Thus, physics says that 'that table over

there' is *really* made up of 'empty space' and 'whirling particles' that we cannot see. Such claims, while they may be
found in the nonscientific writings of some scientists, were
successfully demolished by Susan Stebbing in *Philosophy and
the Physicists.*[49] To say that tables, for example, are really
made up of "empty space" and "particles" is to forget that
those terms carry meaning only because of their function in
ordinary language. What "empty space" does not and cannot
mean is "the space occupied by such things as tables." "Empty
space" cannot be carried over into the theoretical language of
physics. Scientific language, in its proper theoretical form,
does not deny or call into question the reality of *what we see*
when we use such expressions as "that table over there." It
does not supply ordinary language with alternatives to its
ordinary mode of macroscopic description—it does not operate
within ordinary language at all. As Ernest Nagel remarks:

> . . . the word 'table' signifies an experimental idea that does
> not occur in the language of electron theory; and the word
> 'electron' signifies a theoretical notion that is not defined in
> the language employed in formulating observations and
> experiments. Though the two languages may be coordinated
> at certain junctures (by means of correlative definitions),
> they are not intertranslatable. Since there is thus only one
> *table*, there is no issue as to which is the 'real' one. . . .[50]

There are not two *tables*, one made up of solid stuff, and the
other made up of empty space and particles; there is only *that
which we see* (i.e., the external object of our nonintentional
sensory experience) when we say "that table." *What we see*
(external reality) may be informed and described *either* in
terms of ordinary language, with its macroscopic primary entities, *or* in terms of theoretical language, with its microscopic
primary entities. It cannot be described simultaneously in
both terms within the same linguistic framework. Given the
present state of theoretical science, the description in purely
theoretical terms of *what we see* presupposes the ability to
correlate the theoretical language at certain junctures with

[49] S. Stebbing, *Philosophy and the Physicists* (London, 1937).
[50] *The Structure of Science*, p. 98n.

the ordinary language of experimentation and observation. The language of scientific theory depends at present for its referential and explanatory power on the unquestioned status of ordinary language and the unquestioned privilege of referring to the public world of ordinary experience. Even if we grant that scientific language has ultimate ontological priority over ordinary language, we are not challenging the reality of *what we see*, but only claiming that it may ultimately be possible, at some future stage in the perfection of scientific language, to inform and describe *what we see* in scientific terms without the mediation of the ordinary experimental language.

Religious language can never be fitted to that model. If religious language were a kind of theoretical explanation of observable events, then either God himself must be directly sensible, or the concept 'God' must be definable in terms of a conceivable and commensurable relationship to other entities or forms of the system which can be used to describe sensible reality (whether directly or by means of correlation through correlative definitions with descriptive terms in ordinary language). Unlike the theoretical language of physics, which at most *analyzes* or *describes* what we see in terms of unperceived theoretical entities, such a theological explanatory language would posit an unperceived reality *over and above* what we see.

Attempts to make the language of faith straightforwardly explanatory in some theoretical sense have been largely abandoned. Attempts at assimilation to straightforward instances of meaningful language have not. Thus, in place of the claim that the language of faith exhibits a kind of theory about the world, more and more theologians are adopting devious modes of saying approximately the same thing. There has been an outbreak of attempts to show that, while religious language does not possess the conceptual clarity of a scientific theory, it can be assimilated to the function and status of nonmathematical *models* of scientific theory. Ignoring the fact that a model *contains* the theory, it is assumed that one can possess and use the model without knowing the theory. The suggestion has enough prima facie plausibility to require further analysis of our 'man-in-the-street' and his 'understanding' of an ordinary-language interpretation or model of scientific theory.

It would seem that a model *can* be possessed and used without knowledge of the theory itself. The man unlearned in scientific concepts can often follow an explanation of scientific theory in terms of a nonmathematical model. He may not possess the conceptual framework necessary to understand the proper language of atomic physics, but he can get some idea of the kind of claim being made when he is told to "picture a little piece of stuff with a number of other little pieces of stuff moving around it." The 'model' is, of course, highly misleading, but it does correspond in some relevant ways with some of the moments in the development of submolecular theory. Some of his misconceptions can even be corrected: "Now, when I say 'little pieces of stuff,' you must understand that some of the things that I refer to act much of the time more like little waves in a trough of water." The awe-struck believer in the authority of science cannot himself see the formal relation between the picture in his mind and some of the theoretical statements of physics; but, so long as he holds on faithfully to the picture, there *is* a tenuous conformity that the scientist can see. Does this not parallel the condition of the man of faith, who has, as it were, a model of God in a language other than that proper to God himself? As Aquinas repeatedly states, the believer does not see *how* the language that he uses—his empirical-language model—is true of God; he does not see how it is formally related to God's knowledge of himself; but so long as he holds faithfully to the language, there is a more or less tenuous conformity that God can see. His model is, of course, misleading—like all models—but misconceptions can be at least partially corrected: "Now, when I say 'three persons,' you must understand that I do not mean 'three substances,'" or, "You must learn to ignore certain aspects of the model, such as the finitude of human persons, which could not apply to God." Some even see this as the true nature of analogy (whether *analogia entis* or *analogia fidei*): one can get some idea of the nature of God by 'cleaning up' a human concept—by denying those aspects of a human concept that cannot apply to God, until all that is left is a perfect and formal 'idea' that corresponds to something in God.[51] The process appears no more mysterious than teaching a novice in science what parts of a physical model to ignore. The difficulty, however, is that the scientist corrects the novice's use of a model on the basis of his own understanding *of the theory*; how are we ourselves to correct and refine our own use of the religious model without possessing and understanding the theory? Without knowing what God is like in his own terms? For that reason, other theologians[52] do not think that the analogies of faith can be perfectly corrected or refined, but that one aspect of a model may be corrected by another aspect of the model. The models of revelation correct one another, by emphasizing disparate and incommensurable model-images, without supplying theoretical knowledge of what God is really like. Thus, "God is one" is balanced by "God is three." Holding on to the tensions created by the religious model conforms the mind in some way to God.

Certain parts of the description of the man of faith in the 'theory-model' account are valuable as a means of emphasizing the disjunction between God's language and our language. It does not succeed, however, in giving an adequate account of the language of faith, and it certainly does not succeed in assimilating religious language to scientific language in such a way as to justify or render intelligible the claims of religious language. The major problem is again that of reference. The language of faith, it would seem, is *about God*. The model itself—religious language—conveys analogous knowledge about God through a formal correspondence (which only God can see) to God's knowledge of himself. So far, however, we have only two elements: the theory proper (known only to God), and the imperfect model (known to man). In the case of scientific language, however, there are three elements: the theory proper (known only to the scientist), the imperfect model (known to the man-in-the-street), *and* that to which they *both refer*—the world. The novice in science, who holds

---

[51] Cf., Garrigou-Lagrange, *God: His Existence and His Nature*, Vol. II.
[52] An example might be Austin Farrer's "Revelation," in *Faith and Logic* (Beacon Press, Boston, 1957).

faithfully to the imperfect model, learns something about the theory only when he understands that the model is meant to be applied to *that which he experiences.* In learning how (misleadingly) to look at the world in terms of the model, he learns something about the way in which a scientist applies his theory to the objects of human experience. Unless he understands how the model purports to be about such ordinary things as the table in front of him, he does not learn anything about the theory as an explanation of what is there when man says "There is a table." The status of theories and models may not be exhaustively explicable in operational terms, but an operational element is a *sine qua non* of the referential and explanatory power of a theory and of its models. The usefulness of a model in teaching science to a novice is precisely due to the fact that its referent is co-extensive with that which is experienced in ordinary human experience. In order to be (misleadingly) *rethought* as a 'bunch of little pieces of stuff,' the table had first to be thought in another way. The role of the model is eventually to help us move from the object language to the theoretical language. In order to be able to apply a model, one must be able to refer to its referent independently of the model.

If God himself is the common referent *both* of religious language *and* of God's knowledge, then we can only gain analogical knowledge of God's real (theoretical) nature if we know how to look at *God* in terms of the model of religious language. Unless we can refer to God independently of the model, however, we cannot *apply* the model to him; unless, then, God is already known in some nonproblematic (if imperfect) manner, religious language cannot serve as a model of his knowledge of himself. I can hold in my mind the images of "trinity" and "unity," but the application of these images *to God* is impossible unless I know what God is independently of the images. A *common* and *available* referent is needed, if religious language is to be *assimilated* to empirical models.

The obvious solution is to maintain that religious language is about the world, and reflects or models God's knowledge of the world. The believer, in seeing the world in terms of the 'model,' learns something analogous to God's 'theoria' of the world. The wording is attractive on several grounds. It does not explicitly state that the world appears intelligible to the one who uses the language of faith, any more than the table appears intelligible to the scientific novice who rethinks it in terms of his imperfect model: both may be rather confused and disturbed by the nature of the rethinking; both may have the preconceptions of ordinary thinking somewhat shaken. The wording is attractive too, because it takes account of the fact that the language of faith contains so many propositions which are quite clearly about the world, including some rather straightforward empirical descriptions of historical events. There is even a parallel to eschatology. Just as the scientific novice goes through with the task of rethinking the world in terms of his misleading model, with the faith that he is doing something analogous to what the accomplished physicist does, and with the hope that one day he too will be able to analyze the world in terms of the rigorous mathematical model: so also the believer applies the 'model' of religious language to his experience, with the faith that he is looking at the world in a way somehow analogous to God's knowledge of the world, and with the hope that one day he too will see the world from God's more theoretical point of view. The novice bases his faith and hope on the authority of the instructor in science, while the believer bases his on the authority of God, who teaches in his revealed Word. The application of the model exhibits belief in a promise.

Unfortunately, this parallel is also incoherent. The major problem is the role of "God" in the model. If the *only* referent of the model—the only reality intended by the language of faith—is the *world*, then the status of those propositions of faith that *seem* to refer to God is highly problematic. One possible solution might be to say that "God" as it appears in the language of faith is not a straightforward and intelligible reference, but is rather the model-equivalent of an explanatory entity—God himself—which is intelligibly related to the world *as known by God*, but not as described in the model-language. Its occurrence in the model reflects the fact that God sees the world as 'explained' or 'illuminated' by himself, but its occurrence is not meant to make *us* see the world in that way. The word "God," in other words, *mentions* the theory of which the language of faith is the model, but does not *describe* it or intelligibly *refer to* it. The proposition of faith, for example, which states that "God is the creator of heaven and earth" is meant only to imply that if we look at the world in those terms we shall be doing something analogous to what God does when he sees how the world is related to himself. The problem, of course, is how on earth we could look at the world as a creation of God, without being able to refer to him and without knowing anything intelligible about him.

The same incommensurability which prevented us from assimilating religious language to an explanatory theory prevents us from applying a crucial aspect of the so-called model to its purported referent. Unless we can think God in some fashion, we cannot use those elements of the language of faith which contain his name, as a model in terms of which to look at the world. The apparent solutions, unique to Christianity, which would avoid the meta-empirical problem by identifying "God" in some way with empirical events, do not in fact circumvent the logical difficulty. The identification can never be complete or symmetrical (even in process theology); the theologically interesting element—that which keeps us from mere tautology in making the identification between "God" and "Christ"—is just that aspect of ultimate transcendence that is logically problematic.

Many theologians pretend that the problem of reference has been solved by the claim that "The man, Jesus of Nazareth, is God." If, however, they really mean to say that Jesus of Nazareth is an exhaustive revelation of that which God *is*, then they must claim that the identification is complete and symmetrical. To say, then, that "God created the heavens and the earth" is to say nothing more than "The man, Jesus of Nazareth, created the heavens and the earth." This either implies that the world was created by something occurring straightforwardly *within* it, or that the man, Jesus, pre-existed in some straightforward sense before he made the world. Aquinas indicates that the relation is asymmetrical when he claims that Christ is entirely divine but not all of divinity. He then denies in rigorous terms that the human nature of Christ pre-existed in any form aside from an 'idea' in the mind of God.[53] The point is not a fatuous one, for it removes the possibility of giving to names applied to God the *same* import that they have when applied to Christ. Those followers of Barth who try to make him assert that God became a finite, empirical object in the Incarnation in such a way that there is no 'hidden' aspect of God apart from Christ, fail to see the full implications of their claim—either God ceased to be God in the Incarnation, or *every* predicate which applies to Christ applies to God as he always was and always will be. The problem is one of logical reference, not of theological rhetoric. Barth's point is that there is no *deus absconditus*, the nature of which is not known by faith, lying behind the *deus revelatus*.[54] The Christ who is seen by faith, however, is a different *logical* subject from the Christ who is seen by man's natural powers of apprehension. There is, again, an element of the 'ontological school' at work: in faith God becomes an object of the intellect in as straightforward a way as a table can be an object to natural modes of apprehension. "God in Christ" cannot be identified with what men see in Christ in the light of natural reason. The expressions are not co-extensive. Thus, God has not become an *empirical* object, but an object of *faith*, which apprehends a totally new kind of immediate object.

Aquinas prefers another formulation. The object of faith (which is not directly an object of the intellect) is not the empirical substructure of dogma—natural events. The primary object is the meta-historical, meta-empirical *God*; empirical events are *indirectly* objects of faith.[55] What men could see, in an empirical sense, is not what they believe. Men might *see* the resuscitation of a dead body—they believe the Resurrection, an act of God and a principle of human salvation. A reference to the object of belief includes a reference to an empirical fact or event, but a reference to an empirical fact or event does not solve the problem of how to refer to the object of belief. Once again, in order to *solve* the problem of

[53] *C. G.*, IV, 43.
[54] K. Barth, *Church Dogmatics*, II, 1, pp. 210, 541ff.
[55] *S. T.*, II-II, 1, 1.

reference, it must be presupposed that reference to God has become possible—and apparently so—or that reference to strictly nonempirical events has become possible. Thus, a religious model will differ from any scientific counterpart at precisely the crucial point of the nature of *unquestioned* reference.

To effect an assimilation to empirical models, the reduction of "God" to an empirical object must be radically carried out. Such attempts have been made.[56] It might be said (in terms of our analogy) that the word "God" does not occur *in* the model proper. The propositions which seem to refer to God are meta-linguistic accounts of how we are to use empirical elements in the model. The central meta-linguistic rule is the so-called doctrine of the Incarnation. It states in fact the simple rule, "For 'God' read 'Jesus Christ.' "[57] This time the reduction is complete. Jesus Christ, and other empirical objects and events related to him, constitute the model of faith. We are to rethink the world in terms of what we find in Christ. The object of faith is nothing but the empirical, historical, describable, observable, touchable *man*—Jesus of Nazareth. If we confess him "Lord of Creation" we are doing all that we can to model forth the truth about reality. To say that "God is the creator of heaven and earth" is to commend or confess[58] the view that Christ is the key to authentic existence in the world as it really is—that all reality finds its focus and its meaning for man in the life and death of one man.

If such a program is carried out consistently, it will in fact eliminate any referential problem, for it will eliminate "God" as anything more than a devious mode of commending or confessing certain forms of behavior and certain attitudes toward the world and toward other men. As Paul Van Buren asserts, we ought to eliminate the notion that "God" is a pseudo-empirical 'tag-name' for an existing reality. All that men thought they were looking for when they projected an impossible 'God' onto reality can be found in Christ.

It is not quite clear, however, whether the empiricists and

[56] Cf., esp. P. Van Buren, *The Secular Meaning of the Gospel* (Macmillan, New York, 1963); and, R. B. Braithwaite, *An Empiricist's View of the Nature of Religious Belief* (Cambridge Press, Cambridge, 1955).
[57] Van Buren, *op.cit.*, p. 147.
[58] Van Buren 'confesses,' Braithwaite 'commends.'

secularists are really intending only that. A number of their expressions seem to suggest that there is something 'meta-empirical' going on under the surface of their apparently empirical language. Faith, for example, may be said to be the possession of a 'blik' about the world. The way that one sees the world when he has faith in Jesus Christ is not a matter of *merely* commending a certain form of behavior in it. One sees the *world*—all of reality—in terms of Christ. There is an attitude *toward the world* that is not justifiable as a pure matter of empirical generalization about the world: in the "contagious freedom" that one catches from Christ, the world is known as it *really is*. It is at least probable that a mode of apprehension is being introduced which is no less problematic or more empirical than that claimed by more 'supernatural' interpreters of religious language. Van Buren *seems* to be introducing a new kind of 'fact' into the world. If not, it can only be said that his interpretation of such concepts as Creation does not take account of what most theologians *think* they are doing when they use them. Far from giving an account of religious language as it exists in use among men, Van Buren and Braithwaite create *another* language which they desire to substitute in its place—a language that can only be called "religious" in a Pickwickian sense. The attempt does make clear, however, the unavoidable conclusions of any honest attempt to assimilate the language of faith to the language of empirical observation. The word "God" must either remain *flatus vocis*, and without use, or it must be interpreted as a general name for purely empirical aspects of the world observable in theory by all men.

The parallel of religious language with scientific models— or any other analogous mode of human speech—fails to note that models contain their theories. The man who uses an imperfect model of atomic physics is not ignorant of the theory; he has an imperfect knowledge of the theory to the extent that he can correctly apply the model. There are no 'pure theories' existing in minds. Even the mathematical version of atomic theory is a *model* of that theory. In using a model a man must be able to make all of the references implied by the theory. In using religious language, a man must be able to make the references implied by religious 'theory.' To do that, he must have a meaningful intention of every entity referred to in it—he must know the syntax of every term. To try to *use* religious language without theoretical knowledge of that to which it refers, is like trying to believe propositions without understanding them. To have that knowledge, to understand the language, presupposes an apprehension of God or of some nonempirical 'fact.'

There are two fundamental differences between religious language and scientific language, and thus between religious and empirical modes of apprehension: 1) the referential power of scientific language is exhausted by the world, while religious language purports to refer beyond the world; and, 2) scientific language contains no concepts incommensurable with concepts that can be correlated with referential terms in the observation language. The entire model of any scientific theory has reference to the world—to what we experience. Scientific explanation or illumination is by way of co-extensive analysis. Event *E* occurs at the observable level because events *x,y* occur at the analytic level. The claim is not made that *in addition to* event *E*, there are *also* events *x,y*—the distinction is one of descriptive levels. Events *x,y* *are* event *E*, as seen or described from the noetic standpoint of the model or theory. Or better, events *x,y* are that which we are looking at when we say in *our* language that event *E* is occurring. ("Looking at" is clearly meant in its nonintentional or material sense.) The two levels are co-extensive in a way in which 'what is believed' in religious theory cannot be co-extensive with what is empirically observable—unless, of course, God *is* the world. Such elements in scientific theory as might appear to be transcendent—such as gravity or fields—are only transcendental: that is, they are exhaustively definable in terms of the operations and relations of analytic entities or macrocosmic objects. They do not transcend the world. The co-extensive referential range of scientific theory and ordinary descriptive language is the ground of the ability to correlate the two by means of correlative definitions. Nothing is referred to in empirically meaningful language systems that cannot be related intelligibly to statements about observable reality. Either those words in religious language which intend to refer beyond empirically observable things and events, and which are not alternative modes of analyzing that which can be referred to in ordinary language, are merely *flatus vocis*, or they derive their meaning and referential power from a new mode of apprehension which has as its object that which already transcends empirical reality or the public world. Since the world is the only *unquestionable* object of natural human reference, and since the references of empirical theories are explicable in terms of references to the public world, it follows that empirical theories have a nonproblematic mode of intelligibility and a natural communicability not possessed by the language of faith. Even granting, therefore, the possibility of receiving a revealed language of faith (from the Bible, for example), the meaning of that language could never be expressed in the natural universe of human discourse; it could never be made intelligible to the majority of men what faith proposes for belief.

C. The ordinary and public world, it has been argued, is the sole source of the referential power of both the epistemic claims of ordinary language and the theoretical explanations of scientific language. The only prime and unquestionable referent of any form of natural human language is the public world of ordinary experience. On the other hand, it has been maintained that the language of faith can neither intend nor refer unless there is some other mode of human experience having as its object a meta-empirical entity or nonempirically observable events. It remains then to raise the question of whether there might be another mode of human speech which intends and refers in such a way that the ordinary world of common experience is not a sufficient ground to explain its intentional and referential power.

A possible candidate might be language about persons. If a notion of "God" cannot be extrapolated from our ordinary language about observable states of affairs, it might be extrapolated from our ordinary language about persons. We have said, after all, that the language of 'physical states' is incommensurable with that of 'mental states.' Neither is reducible to the other, and yet mental states are not part of the public world of ordinary experience. Do we not already possess a notion of a nonmaterial entity that transcends a purely empirical description of *what we see?* The answer is "No." We do not possess an intelligible notion of what the 'mind' really is—of what we are naming when we use the 'mental-state language.' We find it necessary, in order to describe and explicate intentional human behavior and overt linguistic behavior, to use the language of 'intentions' and 'concepts.' This vocabulary is derived from meta-linguistic analyses of overt verbal behavior, and is used to name a power of the thinking animal of which we have no essential and coherent knowledge. Insofar as we might be said (in misleading terms) to construct in that fashion a notion of 'immaterial reality,' it is a notion of 'immateriality' which is symbiotic with our notion of 'materiality' and possesses no logical or epistemological independence from the 'physical-state language.' Meaningful references to 'internal' states and 'spiritual' acts presuppose meaningful references to the material order and are incoherent in abstraction from such references. Whatever the 'soul' really *is*—whatever we are naming when we use the 'mental-state language'—it is certainly part of the natural order which we experience in ordinary human experience. That is why, for Aquinas, the abstraction of the notion of 'immaterial intentional existence' from that of a 'thinking *animal*' would result in a highly confused notion of an *angel,* not of God. An angel is at least *generically* part of the same created order that we *sense.* A 'pure' Thou, independent of *all* natural entities, is just as referentially problematic as a nonempirical transcendent entity—which is why the I-thou model is a good one for theology *proper.*

A more popular candidate for near-relation to religious language is poetry—the free creation of a *sui generis* mode of symbolic speech. The point at issue, of course, is not whether the language of faith can, or even must, use poetic language, but whether the language of nonreligious poetry constitutes a natural analogue to religious apprehension and language. We shall therefore not take into account poetry which incorporates self-consciously religious or dogmatic language, and thus depends for *its* meaning on that of religious language. Once again, certain formal similarities between religious and poetic language are easy to find: the poet, it is said, sees things that other men do not see; he states truths in a language that cannot be reduced to ordinary conceptual language without the loss of the meaning he intends to convey; he creates 'new meanings' and sees possibilities not suggested by ordinary experience; he offers a vision of reality that could never be contained in descriptive tracts on the nature of the world. All of these claims are true—in a sense.

The poet sees things that other men do not see. It would be better to say that he notices things that other men do not notice. And not just facts. He notices ways of looking at things, which pinpoint more clearly the way that things are. He makes the reader notice things by insinuating ways of taking things. Gerard Manley Hopkins makes us notice the particular dynamism of each 'ecstatic' existent thing by creating in us the sudden in-take of breath produced by the sight—the noticing—of a falcon banking against the sudden "big wind," like a horse in full stride circling, controlled, at the end of its rein, then breaking off in a new arc and a new image:

> I caught this morning morning's minion, kingdom of
>   daylight's dauphin, dapple-dawn-drawn Falcon, in his
>   riding
>   Of the rolling level underneath him steady air, and
>   striding
> High there, how he rung upon the rein of a wimpling wing
> In his ecstasy! then off, off forth on swing,
>   As a skate's heel sweeps smooth on a bow-bend: the hurl
>   and gliding
>   Rebuffed the big wind. My heart in hiding
> Stirred for a bird,—the achieve of, the mastery of the thing!

He calls our attention to what things *do*—even to what *stones* do: "As tumbled over rim in roundy wells/ *Stones ring;* . . . ." And they do! And that is why poetry works—it makes us see what is there to be seen. It does so, however, not by calling our attention away from our experience, but by forcing our attention more intently on our experience. To achieve its end, it uses every *natural* meaning packed into language by the common experience of a richly manifold world. If it is good poetry, it intends its ambiguities (like the aural and spatial "ring" of a stone in a well), and controls its deviant uses of language (like the near contradiction of "rolling level"). It is not *another* world that the poet sees—which is why we are often so surprised by what has been there all along.

The poet has his own irreducible language. He has his own way of using language which is not the way of ordinary prose. That is not to say, however, that *what* the poet says (the *information* he primarily or secondarily communicates) could not be said in "ordinary conceptual language." It could. But it would not then *do* the same thing. The language of the poet is not only meant to convey information by means of intelligible intentions; it is meant to create an intentional state within the reader more akin to an immediate grasp on some aspect of reality or experience, with attendant state of mind *and* emotions,[59] than to a consideration of possible ways of looking at things. A poem not only tells us that it is *possible* to look at a bird in flight as though it were a horse at rein— it creates that "taking" within us. To achieve a more than accidental result, however, the poet must be able to depend upon the words he uses to *mean* in some predictable way. They do that, within the limits imposed by the porosity of concepts, because the world is there to be seen, and men have predictably common natures within communities sharing intentions.

The poet creates new meanings. New meanings, of course, are being created all the time—not only by poets, but by farmers and minor bureaucrats. Meanings are shifted, new words are created, new distinctions are found—and the poet quickens and livens the process. But he does more than that. He sees possibilities of interpretation not suggested by straightforward descriptions of ordinary experience. Hopkins not only calls our attention to what things do—sometimes with "brute beauty and valor and act . . ."; he suggests an image, rooted historically (though not crucially) in Scotist theology,

---

[59] I am using 'emotion' here to refer to all noncognitive (noninformational) aspects of the way in which we take or interpret our experience.

in terms of which more general questions may be raised about 'the way things are.' Each thing, he suggests, *is* what it *does*; what a things does constitutes its 'self'—it is its 'selving forth.' Hopkins sees the *esse-operatio* of nature as a mode of self-expenditure. What things *do* in the world is to blaze forth in a more or less lavish and expensive display of their potency, and then die out in a brilliant trail of "blue-bleak embers" which "fall, gall themselves, and gash gold-vermilion." The most stunning operations of nature are, for Hopkins, those which use themselves up in their act of being—like the "flaunting forth" of a "cloud-puffball," which is the beginning of its dissolution. Hopkins has introduced no new 'facts' into his description of reality; and yet another poet might disagree with him. They would not be disagreeing about the empirical fact that objects come into being and disintegrate: they would be disagreeing about the proper mode of *taking* that fact. To say that things "gash gold-vermilion" is to say something about man's subjective reaction to the flux or "bonfire" of the world: shifting the images to cold and dark would produce a different taking of the same aspect of reality. Hopkins sees the world as saying something *to* man's state of longing for permanence of beauty, just as the 'contingency' of the world for Aquinas says something *to* man's longing for complete intelligibility. Each taking raises a question to the judging, intellect (and emotions):

> How to keep—is there any any, is there none such, nowhere known some, bow or brooch or braid or brace, lace, latch or catch or key to keep
> Back beauty, keep it, beauty, beauty, beauty, . . . from vanishing away?

As in Aquinas, there are two possible answers. The first is a "beginning to despair" of man's desire. The second is an affirmation: "There is one, yes I have one." The affirmation, however, is not of that which can be presented as an object or communicated to us by the poet—it is an affirmation of that which remains "yonder," like the Unknown God of Aquinas' theology:

Only not within the seeing of the sun,
Not within the singeing of the strong sun,
Tall sun's tingeing, or treacherous the tainting of the
    earth's air. . . .

The affirmations are all negative, aside from the mere *claim*
to have "one." Hopkins has so *taken* the doing of the world
that it is possible for him to use religious language in his
poetry as an 'answer' to a question his *taking* of reality has
itself raised: he can *assert* that self-expenditure is sacrifice—a
yielding by nature of beauty back to God—to be understood
only in the light of Christ ("my chevalier!"). Hopkins suggests that the flux of the world can only be understood, that
is, in the light of faith. He cannot produce that faith or exhibit the meaning of religious language—he must depend upon
the meaning of the language of faith when he uses it in his
poetry. If the language of faith has no meaning, then Hopkins'
more confessional poems lose a level of meaning that he intended to give them. The mere fact that a poet might *use*
religious language does not mean that religious language is no
more problematic than the language of ordinary poetry. To a
reader who has not seen reality in the light of faith, there remains from Hopkins' poetry only the question: "Is there any?"

Other poets, of course, have claimed to know or see a realm
of reality surpassing that of the world. In each case, however,
they convey the notion of transcendence either by negations
(as did Hopkins) or by a heightening of the isolated "takings"
of beauty in this world (as in Yeats). In either case, the 'cognition' conveyed to the reader of the "really real" involves the
use of predicates—denied or heightened—whose meaning is
dependent upon ordinary reference to the public world. The
heightened sense of beauty, order, or even futility, which characterizes the poet's "vision" of reality, is never sufficient to
produce an *intention* of transcendent being. It is basically non-
cognitional. For that reason, many more mystically minded
poets (such as Blake), who have 'in mind' a *wholly other*
beauty or order, resort to the technique of the mystic himself—
the introduction of contradictory epithets, which is itself the
despair of communication.

Poetry, then, like scientific language, *communicates meanings* and *makes references* only because it relies upon the ordinary usage of language to refer to the world and describe its contents. That is why the *meaning* of a poem, like the meaning of an esoteric scientific proposition, can be taught, with no mystical appeal to special modes of intelligibility or transcendent objects. Even the devious poetic uses of ordinary language can be explained, precisely because they are uses of ordinary language and dependent upon the residual ordinary meaning of the terms used. Emotive or subjective *takings* (the 'feel' of the noncognitive element of a poem) are not so readily taught—although we have all learned our emotional responses in society—and it is conceivable that there may be many people, who, because of a temperamental insensitivity, can *explain the meaning* of a poem, but cannot *read* one. That is unfortunate precisely because the most important aspect of poetry may not be the *meaning* of a poem. In any case, insofar as a poem *has* meaning, its references and explanations are as restricted as those of ordinary language: when a poem transgresses those limits and attempts to *mean* something that cannot be meant on the basis of reference to the common object of human experience in the context of a common logical space, to that extent it shares in the problematic of religious language and cannot be used to explain it.

There is then no reason to suppose that any other form of human language shares the same referential and significational problem as the language of faith, unless it is itself without meaning in the natural universe of human discourse. Attempts to describe or even refer to a transcendental object are claims to have experienced nonuniversal modes of apprehension, and give rise to propositions the meaning of which cannot by definition be made clear to one who does not share in the alleged experience. In terms of the natural universe of human discourse, the claims of faith must remain unintelligible, as must also the claim to possess a new mode of understanding in terms of which the claims of faith are intelligible. The very possibility of faith remains problematic to the natural understanding of man. It may be possible in intelligible terms to indicate the bare, negative possibility of other modes of understanding, in the same negative sense that it is possible to admit that there might be that of which I cannot conceive; such meta-empirical possibilities, however, cannot be said to be significant possibilities. "I possess a mode of understanding given by faith" has, as a proposition, no more significance within the natural universe of human discourse than, "There is a God." They do not describe *apparent impossibilities*, but they also do not describe *apparent possibilities*—there could in theory be no evidence on the basis of which to decide their truth.

THE CLAIMS OF FAITH

A cursory analysis of the first article of the *Summa Theologiae* would seem to indicate that Aquinas does not make any special claims for faith except with regard to the source of the propositions to which it gives assent. The article is an attempt to explain why another doctrine beside philosophy is needed in order to teach men about God. The implication seems to be that human reason is able to discover some truths about God without the help of grace. Since, however, most men are not able to see the reasons for asserting the conclusions of natural theology, and since there are some further truths about the inner nature of God which human reason cannot discover, it was necessary that men be instructed by divine revelation, in order, as he says, that salvation might be more conveniently and certainly provided![60] Faith, it would appear, is but a convenient antidote for the limitations of human reason.

It is dangerous, however, to take Aquinas at surface value in his first statement of any profound question. His primary concern is to find a suitably broad basis of agreement from which he can proceed to more exact distinctions and argumentation.[61] Philosophy and Sacred Doctrine may both be said to discover, in some general sense of the word, *cognitiones* of God; but the nature of the "cognitions" discovered by philosophy is radically different from the nature of the "cognitions" of faith (which both, in turn, differ from the cog-

[60] S. T., I, 1, 1, *respondeo.*
[61] As in his discussion of the *imago dei* (see below, pp. 255f.).

nitions of ordinary experience). Some indication of future distinctions may be found in the article itself. In the reply to the second objection, for example, Aquinas suggests that sacred theology treats of 'being' in a "different light" from that available to philosophy. In a later article,[62] he will indicate that sacred theology, unlike philosophy, considers things precisely *as* they are ordered to God, and considers God in himself. As we shall see below, this means that God is the proper *subject* of theology, while he is treated only obliquely in philosophy. Again, in the first article, Aquinas refrains from calling philosophy a "science"; he consistently uses the word "discipline," while referring to Sacred Doctrine as a "science." In other contexts, Aquinas is quite willing to call philosophy a "science"—indeed, a *divine* science; in this article, however, *scientia* is too closely linked with *scientia dei* to be applied to philosophical theology, which, while it is a science which indirectly refers to God, is not a source of *scientia dei* (the conformation of the mind to God as object). The 'science of God' can only be found in Sacred Doctrine, under the formality of revealed truth.

The point is clearly made by Aquinas in his Commentary on the *De Trinitate* of Boethius. There he bluntly denies that God is the subject of natural or philosophical theology:

> And thus theology, or divine science, is twofold. There is one kind in which divine things are considered, *not however as the subject of that science*, but rather as the principle of its subject matter; and such is the theology which philosophers pursued.

> [Sic igitur theologia, sive scientia divina, est duplex. Una in qua considerantur res divinae, non tamquam subiectum scientiae, sed tamquam principium subiecti, et talis est theologia quam philosophi prosequuntur.][63]

God is *not* the subject of philosophical theology, although philosophical theology terminates in an indirect and opaque reference to him as the extrinsic principle of the connatural subject of the science—contingent or physical being. Within

62 S. T., I, 1, 7.   63 De Trin., 5, 4, respondeo.

the science God remains unknown (*ignotum*), although it is known that there exists a common first principle of all reality. Abstractly speaking, God may be said to be proper matter for the investigation of metaphysics, since God is 'being itself' and metaphysics *intends* to consider all 'being' insofar as it is;[64] metaphysics, however, does not *actually succeed* in considering God in himself, but takes cognizance of him only by referring the world to its unknown and final context of existence and intelligibility. Only in Sacred Doctrine does God become the proper subject of human science:

> There is another kind of theology which considers divine things in themselves, as the subject matter of the science; and that is the theology which is called Sacred Scripture.

> [Alia vero quae ipsas res divinas considerat propter seipsas, ut subiectum scientiae; et haec est theologia quae sacra scriptura dicitur.][65]

In metaphysics, contingent reality is considered as it is in itself, and God is considered only as related in some fashion to contingent reality; in Sacred Doctrine, however, God is considered as he is in himself, and all other things are considered as ordered to him. That which is obliquely *mentioned* in natural theology becomes the formal object of Sacred Doctrine. God is extrinsic to the proper subject of 'first philosophy,' but intrinsic to that of the Science of God.

Even those propositions concerning God which philosophy investigates function quite differently as part of Sacred Doctrine. The proposition, "God exists," for example, takes on such utterly new significance for faith that Aquinas is willing to say that the pagans (who after all proved the truth of the proposition "God exists") cannot be said to believe in God.[66] The reason that Aquinas gives for this claim is rather complex. In the body of the article, he argues that the act of faith establishes a threefold relationship to God:

1. The matter or content of faith is either God himself or other things as ordered to him. Nothing is proposed for belief except insofar as it pertains to God. In giving assent to the

[64] *Ibid.*   [65] *Ibid.*   [66] S. *T.*, II-II, 2, 2, ad 3.

propositions of Sacred Doctrine, the intellect of the believer is related to God (or acknowledges him) by the very nature of the matter to which it assents. By the mere fact of assent, therefore, the believer may be said to "believe in God" (*credere deum*).

2. The contents of faith share materially in common the mere fact that they pertain in some way to God. Formally speaking, however, they possess another and more profound character: they have been revealed by God. In giving assent to Sacred Doctrine, the believer submits to the teaching authority of God himself. He adheres to God precisely as the *veritas prima*—the first truth—the highest and most authoritative object of the intellect. He may thus be said to "believe God" (*credere deo*).

3. The will is also related to God in the act of faith in that the intellect is moved by the will to give its assent. "The first truth is referred to the will because it has the nature of a final end." The will adheres to God as *summum bonum*. According to the volitional aspect of the act of faith, a man is said to "believe in (or be motivated by) God" (*credere in deum*).

It should be noted that *credere deum* translates almost exactly as "believe that God exists." Aquinas does not even consider the notion that a pagan might believe in God in either of the *other* senses. Since, however, even the pagans may be said to believe that a God exists, Aquinas does consider the charge that *credere deum* ought not to be included in a formal definition of *faith*. His answer is that the pagan *cannot* be said to believe that *God* exists, since he does not believe that God exists "under the conditions that faith determines." If all that we understand by *his conditionibus quas fides determinat* are such matters as the Trinity and the Incarnation, we might feel that Aquinas is splitting hairs. True, as Aristotle remarked (and as Aquinas quotes him), "deficiency of cognition in simple matters is to fall entirely short of knowledge"; but is it a *deficiency* of cognition to know that there is *one* God, but not to know that *that same one God* exists as three persons? If that is indeed the case, then none of us can be said to believe in God, for there are surely true propositions about him that we do not know. Aquinas himself admits that the cognition of *faith* is imperfect. Should we not say, then, that even those with faith do not believe that God exists?

Both the interpretation and the rejoinder, however, *completely* miss the point. It is not a question of how many 'facts' we know about God. In a strict sense we do not know *any* facts about him. It is a question of *how* the intellect is related to God in the act of believing. As Aquinas points out, *credere deum, credere deo* and *credere in deum* are "not designations of *diverse* acts of faith, but of one and the *same* act having a diverse relationship to the object of faith."[67] Only when God is believed to exist under the formal aspect of *one who has revealed himself in Christ* does *credere deum* form an inseparable unity with *credere deo* and *credere in deum*. It is only because of the latter two aspects of the act of faith, however, that the intellect may be said to adhere to the first truth, or the will to incline to its final end. Thus, in that form of 'belief' produced by natural theology (and present in the pagans), the mind is not conformed to God and the will is not motivated by God—the 'beliefs' of natural theology do not terminate in God, but in the world. God is not the formal object of the "proofs for the existence of God" in natural theology. Furthermore, the act of faith is not a partial or deficient cognition of God in the sense that the rejoinder implies. Faith is not imperfect because it only knows certain 'facts' about God; it is imperfect because it is not a direct and intelligible *comprehension* of God. Such imperfection, however, is not *deficiency* in the sense defined; unlike natural theology, faith *does* terminate in God, and in the *whole* of God; there is no *deus absconditus* to faith; the whole of God is *deus revelatus*, but not *revelatus* in the sense of intelligibly *comprehended*.

It remains to be shown, however, in what way the language of faith is or even could be about God. How is it possible that through an act of faith the mind of man is conformed to God, when even in Sacred Doctrine "we use his effects . . . in place of a definition"?[68] That is Aquinas' way of stating that the words

[67] S. *T.*, II-II, 2, 2, ad 1.   [68] S. *T.*, I, 1, 7, ad 1.

used in the propositions of faith are drawn from ordinary language and apply primarily and intelligibly to the world and not to God, according to that mode of significance that they have for man. If the analysis of the preceding section was correct, it will not be possible to show how the language of faith is about God in anything like intelligible terms. For reasons that will emerge at a much later stage of the argument, such a consideration need not deter us. The claims of faith may be examined independently of their possible meaninglessness in terms of natural reason.[69] Our interest for the moment is what Aquinas *says* about Sacred Doctrine.

He clearly claims that Sacred Doctrine is about God; the act of faith is directed toward God as its prime and formal object. It is also clear, however, that many other things beside God are in some way the objects of faith and are included in the matter of Sacred Doctrine. Thus, in addition to talking about God, Sacred Doctrine also talks about the sacred humanity of Christ, the sacraments of the Church, and innumerable other created things apprehended by faith as related to God.[70] Sacred Doctrine also includes, as a *kind* of object, the propositions in which the material objects of faith are proposed to man for belief or assent.[71] Most analyses of faith suffer from a failure to distinguish between the kinds of 'objects' or 'subject matter' included in Sacred Doctrine; as a result there is a tendency either to reduce faith to belief in one kind of object or to assume that all kinds of religious objects are believed in the same way by means of a similar act of consent. Aquinas distinguishes radically between the kinds of objects included in faith, and the mode of assent proper to each.

Strictly and *formally* speaking, faith has one object only:

---

[69] Cf., S. Hampshire, *Thought and Action*, p. 205: "The actions of another may compel me to refer, in properly interpreting his intentions, to things and events that do not exist in fact, as I believe, and also to things that could not possibly exist, according to the implicit or explicit philosophical principles that govern my recognition of the existence of things. I may learn to understand what he is trying to do, even though I believe that what he is trying to do is something that could not conceivably be done. . . ." We, too, are trying to understand something that cannot *conceivably* be done.

[70] S. T., II-II, 1, 1.   [71] S. T., II-II, 1, 2.

God himself. The expression "object of faith" is, then, analogical in the strict sense; it has a number of uses all of which are dependent upon a relationship of derivation from a prime analogate. An appropriation of the expression "object of faith" to anything other than God, is dependent upon an ordination of that object to God as source and final referent.[72] So also, the expression "Sacred Doctrine" is itself essentially analogous. Any speech which is ordered by faith to God can be included under the designation of "Sacred Doctrine." Normally, Aquinas uses the expression *sacra doctrina* interchangeably with *sacra scriptura*—and that is clearly its primary use;[73] he also applies it, however, to the Apostles' Creed,[74] the ordinary teachings of the Church,[75] and the speculations of the theologian.[76] As in all analogical sets, there is a distinct order among the analogates. The prime and radical locus of *sacra doctrina* is the Word of God.

In his *Commentary on the Posterior Analytics*, Aquinas defines *doctrina* as the *actio eius qui aliquid cognoscere facit*— "the action of him who makes something known."[77] *Sacra doctrina* is the action of God who makes himself known. The prime locus of God's act of self-communication is God himself—the eternal and immanent expression of his personal intentional state, terminating in the eternal Word (the Image of God, or the second 'Person' of the Trinity). That act of self-expression is not *denominated* an act of "teaching," since the mode of signification inseparably bound to the name of "Teacher" connotes, like "Lord," a temporal relationship between the creature and God. All revelation, however, and thus all *sacra doctrina*, is an extension of the eternal procession of the Word; it is, in theological terminology, the temporal *mission* of the eternal Person.[78] The central historical locus of the temporal mission of the Word of God is the sacred humanity of Christ.[79] Therefore, the prime locus of "speech about God" is *sacra scriptura*, the primary subject of which is Christ. Scripture is itself a created analogue of God's act of self-

[72] S. T., I, 1, 7.   [73] S. T., I, 1, 9.
[74] S. T., II-II, 1, 6.   [75] S. T., II-II, 5, 3.
[76] S. T., I, 1, 8.   [77] Post. Anal., I, 1.
[78] S. T., I, 43, 2.   [79] Ibid.

knowledge as expressed in his Word or inner speech. Conformation of the mind to the intention of sacred scripture effects the conformation of the soul to the Second Person of the Trinity.

That which is communicated in an act of teaching is a mode of *scientia* or knowing. *Scientia*, for the medieval theologian, signifies both an immanent act or disposition of the knower, and an expression of that intentional state in intelligible propositional terms, unified under common principles of understanding. In human terms, a "science" is both a dispositional state of the scientist, and, by extension, the written or spoken expression of that state. *Scientia dei*, which is the knowledge communicated in Sacred Doctrine, is primarily and radically God's own eternal act of knowing, both as possessed immanently by God, and as directly and intrinsically participated in by the *beati* through the *visio dei*.[80] Intrinsic participation in the life and intellect of God himself is wholly and strictly confined by Aquinas to the state of Beatitude. The formal principle of the knowledge of the *beati* is the very form of God's own self-knowledge.[81] In human and analogical terms, we might say that the *beati* possess an adequate intention of the very nature of God. Far from being able to state how this is possible, Aquinas postulates a new mode or power of knowing, the *lumen gloriae*, which enables the *beati* to internalize that which man *in via* can in no way conceptualize—the 'whatness' or form of God. Since only the *beati* possess the Science of God in intelligible form, it must be viewed as a radically eschatological concept.

The believer *in via* may be said to receive *scientia dei* by means of causal participation. The formal *scientia dei* shared by God and the *beati* is the principle or cause of the intentional state of the believer *in via*;[82] that intentional state is itself the immanent cause of the believer's ordination to the *visio dei*. The knowledge of God and the blessed is thus the efficient and final cause of the faith of the believer. Since, however, the believer does not possess the *lumen gloriae*, he does not comprehend the Science of God. In place of an intel-

---

[80] S. *T.*, I, 1, 2; and I, 12, 1 and 9.
[81] S. *T.*, I, 12.　　　　　　　　　[82] *Ad Heb.*, XI, 1.

ligible science, the believer possesses only nonintelligible 'articles' of faith, which he believes to be created analogues of the knowledge shared by God and the blessed. Although he cannot himself see how the articles of faith are true of God,[83] he believes that they express the proper intentional state of one whose mind has been directed to God, and in some fashion conformed to his nature. He *hopes* to see, *in patria*, how his present 'state of mind' when he assents to the articles of faith is intelligibly related to the eternal essence of God.[84]

Thus, while it was correct to say that God is intrinsic to *scientia dei*, and so intrinsic to *sacra doctrina* considered as an action of God, it is not the case that he is intrinsic to or intelligibly contained in the participated "science of God" received by man through the teaching of sacred scripture, the Church, or the creeds. The problem, then, is to ascertain in what way God can be said to be the formal object of the participated science, while remaining unintelligible to the mind of one possessing the science. In order to answer that question, it is necessary to determine how man is related by faith to the secondary or "analogical" objects of faith—the sacred humanity of Christ, the events and objects described in sacred scripture, the Church and the sacraments, the articles of the creeds, the ordinary teachings of the Church, and the propositions of systematic theology. These may be considered in two general categories: words and things.

The Science of God as an expression of the intentional state of God may be considered in two forms: eternal and created. The eternal expression of *scientia dei* is, as we have said, the Eternal Word of God. That Word—the unknown conceptual framework of God—is the only perfect and intelligible expression of God's science.[85] There is, however, an expression of the science of god which is extrinsic to God, and that expression is contained in the linguistic form of sacred scripture. To faith, the scriptures are the Word of God. The entire linguistic system of faith—creeds, dogmas, and theological propositions —is derived from and dependent upon the language of scrip-

[83] S. T., I, 12.   [84] S. T., II-II, 1, 6, ad 1.
[85] S. T., I, 34, 2; and 35, 2.

ture.[86] In that the language of faith does refer the believer to the language of sacred scripture, it too is Sacred Doctrine—an expression of the science of God. Considered as *propositions*, however, the language of Sacred Doctrine may not be said to be the formal object of faith: propositions are the natural human mode of *receiving* truth, but they have as their proper end the reference of the intellect to a *nonpropositional* object, in this case the *veritas prima* or God himself.[87] Furthermore, the *mere* reception of the propositions of faith, even in a humanly achievable positive volitional state, is not sufficient to relate one to the *veritas prima*.[88] According to the natural significance that words have for man, it is impossible that God be intentionally contained in them; as open to the understanding of man, the language of faith does not refer to God. God is, then, extrinsic to the language of faith in so far as it is *conceptually significant* to the believer. For that reason, faith can never come from the mere hearing of the language of faith.

In his *Commentary on the Epistle to the Romans*, Aquinas distinguishes between *fides ex auditu* and *fides infusa*.[89] The function of *fides ex auditu* is the "determination of the credible";[90] it is through exposure to the language of faith that man comes into intellectual possession of the material objects of faith and the nonintelligible claim that they are ordered to or pertain to God. Since man cannot see the truth or significance of the propositions, he is not able through hearing to *believe* them (to *think* them with assent). Should he attempt to assent to their truth on the basis of hearing alone, he would not thereby be related to the *veritas prima* as formal intellectual object or as the final determinant of his will. Such assent to the unintelligible would be of the nature of "common faith"— the sort of faith or opinion that people normally have in matters of empirical truth—but not of the nature of "proper faith," or the mode of believing appropriate to divine matters.[91] It would not have even the coherence or intelligibility of ordi-

---

[86] *S. T.*, II-II, 1, 9, ad 1. [87] *S. T.*, II-II, 1, 2.
[88] *Ad Rom.*, x, 2. [89] *Ibid.*
[90] *Ibid. Determinatio de credibili* means, of course, the determination of the proper matter of belief, not the determination of its 'credibility.'
[91] *Ad Heb.*, x, 1; and *S. T.*, II-II, 4, 1.

nary belief in undetermined matters of empirical fact, since it
is not clear what would count as determinate evidence for the
truth of theological claims which cannot be comprehended.
For belief in the propositions of faith there is required an
"inclination of the heart to believe."[92] *Hoc non est ex auditu,
sed ex dono gratiae.*[93] The gift of grace which allows man to
assent to the matter proposed *ex auditu* is *fides infusa.* If faith
were a mode of *knowing* (in the ordinary sense), its 'infusion'
in the mind would allow the believer to see or to know the
way in which the propositions of faith refer to God and specify
his nature. In a strict and straightforward sense, man could
then be said to understand the propositions and to believe
them by "thinking with assent." To say "God is the formal
object of faith" would imply that God is the object of the
knowing intellect. Faith would then be the gratuitous communication to man of a new mode of conceptualization (presumably coupled with a new sort of experiential state) within
which "God" would occur as an intelligible form. Aquinas'
seemingly impossible claim, however, is that God *is* the object
of faith, that faith is an intellectual virtue or power, but that
God is *not known* by faith.[94] In this life, therefore, one cannot
see the truth or significance of the propositions of the faith;
nevertheless, the propositions of the faith are believed or
"thought with assent"!

Aquinas' most rigorous statement on the nature of faith is
contained in his *Commentary on the Epistle to the Hebrews,*
and is in explication of the text: *Est autem fides, sperandarum
substantia rerum, argumentum non apparentium.*[95] He takes
as his starting point the following claim: "The act of faith is
believing, which is an act of the intellect determined to one
thing by the command of the will."[96] Quoting Augustine, he
again repeats the claim that believing is "cogitating with
assent." (It may be significant that in this context he uses

[92] *Ad Rom.*, x, 2.
[93] "This does not come about through hearing, but through the gift of
grace."
[94] "Known" in this context means, of course, "intelligible in the light
of natural reason."
[95] *Ad Heb.*, xi, 1.
[96] *Ibid.*; cf. also *Comm. in Sent.*, iii, xxiii, 2, 1.

cogitare rather than *intelligere*.) When Aquinas goes on to
say that the first truth is the object of faith, we might expect
him to claim that the first truth is thought or possessed by the
intellect. That is precisely what he denies. In the act of believing, "the object of faith and the motivating end of the will
are the same." That object and end is the *veritas prima*, which
Aquinas equates with "Beatitude." Man's relationship to the
veritas prima differs, however, *in via* and *in patria*, since "*in
via*, the *veritas prima* is not possessed, and consequently not
seen, for in those things that are above the soul, it is the same
thing to possess and to see."[97] The first truth is merely "hoped
for." Aquinas concludes his comments on the first phrase of
the Hebrews text with the astounding words, "Thus, the *veritas
prima*, not seen, but hoped for, is the motivating end of the
will *in via*, and consequently the object of faith." Thus, God is
the object of an 'act of the intellect' *because* he is the object
of the will; and he is the object of the will because *he* moves
the will to command the intellect to assent without comprehension to the propositions received *ex auditu*.

So barely stated, Aquinas' position does not seem to differ
from the radically untenable claim to believe that which is in
no way understood. The submission of the *will* to the grace
of God might be considered sufficient ground for claiming to
believe on the authority of God (*credere in deum*), and the
resultant acceptance of the truth of the propositions of faith
might be sufficient ground for claiming to believe *that* what
God reveals is true (*credere deo*); but, unless the propositions
are rendered in some way lucid, neither aspect of faith would
seem to justify the claim to believe the articles of faith themselves (*credere deum*), by which act we believe God to exist
under those conditions specified by revelation. If the propositions of faith are absolutely opaque to the understanding, they
cannot conform *the mind* to the nature of God, regardless of
the presumed 'state of the will.' The believer could not be
said to believe anything *about* God. There must be present 'to
the mind' *some substitute* for a meaningful intention of God;
meaningless propositions would not seem to be a sufficiently intentional basis for any conformation of the mind to God.

[97] Until otherwise stated, all citations are from *Ad Heb.*, xi, 1.

Aquinas goes on, however, to examine the import of the Apostle's claim that "faith is the *substance* of things hoped for." How can things "hoped for" be substantially present to the mind through an act of the will? His first two explications are causal in nature: they are ways in which faith "makes the things hoped for to be present (*substare*) in us." Firstly, the submission of the will to the teaching authority of God may be said to 'merit'—through God's graceful decree—the ultimate vision of God. Thus, the things "hoped for" are present only in the weak sense of being "assured" in the future. Then, says Aquinas, it is as though "by its present nature, faith brought it about that what is believed as really in the future (*futurum in re*) is already possessed in some way, as long as faith believes on the authority of God (*credat in deum*)." It is uncertain whether Aquinas merely means to speak again of the assurance of faith that the things hoped for will at some future time be possessed, and are thus 'as good as already present'; or whether he means that as a result of that assurance, there is actually in the mind a kind of intention of those things—a sort of 'noema' of the things hoped for. If he intends the latter, although we cannot speak of a *knowing* by faith, we might speak of a 'knowing-by-*faith*'—a peculiar kind of intellectual apprehension unlike all other modes of cognition, and thus proper to faith alone. The remainder of Aquinas' comments commit us to such a view.

The third explication of faith as the "substance of things hoped for" is 'essential,' rather than merely 'causal':

In another way, *substantia* may be explicated essentially; as if faith *were* the substance, that is, the essence, of the things hoped for. Thus, in Greek it appears 'hypostasis of the things hoped for.' For the essence of Beatitude is nothing else than the vision of God. . . . The full vision of God is itself the essence of Beatitude.

[Alio modo exponi potest Substantia essentialiter; quasi fides sit substantia, idest essentia, rerum sperandarum. Unde in graeco habetur, hypostasis rerum sperandarum. Essentia enim beatitudinis nihil aliud est quam visio dei. . . . Ipsa ergo plena visio dei est essentia Beatitudinis.]

Faith, of course, is not itself the "full vision of God." It is, he says, "a kind of beginning, as it were," of the vision of God (*quasi quoddam inchoativum*). A more guarded statement would be difficult to imagine: *quasi* is 'as-if' language; *quoddam* is 'sort-of' language; and *inchoativum* signifies a first movement or a "germ of a beginning."[98] Aquinas uses the "science-principle" distinction to illustrate his claim. If a man knew the first principles of geometry, he would "in essence" possess the entire science, although he was not aware of the many conclusions he might draw from them. So also, in believing the articles of faith (and particularly those concerning the Trinity), man possesses the principles which "contain the complete sum of that science" that *will* one day beatify him. The articles of faith are the principles of the science or knowledge of the *beati* in heaven:

> Our faith is that we believe that the *beati* will see and enjoy God. And so, if we wish to arrive at that, it is necessary that we believe the principles of *that* cognition.

> [Fides autem nostra est, ut credamus quod beati videbunt et fruentur Deo. Et ideo si volumus ad hoc pervenire, oportet ut credamus principia istius cognitionis.]

Such a "rationalistic" view would hardly seem to be in keeping with Aquinas' denial that the cognition of faith is of the nature of science,[99] or with his claim that the *beati* see God, not through created forms, but through God himself.[100] How can we, possessing only *created* forms, be said to believe the principles of the science of the *beati*? Aquinas makes it clear, however, that the form in which the man of faith possesses the principles of *scientia dei* is a mode appropriate to faith alone, and not to *vision*. We, unlike the *beati*, do not possess those principles in intelligible form; we possess only created and nonintelligible propositional analogues of those principles. Thus, Aquinas modifies his claim by stating that "the whole [science of the *beati*] is contained *quasi* essentially" in the articles of faith. Insofar as faith "sees," it sees "by means of a

---

[98] Cf., Deferrari, *A Lexicon of St. Thomas Aquinas*, entry under *inchoo*.
[99] *S. T.*, I, 12, 13, ad 3.   [100] *S. T.*, I, 12, 9.

mirror, and in an enigma." Since the articles provide a *kind* of vision, however, they must be said to give rise to a *kind* of 'intention' or 'noetic' appropriate to faith and not to science. To possess the essence of a thing, in a mode appropriate to a particular sort of 'cognition,' is to apprehend that thing in some way.

Aquinas goes on to distinguish the 'cognition' of faith from all other modes of cognition. Its uniqueness is suggested by the Apostle's phrase, "the argument of nonapparent things." Aquinas insists that "the act of faith proper, although it is connected with the will . . . , is nevertheless in the intellect as in its subject, since its object is something true." It is not, however, a kind of science properly speaking: "habits of science bring all modes of certitude to the complete vision of that which is thought (*intelligitur*)." In science, "the intellect is moved by the evidence of an object, which is either *per se* knowable, through the possession of first principles, or which is known (*cognitum*) through another, which in turn *is* per se knowable." In claiming that faith does not know in this fashion, Aquinas excludes all naïve notions of faith as "knowing God through his creatures" or by means of an interpretation of ordinary events or objects. On the other hand, faith is neither a state of *doubt*, produced by a lack of evidence, nor an *opinion*, based on probability. Through faith the mind is determined to one alternative with a "*kind* of certainty and firm adhesion, by means of a *kind* of voluntary choice." The "kind"'s are inserted, not as denigrating qualifications, but in deference to the source of certainty: "Divine authority makes the choice in us." Because of God's operation on the soul of the believer, he possesses a *kind* of intention, a *kind* of certainty and a *kind* of cognition proper to the act of faith and not to any other act of the intellect:

> In that it is called 'argument,' faith is distinguished from opinion, doubt and suspicion. . . . And in that it is called 'of nonapparent things,' it is distinguished from the possession of principles and science. And in that it is called 'of things hoped for,' it is distinguished from faith as it is commonly "taken," which is not ordered to Beatitude.

[Per hoc enim quod dicitur argumentum, distinguitur fides ab opinione, dubitatione et suspicione. . . . Per hoc autem quod dicitur, non apparentium, distinguitur ab habitu principiorum et scientia. Et per hoc quod dicitur, rerum sperandarum, distinguitur a fide communiter sumpta, quae non ordinatur ad Beatitudinem.]

In final summary, Aquinas reaffirms his opinion that neither the conclusions nor the principles of faith possess intelligible *evidence* for the believer; thus, "the intellect does not assent to its conclusions either as known or as seen."

Nevertheless, faith provides its own inexplicable mode of 'apprehension,' which is the apprehension enabling the believer to assent to propositions that are nonintelligible in the light of conceptual reason. Man 'apprehends' because grace *makes* him apprehend in a new and unique way. The formal referent of that apprehension is not possessed in an immanent mode, as are the objects of science: God does not exist in his formal clarity in the intellect of the believer. The mode of faith's participation in the science of God is causal and analogical. The first truth is both the first and final cause of the existence in the soul of the intentions of faith. The form in which we possess the science of God is not the form in which God himself possesses that science, but an *analogue* of that form. The manner in which that 'state of mind' called "faith" exemplifies or is isomorphic with the intentional being of God is known only to God and the *beati*. The language of faith—in so far as the words have meaning to us—is analogous to the language of God by an analogy of extrinsic attribution: it is claimed that there exists in the eternal Word of God an analogical counterpart of the linguistic system of faith, such that it is in all aspects intelligible and unified by the *per se* principles of intelligibility governing the conceptual framework of God himself. It is further claimed that in terms of the conceptual framework of God himself, there exists a *per se* causal relationship between the intentional state of God and the state of mind produced in man by *fides infusa*. That created state of mind and will is said to be the immanent cause in us of the future possession of the intelligible knowledge or intellectual vision of God: it may therefore be termed a 'proleptic participation in *scientia dei*.'

Through the gift of faith, then, man intends *toward* a truth which he does not naturally comprehend, in the way that a man might strain to hear a spoken word that he did not catch. To use Hayen's suggestive phrase, the intellect is "seized by God,"[101] in such a way that the intellect cannot "get a hold" on him. The logical problem does arise of how man knows that it is in fact "God" toward whom he is intending or responding in faith. There is no question of a direct "I-Thou" encounter in faith; God in his "pure subjectivity" is not present to the mind. But there is an element of *taking* that could logically be a *mis*-taking: faith does not *know* that it is "God" to which it is ordered, for that would imply a formal knowledge of the nature of God; it does, however, claim to believe that it is ordered toward the beatitude of man—the final resolution of the natural frustrations of the intellect and will. It is not clear, of course, how a *foretaste* of beatific complacency could afford unmistakable *evidence* of an efficacious movement toward *complete* complacency—toward the final saturation of man's natural longing for total intelligibility and volitional fruition. It is not clear what sort of object would in fact afford such saturation; if it *were* clear, we should know what God is. To name God "Beatitude"—the objective correlate of the postulated human state of knowing and loving beatifically —is to name God on the basis of an unknown state. Aquinas, of course, is aware of the problem. The "evidence of things not seen" is not the "evidence" of science—it is evidence only in the light of faith. It is evidence "on divine authority"; it is *taken* as "evidence" only because "divine authority makes the choice" in man. The "argument" is, of course, circular and confessedly so: for there is no real argument. The Apostle, says Aquinas, uses the word "argument" to signify the normal conclusion of an argument, which is "certainty." In this case, however, the "certainty" is not really *argued*, since the assurance of faith is, for the believer, beyond argument.

The nature of the 'apprehension' involved in faith, and of

[101] A. Hayen, *La communication de l'acte de l'être d'après Saint Thomas d'Aquin* (De Brouwer, Paris, 1957).

the peculiar 'intention' created by faith, may be somewhat clarified by an analysis of the analogy developed by Aquinas between the intentionality of faith and that of natural reason. It is an analogy in the purely formal sense—there is no relationship of intrinsic attribution. Certain formal similarities are noted between science and its object on the one hand, and faith and its object on the other. Such similarities are made the basis of the appropriation of the *language* of science to the acts of faith. It is not thereby claimed that faith is a subspecies of science or that the formal similarity renders faith any more natural or less problematic—the appropriation of language is an equivocation pure and simple, although its appropriateness can be seen. Such analogical appropriations of language from one context to another may be quite illuminating, although they have their own intrinsic dangers. The similar analogy established by Aquinas between sensation and conceptual judgment has, in fact, been the source of many confusions in the analysis of Thomas' epistemology. There is a purely formal similarity of relationship between sensation and its objects on the one hand, and conceptual judgment and its objects on the other. Thus, Aquinas appropriates the language of 'sight' to the acts of reason. A great deal of epistemological nonsense has been generated by the failure to see that such analogies are *appropriate equivocations*. While Aquinas will say that intellection involves a kind of seeing, he does not mean that the mind 'takes a look at' the world, as though the formal intelligibility of the world 'lay at hand' to be passively observed. The words "kind of" in this context do not imply a subtype or subspecies, but function as 'sort-of' language. The dangers of the science-faith analogy are equally real. If faith is said to afford a *quaedam cognitio*, it must not be thought that faith gets a *special type* of conceptual grasp on its object, so as to move to a "higher level of intelligibility." *Quaedam* is 'sort-of' language, signaling an appropriate equivocation. We must always bear in mind Aquinas' claim that "in the cognition of faith is found a most imperfect operation of the intellect."[102] In his more guarded moments, Aquinas distinguishes between faith and cognition; quoting with approval from Gregory, he

[102] *C. G.*, III, 40.

remarks that "apparent things yield *cognition*, not *faith*."[103]
And so, technically speaking, nonapparent things yield *faith*,
not *cognition*.

Nevertheless, the parallel between faith and science can be
helpful. It rests primarily on the analogy between the "light
of natural reason" and the "light of faith." In ascertaining the
status of the first principles of natural reason in Aquinas' epistemology, it is necessary to take account of conflicting texts.
Some of those texts assimilate the first principles to *per se nota*
(analytic) propositions; others merely claim that they arise
automatically from sense experience; a third group speaks of
a 'natural tendency' of the mind. A clue to the proper reading
is found in such statements as: "Cognition of first principles is
received *by way of* sense experience, and yet the light by
which those principles are *known* is innate. . . ."[104] The innate
"light" constitutes a natural disposition to utilize syntactically
significant forms and rules in judging the objects of human
experience. Intelligibility consists of the formal correlation between the material of sense experience and *innately generated*
categories of judgment. In abstraction from sense experience,
the dispositional principle of "the intelligibility of being" (the
natural tendency of the mind to expect reality to be intelligible) is without specific content. In abstraction, however, from
the "light of reason," material reality is not *actually* intelligible.
Material forms—the formal element of the objects of perception—are not themselves universal in character. They must be
'abstracted' by the intellect and rendered intelligible in a formal judgment that terminates in *per se nota* intelligibility. The
judgment is made in terms of categories produced by the mind
for the matter at hand, but determined *in form* by the universal requirements of intellectual clarity. Thus, on the basis
of perceiving several objects with the same important accidental properties, the intellect judges that each possesses the
same substantial form or essence, although that form cannot
be passively observed or known through empirical observation.
The substantial form is *named* from abstracted accidents—
taken to be essential properties—while the notion of 'form' is
itself produced by the agency of the "light of reason," which

---

[103] *Ad Heb.*, XI, 1.　　　　　　　[104] *De Trin.*, 3, 1, ad 4.

judges the objects to possess in themselves the *real* counterparts of its own *ideal* forms of intelligibility. To "conceive of an object" is to "conceive" its form in the immanent operations of the mind itself.

Aquinas states the parallel between reason and faith as follows:

> This habit of faith, nevertheless, does not move us by way of intellectual understanding, but more by way of the will; therefore it does not make us comprehend those truths which we believe, nor does it force assent, but it causes us to assent to them voluntarily. And thus it is evident that faith comes in two ways: namely from God by reason of the interior light that induces assent, and also by reason of those truths which are proposed exteriorly and take their source from divine revelation. These latter are related to the cognition of faith as things known by the senses are to knowledge of first principles, because in both cases there is a certain determination of cognition. Therefore, as *cognition* of first principles is received by way of sense experience and yet the *light* by which those principles are known is innate, so faith comes by way of hearing, and yet the habit of faith is infused.[105]

Just as the contents of sense experience are not intelligible until the "light" of the intellect judges them really to possess the formality it conceives in its own intentionality, so too the material objects of faith do not refer the mind to God until the "light" of faith judges them really to possess the formality it finds in its own intentionality—order to the *veritas prima.* Just as the natural intentionality of the mind is nonspecific without the matter supplied by sense experience, so also the internal "inclination of the heart to believe" is "inchoate" without the matter supplied *ex auditu.*[106]

The mere possession of an innate tendency toward the discovery of intelligibility is not in itself the possession of intelligible truths, even if it provides a natural light in which intelligible truth may be recognized. Likewise, the mere posses-

105 *Ibid.*
106 On *fides infusa* without *fides ex auditu,* see *Ad Rom.,* x, 2.

sion of an infused tendency to rest in God as in one's beatitude is not in itself the possession of saving truths, even if it
provides a supernatural light in which the salvific may be
recognized. On the other hand, just as no object in the world
can be judged intelligible without the natural light of reason,
so also no particular object can be judged salvific without the
supernatural light of faith. Both *fides infusa*, which constitutes
the light, and *fides ex auditu*, which proposes the object, are
strictly required in order that the intellect possess the *sui generis* 'intention' of faith which allows the believer to 'apprehend'
the "substance of things hoped for" and to refer to God in a
nonvacuous way.

We have thus defined the role of *words* in the communication of the participated science of sacred doctrine: in the light
of infused faith, they refer the intellect to the nonpropositional objects of belief. The propositions of the language of
faith can be believed in the formal sense only when the intellect possesses an intentional orientation to its final end under
the formality of salvation and beatitude. That intentionality is
supplied by God in the infusion of faith; and so it is God who
makes the propositions really refer to their supernatural objects. Any attempt to 'believe' the propositions without the
formality supplied by grace will result in a state of false or
dead faith[107] which lacks the gift—as we shall see—of the
mode of 'understanding' proper to faith.

In order, however, to refer us to a nonpropositional object
which we can take to be salvific, the propositions of the language of faith must contain at least one straightforward and
nonproblematic empirical referent. If the propositions of faith
purportedly referred directly and exclusively to God himself,
the intellect would be left with only the inner light of faith.
Something must be communicated *ex auditu* before the light
of infused faith can judge it to be a cause of salvation and
thus a proper object of formal faith. The propositions of faith
must in some way make or imply at least one reference to an
empirical fact.

Many of the propositions of Sacred Doctrine would appear
to be straightforward historical references to theoretically ob-

[107] Cf., S. T., II-II, 5, 2.

servable objects or events. One such proposition contains the claim that "Jesus Christ was resurrected from the dead." To the light of natural reason, it is impossible to see how such a proposition could be saying anything about the final end of man or the particular destiny of anyone other than Christ himself. Its conceptual content, even for the believer, is commensurate only with a logically possible but unlikely event within the physical world: the resuscitation of a dead body. The empirically meaningful content of the proposition is incapable of conveying any information whatever about "God." When man assents in faith to the proposition, however, he assents implicitly to a claim about the resuscitation of a dead body—he assents to the claim that the occurrence is a cause of his own still future beatitude:

> Now, since faith is principally concerned with what we hope to see *in patria*, that is, God himself . . . therefore those things pertain *per se* to faith which directly order us to eternal life.

> [Quia vero fides principaliter est de his quae videnda speramus in patria . . . ideo per se ad fidem pertinent illa quae directe nos ordinant ad vitam aeternam.][108]

In the light of faith, the resuscitation of that particular dead body is 'apprehended' or 'known-by-faith' to be an existential correlate of the intentional formality created by the infusion of faith. The inner ordination of the intellect and will to their final end gives rise to the category of soteriological causation, which supplies the intentional form of the judgment that Christ's resurrection is salvific. The 'apprehension' of faith corresponds analogically to the cognition by reason of an existential correlate of an internally conceived category of understanding—as, for example, "I see that A is causing B." The judgment of faith, however, is not a judgment of science since the reason cannot see how the purported cause is related to the postulated effect. The believer does not possess a form of intelligibility which corresponds to the judgment of faith, but only a form of faith itself, conceived *by God* within

[108] S. T., II-II, 1, 6, ad 1.

the soul of the believer—not by the believer himself. How the resuscitation of a dead body could possibly cause his own beatitude, the believer cannot conceivably comprehend—although he hopes to comprehend *in patria*. In that respect, the apostles—who saw the empirical result of the resurrection—were no better off than the contemporary believer:

> Demonstration may be taken in two ways. Sometimes demonstration means any kind of a reason for a thing which reduces doubt to belief. . . . In the first sense of demonstration, Christ did not prove his resurrection to the apostles by demonstrating it to them. For such demonstrative proof proceeds from certain principles: from which, if they are unknown to the apostles, nothing could be manifested to them, for from ignorance nothing can be made known. If the principles were known, however, they would not transcend human reason, and thus they would not be efficacious in establishing faith in the resurrection, which exceeds human reason. . . . Therefore, he proved his resurrection to them through the authority of sacred scripture, which is the foundation of faith. . . .

> [Argumentum dupliciter dicitur. Quandoque dicitur argumentum quaecumque ratio rei dubiae faciens fidem. . . . Prima igitur modo accipiendo argumentum, Christus non probavit discipulis suam resurrectionem per argumenta. Quia talis probatio argumentativa procedit ex aliquibus principiis; quae si non essent nota discipulis, nihil per ea eis manifestaretur, quia ex ignotis non potest aliquod fieri notum; si autem essent eis nota, non transcenderent rationem humanam, et ideo non essent efficacia ad fidem resurrectiones adstruendam, quae rationem humanam excedit. . . . Probavit autem eis resurrectionem suam per auctoritatem sacrae scripturae, quae est fidei fundamentum. . . .][109]

Christ appeared to the apostles to establish the fact of the resuscitation, which is what is taken by faith to be a cause of salvation. As an article of faith, however, the resurrection cannot be seen, but must be believed; for the object of faith is

[109] S. T., III, 55, 5.

not the fact, but the causal efficacy of the fact in the order of salvation—in Heilsgeschichte. That must be proved out of scripture, even with the resuscitated body standing before the believer. To prove by scripture is to presuppose the intentionality of faith. Ultimately, that which is believed is God himself, since he is the principle of that causal order known-by-faith as the "order of salvation."

The central empirical referent of Sacred Doctrine is the humanity of Christ: "The mystery of Christ's Incarnation and Passion is the way by which men come to beatitude."[110] All other empirical referents depend for their soteriological status on their relationship to him:

> On the other hand, certain things are proposed in Scripture to be believed, not as principally intended, but for the manifestation of those things that are *per se* of faith: for example, that Abraham had two sons.

> [Quaedam vero proponuntur in sacra scriptura ut credenda non quasi principaliter intenta sed ad praedictorum manifestationem: sicut quod Abraham habuit duos filios.][111]

It is, however, the *mystery* of Christ's incarnation and passion that produces beatitude. Just as the empirical fact of the resuscitation of a dead body is not itself the formal object of faith, so too the humanity of Christ considered simply as a series of historical events is not itself the formal object of faith. It is the causal soteriological efficacy of the humanity of Christ that is strictly speaking believed. The formal object of faith is that which begins in man the movement toward beatitude:

> Those things which pertain to the humanity of Christ and to the sacraments of the Church or to any creatures whatsoever, fall under faith insofar as by them we are ordered to God. And to those we assent on account of divine truth.

> [Ea quae pertinent ad humanitatem Christi et ad sacramenta Ecclesiae vel ad quascumque creaturas cadunt sub

---

[110] S. *T.*, II-II, 2, 7, *respondeo*.   [111] S. *T.*, II-II, 1, 6, ad 1.

fide inquantum per haec ordinamur ad Deum. Et eis etiam assentimus propter divinam veritatem.][112]

The humanity of Christ is then an "indirect" object of faith: it is included in the reference of faith, but subordinated to the mystery operative in that humanity—the efficient causal order of salvation. For Aquinas, however, it is the humanity of Christ that justifies or begins salvation in man—it is not some supra-historical 'event' in an idealistic salvation-history:

> The interior influx of grace is from no one but Christ alone, whose humanity, in that it is joined to divinity, has the power of justifying.
>
> [Interior autem effluxus gratiae non est ab aliquo nisi a solo Christo, cuius humanitas, ex hoc quod est divinitati adiuncta, habet virtutem iustificandi.][113]

All other empirical events or objects, including the sacraments of the Church, justify man or produce beatitude only as instrumental causes making available to man the salvific grace of Christ's historical humanity.

The act of taking the humanity of Christ—as an empirically observable object—to be the efficient cause of salvation is a judgment that there exists in Christ the correlate *in re* of the intentional category of divine soteriological causality, a category conceived immanently by the 'light of faith.' The power of justifying is the power of beginning in the believer a real or existential movement toward beatitude or God—a movement traditionally called "sanctification." It is the existential correlate of the intentional ordering of the intellect and will to God as the intended object of beatitude. That inner ordering is taken to be the soteriological agency of God himself, operative in the *ideal* order: the efficacious or existential ordering of man to his final end, as judged by faith to be caused by the humanity of Christ, is taken to be the soteriological agency of God, operative in the *real* order. Faith takes the agency of Christ to be simultaneously the agency of God. God is the subject who justifies in and through the humanity of Christ.

[112] S. T., II-II, 1, 1, ad 1.   [113] S. T., III, 8, 6.

Ultimately, then, the formal object of faith is always God himself, as the principle establishing the efficacious order of soteriological causality operative in the empirical referents of the language of faith and effecting the beginning in the believer of a proleptic participation in the beatific vision. It is important to note that two 'apprehensions' are presupposed by the recognition of Christ as God: 1) the 'apprehension' of the intentional ordering of the intellect and will to God, as itself an expression of the agency of God; and, 2) the 'apprehension' of the empirical events in the life of Christ as the efficient cause of that real ordering of the intellect and will toward beatification. Both of those 'apprehensions' result immediately and unarguably from the gift of grace which establishes the intentionality of infused faith. It is the given function of the light of faith to recognize in any ordering—intentional or existential—of man to God, the agency of God himself. This too is immediate and unarguable—it is "divine authority making the choice within man." As Kierkegaard so clearly saw, God could never emerge as an interpretation of the history of Christ: he must be there from the very first moment of faithful 'apprehension.'[114]

It is Christ's humanity that we 'apprehend' to be "justifying"; but we immediately know-by-faith that only the final end of man can "justify": thus, we immediately know-by-faith that Christ's humanity is expressing the agency of God himself. In the act of faith, one sees or knows the humanity of Christ, and believes the divinity. All further language about the incarnation is an articulation of the basic faithful taking of the soteriological agency of Christ to be the agency of God himself. The 'one person' (one agency) and 'two natures' (empirical object and object of faith) formulation is what Aquinas would call a 'quasi-conclusion' of faith; it is an analytical deduction which gives further *language* to the primary 'apprehension' of faith, without extending its referential range or making it more intelligible.

To the light of natural reason, the analogical parallel between the intentionality or light of faith and that of reason is

[114] *Training in Christianity* (Princeton University Press, Princeton, 1947), p. 80.

hardly enough to render the claims of faith logically coherent, even if Aquinas' epistemological theory is adopted without qualification. The reason is, of course, that the categories of natural judgment render intelligible the contents of sense experience without a reference beyond the publicly observable world. In the case of faith, however, at least two references are highly problematic: "beatitude" and "God." On the intentional level, infused faith is said to incline the intellect and will toward a nonexperienced beatific state of knowing and loving. "God" is then simply defined as the objective correlate of the beatific state. To name God from creatures is problematic enough—to name him, however, from an unknown created state would seem to be foolhardy.

The 'answer' of faith must fall back on its own peculiar light or intentionality. It would be true, of course, that if we possessed only the light of faith, there could be no explicit naming of any kind. The application of the light of faith to certain empirical events, however, makes present to the intellect nonempirical aspects of those same events, their soteriological efficacy. Just as reason conceives immanently out of its own intentionality an intelligible form when confronted with empirical objects through sense experience, so also infused faith conceives immanently out of its own intentionality a soteriological form when confronted with certain empirical objects proposed by the language of Sacred Doctrine. Or, to de-mythologize a bit further, just as we do not know the mechanism by means of which we naturally find ourselves informing experience in terms of the conceptual system we actually possess, so also we do not know the mechanism by means of which we find ourselves informing certain events in terms of the language of faith. Just as reason knows the object of natural understanding in the conceived intentions of the intellect, so also the believer 'knows' the object of faith in the 'intentions' conceived in his mind by faith—which is to say, by God. "My" beatitude is that toward which infused faith inclines my intellect and will at the level of dispositional intentionality; it cannot be said, however, that "my" beatitude is made present to me by the light of faith alone. When, however, Christ is conceived by my intellect through the hearing of the language of faith, the light of faith conceives within me a kind of 'intention' by means of which I 'apprehend' his beatitude—not as seen or known, but as certainly affirmed and 'understood' in a mode proper to faith alone. Christ had to possess 'beatitude,' apprehended by faith, in order to refer the believer to his own beatitude as anything more than a non-significant meta-empirical possibility:

> What is in potentiality is reduced to act by what is in act. . . . Man, however, is in potentiality to the science of the beati, which consists in the vision of God, and he is ordered to that science as to an end: for he is a rational creature capable of that beatified cognition, insofar as he is to the Image of God. But man is reduced to that end of beatitude through the humanity of Christ. . . . And therefore it had to be that that cognition that consists in the vision of God should belong most excellently to Christ of all men.

> [Quod est in potentia, reducitur in actum per id quod est actu. . . . Homo autem est in potentia ad scientiam beatorum, quae in visione Dei consistit, et ad eam ordinatur dicut ad finem: est enim creatura rationalis capax illius beatae cognitionis, inest ad imaginem Dei. Ad hunc autem finem beatitudinis homines reducuntur per Christi humanitatem. . . . Et ideo oportuit quod cognitio ipsa in Dei visione consistens excellentissime Christo homini conveniret.][115]

Thus, although the 'intention' which relates the believer 'noetically' to the beatitude of Christ as an existential 'fact' is highly problematic to natural reason, faith has, in its own terms, sufficient ground for claiming to 'understand' what is meant by "my" beatitude. The 'apprehension' is deficient, and the 'knowledge' which results falls short of vision or scientific comprehension; but if the believer is justified in claiming to possess a kind of intention—a noema of faith—then the reference to "beatitude" is not wholly vacuous, although its non-vacuity could never be publicly proved. The 'nonvacuous' references of the language of faith are based, therefore, on a combination of the eschatological intentionality (or disposi-

[115] S. T., III, 9, 2.

tion) of *fides infusa* and the christological matter of *fides ex auditu*.

There is, however, a further problem. Granting the possibility of a new mode of intellectual judgment emerging immanently from the intentionality of infused faith, and granting the claims based on that judgment to discover a new order of 'soteriological events' in the empirically describable matter of the life of Christ, it is possible to understand the kind of coherence, in its own terms, that statements about beatitude, and about God as the objective correlate of beatitude, might have to one who believes; but the 'noesis' of God in this sense would not seem to account for the specific language about God which appears in Sacred Doctrine. We have given, at best, an account of *some* of the propositions of Sacred Doctrine: namely, those which either make a direct empirical reference to some historical event ("Jesus Christ was resurrected from the dead"), or combine an empirical reference with a reference to the formal object of faith ("Jesus Christ is God"). There is, however, a third category of the propositions of Sacred Doctrine which appear to make a pure reference to the formal object of faith in terms which cannot be deduced from statements about Christ: as, for example, the controlling proposition of all theology, "God is three Persons in a unity of Substance." Trinitarian language cannot be deduced or otherwise derived from language about Christ as perfectly beatified man. If it could, it would seemingly have the status of the propositions of natural theology: it would not only be a naming of God from creatures (which in fact it is), it would also be a reference to God, not as the direct object of faith, but as a kind of meta-empirical ground or cause of what the believer 'apprehends' by faith (the soteriological humanity of Christ). The Trinity would then be judged in terms of a reduction to Incarnational language. Aquinas, however, bases the language of the Incarnation on the language of the Trinity.[116] The point may be made in terms of the order of presentation: while we have been considering the language of faith in an order determined by a philosophical consideration of the problem of reference, theology proper adopts an order of presentation

[116] S. T., I, 43.

predicated upon the solution of the problem of reference by faith. While we began, therefore, with the seemingly nonproblematic references of faith to historical events, Aquinas begins quite properly with references to the object of faith itself, as 'apprehended' in its own integrity with a mode of clarity proper to the intentionality or disposition of faith. He begins, that is, with the Trinity.

While it is true, then, that God is named from beatitude— and particularly from the beatitude of Christ—the solution by faith in its own terms of the problem of reference with regard to beatitude does not solve the problem of reference with regard to God as he subsists in his own nature. The holy Trinity must be the prime and controlling revealed truth, 'apprehended' and 'understood' by the believer in the light of faith. In order, however, to escape the vacuity of a meta-empirical reference to a totally unknown unexperienced object, the propositions concerning the Trinity must contain or imply at least an indirect reference to an apprehended fact, part of which must be susceptible of empirical description. The 'intention' of faith which underlies both the apprehension of and reference to the holy Trinity must, like all other 'intentions' of faith, be conceived immanently in the light of faith as a result of or in conjunction with that which is communicated *ex auditu*. What could there be in that which comes to man by hearing that could supply the matter for an 'intention' of God himself? If there *were* such matter, would we not have to say that God is really *intrinsic* to the participated science of God?

The solution can be found, I believe, in terms proper to the noetic of faith: the 'apprehension' of God by faith constitutes the image of God in man. A review of Aquinas' treatment of the *imago dei* will provide an ideal paradigm of his theological method. The basic principle that God is himself the proper subject of all theology is reflected in the very order in which the Image is treated. The only question of the *Summa* which deals with the Image by name (i, 35, *De imagine*) is part of the treatise on the Trinity. When Aquinas turns his attention to the Image of God *in man*, he does so under the rubric, "On the end or terminus of the production of man."[117]

117 S. T., I, 93.

The image in man is concluded to be a reference of the entire intentional being of man *to God*. It is not something *in* the 'soul'—an element in our conceptual system, for example—that constitutes the image or intention of God in man, but the entire form given to the 'soul' by sanctifying grace.

In Aquinas' first statement of the nature of the image in man, he supplies the key to understanding all of his later references:

> In order to designate the imperfection of the image in man, man is not just said *to be* an image, but is said to be *to the image*, through which is signified a certain movement tending toward perfection.
>
> [Et ideo ad designandum in homine imperfectionem imaginis, homo non solum dicitur imago, sed ad imaginem, per quod motus quidam tendentis in perfectionem designatur.][118]

In the context of the discussion on the Trinity, therefore, the image of God in man is seen as an imperfect tendency or ordination to the eternal image or intentional expression of God. As soon as Aquinas turns his attention in the later question to man himself, his formulations become at first rather misleading. Following the authority of the Augustinian tradition, Aquinas locates the image of God in man in the intellectual soul,[119] and postulates its existence in every man.[120] From such an account, the unfortunate conclusion might be drawn that the human mind *is* the image of God—*tout simple*. Thus, the worst fears of certain antinatural reformation theologians would be realized: the image of God could be seen even in the subtle machinations of the perverted mind of the Grand Inquisitor. Such is the interpretation usually given to such statements as the following, which concern man's "obediential capacity" to experience the beatific vision: "For he is a rational creature capable of that beatified cognition, insofar as he is to the Image of God."[121] The situation is not improved when Aquinas states:

> Thus, first and principally, the image of the Trinity is found

[118] S. T., I, 35, 2, ad 3.
[119] S. T., I, 93, 2.
[120] S. T., I, 93, 4.
[121] S. T., III, 9, 2.

in the mind according to its acts: inasmuch, that is, as from the knowledge we possess, we form by cogitation an interior word, and from this break out into love.

[Et ideo primo et principaliter attenditur imago Trinitatis in mente secundum actus, prout scilicet ex notitia quam habemus, cogitando interius verbum formamus, et ex hoc in amorem prorumpimus.][122]

Presumably, then, *any* instance of knowledge, conceptualization, and love would image on the natural level the very being of God himself. In article 8 of question 93, however, Aquinas excludes such a general interpretation: the conclusion of the article is, "The image of the divine Trinity is in the soul *only* by comparison with the *object* [of the acts of the intellectual soul], which is God." The first objection argues the opposite interpretation:

The image of the divine Trinity is in us according as a word proceeds from a speaker, and love from both. . . . But this can be found in us with any kind of object.

[Imago enim divinae Trinitatis invenitur in anima . . . secundum quod verbum in nobis procedit a dicente, et amor ab utroque. . . . Sed hoc invenitur in nobis secundum quod cumque obiectum.][123]

Aquinas replies:

The divine image is present in man insofar as there is conceived in him a word derived from a noesis *of* God, and a love derived therefrom. Therefore, the image of God is present in the mind insofar as the mind *tends toward God*.

[Attenditur igitur divina imago in homine secundum verbum conceptum de Dei notitia, et amorem exinde derivatum. Et sic imago Dei attenditur in anima secundum quod fertur . . . in Deum.][124]

Although, apart from grace, the mind does not actually tend toward God, it is nevertheless a claim of theology that every

[122] S. *T.*, I, 93, 7.
[123] S. *T.*, I, 93, 8, *obj.* 1.   [124] *Art. cit., respondeo.*

mind is ordered to God as to the Unknown Creator, and thus Aquinas can add that the image of the Trinity may be said to be in man, not only insofar as the mind actually tends toward God, but also insofar as it "is naturally ordered to do so" (*vel nata est ferri in Deum*). There is a kind of potential image in the natural mind since it was created with the passive or obediential power of being moved by grace toward God. The mind has a negative capacity for knowing God, even when it does not know him. The image of God in a positive sense, however, can be found in man only in conformity to grace:

> Wherefore, the image of God can be considered in man in three ways. In one way, insofar as man has the *natural aptitude* for thinking and loving God: and that aptitude consists in the very nature of the mind, which is common to all. In another way, insofar as man *actually* or *habitually* knows and loves God, even if imperfectly: and this is the image through conformity to *grace*. In a third way, insofar as man actually knows and loves God *perfectly*: and thus he attains to the Image according to the similitude of glory.

> [Unde imago Dei tripliciter potest considerari in homine. Uno modo secundum quod homo habet aptitudinem naturalem ad intelligendum et amandum Deum: et haec aptitudo consistit in ipsa natura mentis, quae est communis omnibus hominibus. Alio modo, secundum quod homo actu vel habitu Deum cognoscit et amat, sed tamen imperfecte: et haec est imago per conformitatem gratiae. Tertio modo, secundum quod homo Deum actu cognoscit et amat perfecte: et sic attenditur imago secundum similitudinem gloriae.][125]

The implications of Aquinas' distinctions are far-reaching. While man has a capacity to know and love God, he cannot be said actually to do so (even imperfectly) without grace. Whatever man does in natural theology, he cannot be said to be actually knowing or loving God. Since the knowing and loving of man is meant to terminate in God, we may say that it is ordered to God and thus constitutes in the eyes of faith

[125] S. T., I, 93, 4.

a kind of image of God; apart from grace, however, man actually turns his knowing and loving to the world, and thus does not 'image forth' the knowing and loving of God. Natural theology can be viewed as a mode of reflecting upon the natural aptitude for knowing and loving God, which does not, however, introduce a formal notion, intention, or love of God. Through natural theology, the mind does not actually tend toward God: there is in natural theology no conformity or similitude between the mind and God.

Aquinas' distinctions also make clear the species and imperfection of the knowledge of faith. The 'species' of any act of knowledge is taken from the object of that knowledge. Thus, the knowledge of faith and the knowledge of beatitude are of the same species, while natural 'cognitions' of God differ in species from both faith and beatific knowledge. The 'perfection' of any act of knowledge, on the other hand, is taken from the *form* in which it apprehends its object. Since the knowledge of beatitude takes place through a form proper to God himself, and the knowledge of faith takes place through an extrinsic and imperfect created similitude, the knowledge of faith can be said to be an imperfect instance of its own species.

Aquinas' use of the work "know" in this context is a good example of his nonsystematic and contextual use of words. In the treatise on faith,[126] Aquinas constantly denies that faith results in knowledge; in the present context he asserts rather strongly that it does. The reason for the inconsistency is clear. In the treatise on faith, Aquinas was concerned with the immanent or subjective *form* of the apprehension of faith: compared with the sciences, which know their objects through an adequate form, faith cannot be said to be an act of *knowing*. In the present context, however, Aquinas presupposes a looser and more theological usage of "know," and concerns himself with the *object* of apprehension: in that faith *really* (if not *intelligibly*) terminates in God as its object, it can be said to be a kind of actual *knowing* of God (what I have called a knowing-by-*faith*); natural 'cognitions' of God, however, which terminate in the world, cannot be said to be a knowing of God. The status of faith, therefore, is ambiguous: it rises above

126 *S. T.*, II-II, 1-7.

natural knowledge because of its object, but it falls below both natural and beatific knowledge because of the nonintelligible form in which it knows.

Nevertheless, faith possesses what human science can never produce: a word conceived from a noesis of God, and a love derived therefrom. That entire movement of the soul in faith, from a noesis of God to a termination in love, Aquinas calls the "similitude" of the Trinity—a "perfection" of the *imago dei* in man, which brings the image out of potentiality into actuality.[127] It is that image, begun on its way to complete perfection, that refers man noetically to the Trinity. The noesis, word and love of God in the human soul (created by God's operation on the soul) constitute the 'intention' of faith by means of which the mystery of God may be said to be 'apprehended' and made the object of a nonvacuous reference. It is that directing of man *to* the Image (or eternal Word) of God that controls the entire noetic of Sacred Doctrine.

Once again, however, the entire claim must be read in terms of Christ. What is primarily meant by "the image of God in man" is the image in the soul of Christ—the principle or cause of the imperfect image in the believer. As Karl Rahner remarks, since the Incarnation, all theology has become anthropology—and, we must add, all anthropology has become Christology.[128] It is the knowing and speaking and loving of Christ that truly image and point toward the life of God himself. Christ's knowledge and love are the cause of the birth in the soul of the believer of the knowledge and love of God. Christ's speaking and doing are communicated to the believer in *fides ex auditu*; in the intentional light of faith, there is conceived (by the agency of God the Holy Spirit) an 'intention' of Christ's knowledge and love. They are judged by faith to be both the ground of Christ's beatitude and the cause of "my" future beatitude. The apprehension of faith gives rise in the soul to an imperfect knowledge and love of God, which direct the believer to God himself. They form in him the 'intention' or "similitude" of the Trinity which allows him to

---

[127] S. T., I, 93, 9.
[128] K. Rahner, *Schriften zur Theologie IV* (Benziger, Zürich and Köln, 1964), p. 150.

'apprehend' the image of God in Christ as the terminus toward which his own imperfect image tends.

SUMMARY AND PROBLEM

The language of scripture and doctrine (which is about the sacred humanity of Christ and related matters) is able to refer to God, or to refer the mind to God, only if there is present in the 'soul' of the believer a new kind of intentionality—a new dispositional source of intentional forms—produced by the operation of God upon the soul. A person who possesses such a 'light' is said to have the Gift of Understanding.[129] To comprehend what Aquinas means by "Understanding," it is necessary to recall what understanding is in ordinary intellectual judgments. To say that a person 'understands' some aspect of reality is simply to say that he possesses an intelligible form which he correctly judges to be an isomorphic representation of reality. Understanding is present when man judges that there exists *in re* an existential correlate of the intelligible forms conceived by the intellect in the 'light' of reason—i.e., in conformity with the rules governing our conceptual system. The man of faith possesses (or believes himself to possess) forms of a rather different sort—created or conceived not in the light of reason, but in the light of faith—which he expresses or intends to express through the words and propositions of the sacred doctrine that he confesses. Since it is the claim of faith that there really exist in Christ and in God analogical correlates of those forms, the man who makes an existential judgment about God based on such forms may be said to 'understand' God. Aquinas' use of 'understand,' however, is essentially analogous. The understanding of natural reason is productive of *intelligibility*, since the forms of judgment are created by the innate 'light' of reason—according to the dispositional first principles, whose intelligibility is naturally or *per se* apprehended by man. The first principles of faith, however, which are the 'light' in which theological judgments are made, are *not* intelligible to the believer. To say, therefore, that the believer has the Gift of Understanding is not to say that he understands intellectually

---

[129] On the Gift of Understanding, see, *S. T.*, II-II, 8.

or conceptually that which he asserts 'in the light of faith.' To say that a believer 'understands' in the theological sense is to make a claim *that* there corresponds to his faith-propositions a reality in God, but it is *not* to say that the believer understands *how* his faith propositions make a real claim about the nature of God.[130] In order to understand how a proposition makes a real claim, one must know and understand the syntactical rules which govern the conceptual system upon which the language is formally based. While the believer does not understand the propositions of Sacred Doctrine, he nevertheless believes that his mind is being conformed by God to himself when he assents to the truth of the propositions in a state of real or infused faith. He not only believes that there exist in the language or Word of God analogical counterparts of the propositions of faith, and that, in the Word of God, those counterparts are intelligible; he also believes that, when he is in a state of real or infused faith, he possesses a special sort of 'intention' which gives to his affirmations of the language of faith a real referential and descriptive power that is apparent to God and the *beati*.

There is, however, a crucial problem in the entire analysis. How does a believer know that he is in a state of real or infused faith—in, as we say, a state of grace? It cannot be said that he knows it on the basis of his belief that the propositions of faith are true, since even a person with 'dead faith' shares that belief or opinion. Both 'living' and 'dead' faith are virtues or powers which dispose a man to 'confess' the articles of faith—to say "Yes" to certain propositions which are said to be about God. As Aquinas puts it, 'living' and 'dead' faith are—as virtues of the intellect—of the same species.[131] From the viewpoint of what is consciously or intelligibly 'in the mind,' they are identical powers. Thus, even Satan believes, in the sense of being disposed to say "Yes" to the propositions of the faith—he, however, believes and trembles. To take another example, a man might witness—in the context of Christian preaching—what he takes to be a miraculous or supernatural intervention in the operations of nature. He might, without the action of the Holy Spirit, be led (or psychologically forced) to admit that the

[130] S. *T.*, I, 12, 13.   [131] S. *T.*, II-II, 6, 2.

claims of Christianity—which he cannot comprehend—must be true. He also will say "Yes" to the propositions confessed by the 'true believer.' Similarly, a person might be overpowered by the rhetoric of a clever apologist and assume that the propositions of Sacred Doctrine are to be asserted—"if *he* says so." Unless God 'takes the opportunity' of infusing the intentional forms of live faith, the mind of that 'believer' will not be conformed to the being of God. Aquinas insists that a man cannot really believe, whatever his intellectual disposition, unless God operates inwardly on his 'soul' or intellect. The ground of Aquinas' claim is precisely the natural nonintelligibility of the language of faith. Insofar as the words and propositions of scripture are interpreted in the 'light' of natural reason—according to the meanings that they have in our syntactical system—they do not refer to God or conform the mind to God. God himself must conceive in the human soul the forms which are intended by the language of Scripture. This is not done by the communication of intelligible forms, but by the ordination of the whole soul, intellect, and will, to the Word or Image of God—by the creation in man of the dispositional tendency to 'take' the agency of Christ to be the soteriological agency of God. How, then, can the believer know that his assent to the propositions of faith is based on 'living' faith rather than 'dead' faith? If the supernatural Gift of Understanding is not productive of intelligibility, how does one know that he really 'has the Gift'? It would seem that the 'forms' of faith, the 'intentions' created by God, the 'conformation' or 'adequation' of the mind to God, are all *theoretical* entities or states, named or described by analogy with the operations of the natural intellect. If the claims of faith are correct, then something like them must be present in the 'soul' or 'inner being' of the 'true believer.' If, however, they are not intelligibly grasped or introspectively known by the mind, how can the believer know that they are really there at all? How can he know that he is a 'true believer'? It would appear that he cannot.

I believe that Aquinas wishes us to draw just that conclusion. Indeed, he makes it inevitable. The true form of faith, that which makes faith 'living' rather than 'dead,' is the form

of *charity*, which alone has the formality of salvation in its
'logic.'[132] Aquinas, in a penetrating passage, denies that either
faith or hope contains formally speaking that which is necessary for salvation. The reason that he offers is that both faith
and hope (as they are thought or conceived by man) conceive
or posit God in terms of something that comes to us from
God—an 'intentional' content of our soul or mind. Only
charity, not receiving immanently anything *from* God, goes
out to him and posits him as and for what he is in himself.[133]
Faith and hope appear as tendencies to internalize God—to
make him ours. Charity, however, is a transitive power that
terminates *ad extra*—it affirms the lover as the possession of
the loved one. True faith, then, together with "Understanding," can only be present in the soul which has charity or 'love
of God.' That is also an 'infused' power resulting from the
immanent action of God on the human soul. We could only
know that we had 'living' faith—that we were doing more
than giving assent to totally opaque propositions—if we knew
that we had charity. We could only know that our 'minds'
contained intentional analogues of the being of God if we
could know that grace had 'seized' our will and turned our
affections to the Unknown God. According to Aquinas, however, we cannot know whether we have charity or not:

> That, however, to which charity is ordered cannot be com-
> prehended, because its immediate object and terminus is
> God, the supreme good, to whom charity unites us. There-
> fore, one cannot know from the act of love that he per-
> ceives in himself whether he has attained to the stage where
> he is united to God in the manner necessary for the nature
> of charity.

> [Hoc autem ad quod caritas ordinatur, est incomprehensi-
> bile, quia eius obiectum et finis est Deus, summa bonitas,
> cui caritas nos coniungit; unde non potest aliquis scire, ex
> actu dilectionis quem in se ipso percipit, an ad hoc peringat

[132] S. T., II-II, 4, 3.
[133] S. T., II-II, 23, 6: "Faith and hope affirm God on the basis of what
comes to us from him . . . but charity affirms him as he is in himself. . . ."

ut Deo vivat hoc modo sicut ad caritatis rationem requiritur.][134]

All that we can do is surmise the *possibility* that we may possess charity by observing the kinds of things we find ourselves doing. Aquinas suggests that such essential agnosticism with regard to our own states of grace is a value in that we are not tempted to feel the arrogance and pride of the self-righteous. We might also remark that it is consistent with a theological description of true faith that a man surrender himself to the language of faith out of complete trust in the grace of God manifested in the love of Christ, and not on the basis of a humanly determinable advantage adhering to that surrender.

We cannot, then, *know* that we have truly informed faith—that there is in our 'souls' that intentional image of God which conforms us to him. There is no more in the conscious mind of the true believer than *may* be present in the conscious mind of the nonbeliever. It must also be remembered that it is quite possible that God—in his freedom—has 'seized' the will and affections of men who do not—for one reason or another—assert the truth of the propositions of faith. The *imago dei* may be more truly and actually present in the 'soul' of one who does not consciously believe the propositions of faith, than in the 'soul' of one who affirms their truth. Such judgments must be coupled with a conclusion of our epistemological discussion: what I really am as one being of nature—body-and-soul—is known only by God. What is really going on 'in the mind' or 'in the soul' is adequately represented only in the intentional being or Word of God. Insofar as I hear that Word in the doctrines of sacred Scripture, I know by analogy some of the sorts of things that must be 'going on' *if* I really exist in a state of infused faith and charity. Of that, however, I cannot be certain. In this life God is and remains *ignotum*—the Unknown God whom we cannot grasp or control in terms of the forms of intelligibility created by our intellects. In our language, *the intelligibility of God is not a syntactical matter.*

134 *De Ver.*, x, 10.

THE MATERIAL MOVES OF THE
LANGUAGE OF FAITH

No language springs—like a Goddess of Wisdom—full-blown from the head of man. Learning to use a language wisely is a painful and frustrating process which, if we do not remember, we can observe in the tantrums and frowns of our younger brothers in Adam. In order ultimately to use a language in conscious obedience to the syntactical laws which make it a source of intelligibility and light, we must first learn to respond without understanding to the darkly disapproving countenances of those who lay down the pedagogical laws of semantic association. The law is a taskmaster when we do not comprehend the intention it expresses—when we do not see the intelligible end to which it points. We learn to make the material moves justified by the syntactical laws of our common human language before we learn ourselves to obey those laws.[1] In sheer response to the stimuli of our social environment—like little behavioristic machines—we learn to make the sound of "red" at certain times and to avoid it at others. Our use of the physical token may be correct from the point of view of one who knows the syntactical-semantical laws of the English language—and people may say, "Ah look, he knows what 'red' means"—but we *do not* know what "red" means until we understand the rules which govern the use of "red" and learn consciously to obey those rules. Merely to act in a way that happens to conform to the intelligible laws that someone else understands is not to know what we are doing when we utter "red." It is true that there must be something going on 'in our minds' when we use the word. We are responding in some fashion to the physical state of our sensory system. But we do not yet know what is going on, and therefore nothing is consciously going on. We do not know *why* it is correct to say "red" at certain times or *how* the statement

[1] Sellars, *Science, Perception and Reality*, Chap. 11.

"Red!" signifies an intelligible aspect of our experience of reality. We do not yet know what it means for a thing to be red or what it is that we are naming when we say it. (We do not even know what "naming" means in the language we are learning.)

In support of that claim, Sellars introduces the strange behavior of the honeybee and its syntactical dance of the clover field.[2] Bees have a 'language.' By means of a relatively complex series of bumps and grinds a worker bee can convey to his fellows the distance and direction they must fly in order to denature the clover he has found in his travels. There is even an element of 'translation' involved in such a 'language'— the fellow bees must learn to orient their flight with relation to the position of the sun by 'noting' the orientation of the messenger bee with relation to the axis of gravitation within the hive. We would not say, however, that the bees know the meaning of their dance—that they are consciously following the rules of a syntactical system. Rather, they are going through the material moves of a 'language' physically programmed into their nervous systems by the genetic laws of their strain. So also we, while we were young and fool-like, made the material moves of a language we did not yet know, on the basis of genetically inherited capabilities and dispositions.

Knowledge, Aquinas correctly maintains, is a matter of reflection upon the 'material moves' of the 'mind':

> Truth is known by the intellect in that the intellect reflects upon its own act, not only in that it takes cognizance of its act, but in that it knows its proportion to the thing, which proportion cannot be known unless the nature of the act is known, which in turn cannot be known unless the nature of the active principle, which is the intellect, is known, of which the nature is to be conformed to things; wherefore the intellect knows truth insofar as it reflects on itself.

> [Cognoscitur autem ab intellectu secundum quod intellectus reflectitur supra actum suum, non solum secundum quod

---

[2] *Science, Perception and Reality*, p. 326.

cognoscit actum suum, sed secundum quod cognoscit pro-
postionem eius ad rem quod quidem cognosci non potest nisi
cognita natura ipsius actus; quae cognosci non potest nisi
cognoscatur natura principii activi, quod est ipse intellectus,
in cuius natura est ut rebus conformetur; unde secundum
hoc cognoscit veritatem intellectus quod supra seipsum re-
flectitur.]³

We are able to reflect upon the material moves of the intellect
when we have assimilated enough of the matter of language
for the 'agent intellect'—whatever power or disposition that
names—to take over and conceive immanently in our intentional being the rules of the game we blindly played for so
long. At that moment—or in those periodically recurring moments—a light dawns and we *know* what we were saying and
why. Other members of our human community can and must
teach us the material moves justified (as *they* know) by the
conceptual system, but no one can teach us that insight which
comes with the possession of a conceptual system. That must
be conceived within us by the dispositional nature—the 'first
act,' as Aquinas calls it—of our 'intellect.'

We are now learning, Aquinas would have it, the 'material
moves' of the language of God. Our mode of participation
here and now in *scientia dei* is the making of motions in a
language we do not understand. Submitting to the pedagogy
of *sacra doctrina*—mediated through the teaching *magisterium*
of the Church—we perform the liturgical bumps and grinds
of a syntactical dance that will—we hope—orient us to our
supernatural source of life and delectation once we leave the
darkness of human life *in via*. Still in the dark, however, we
do not possess the key to a translation of our current devia-
tions from the axis of man *post lapsum* into an orientation to
the light. There are, presumably, the periodic glimmers of
light—the beginning to 'understand' at a new conceptual level
what we are doing and why. The *quasi quoddam inchoativum*
of a future intelligibility comes and goes with a 'state of grace'
that we fail to comprehend and that may be there all along
without our reflective awareness. For the most part, the man

³ *De Ver.*, I, 9.

of faith uses the language of faith with no overwhelming sense of cognitive dissonance—and that he attributes without knowing to the internal infusion of 'live' faith. From time to time, however, the seeming rote and lack of intelligible light produce either the catatonic state of theological speechlessness or the temporary aphasia of material heresy. There are, on the other hand, those few who somehow give the impression that they are not simply acting by virtue of the rules, but in conscious obedience to them. Of that, of course, we could never be certain, any more than we can be certain of the precise moment that little Johnnie is following the rules and not simply doing it right. In the case of faith, we would not know what it meant to follow the rules in any case.

We can be taught *ex auditu* what material moves to make. Chief among the material moves are those propositions whose *per se* status is guaranteed by their position in that body of certified language called *sacra scriptura*, and those implicit definitions and unconditionally assertable propositions constituted by officially promulgated dogma. They are the analogues in our natural language of the first principles of *scientia dei*. Faith claims that there are in the intentional being of God elements or forms with syntactically isomorphic status. But what they are or how they occur significantly in the language of God, man cannot know *in via*. Other kinds of material moves are provided by natural theology—which is to say, by the obediential capacity of all human language to be placed at the disposal of *sacra doctrina*. When the vacuous propositions which follow from a recognition of the ordering of the mind to an Unknown God are placed in the context of the propositions of faith, their sentential vacuity is given content, as the unknown meta-empirical referent of natural theology is declared to be the One who was active in the sacred humanity of Christ—the efficient cause of man's eventual participation in that full intelligibility reflected in the intentions of faith "as in a mirror darkly." The way in which the state of mind produced by making the material moves of faith reflects an intelligible unity of conceptual powers is that which man hopes to apprehend *in patria*. The light in which the intelligibility of faith will finally appear cannot itself be given *ex auditu,* but must be conceived within us by the natural locus of that light—the *veritas prima.*

There is a further consequence of note that follows from the theory of language presupposed by our account. When the child makes the leap forward into the intentional realm of self-conscious man—when, that is, he finds himself in possession of a source of formal intelligibility—he becomes something that he was not previously, or something that he was only in potentiality. He becomes a thinking subject. What I am in my own conceptual self-awareness—a person in community—I am because of the intentional language addressed to me by other men, understood by myself, and responded to in kind. Our subjectivity is a transcendental aspect of the language we use and of the conceptual system it expresses. Should we cease entirely to use the language we now use—and the conceptual system it expresses—we should cease to be, phenomenologically speaking, the same 'persons' that we now are. What a 'person' is is not a function of what is nonintentionally given in the 'physical' order, but of what is intended in the 'conceptual' order. It is a function of the words addressed to me and of my response to those words. If our language is distorted—if it does not truly and adequately reflect the intentions of God in creation—then I am not, at the level of conscious self-awareness, what I am intended by God to be, and what I therefore really am as known only to him and expressed only in his Word. It is, I think, a central thesis of the language of faith that I shall only *become* at the level of reflective self-awareness that which I really *am* as a creature of God when my intentional being is constituted by an intelligible 'Word' addressed to me and confirmed by my intentional response in kind. Such a claim can be handled by philosophy: philosophy knows what is involved in references to other possible conceptual systems and intentional frameworks. But the intelligibility of the claim could never be seen unless one were so addressed, learned the material moves of the language used, and had conceived within himself the intentional light by means of which to introspect the contents of his experience and inform reality on that basis. The latter steps of that process are, for Aquinas, strictly reserved to the Beatific Vision *in patria.*

In this life, therefore, the way of remotion reigns supreme. We are closest to the truth when we deny of God that which we have consciously 'in mind'—that which occurs significantly within our language:

When therefore we proceed toward God by the way of remotion, we first deny of him anything corporeal; and then we even deny of him anything intellectual, in the sense that it may be found in creatures; and so also 'goodness' and 'wisdom'; and then there remains in our minds only the notion that he *is*, and nothing more; wherefore he exists in a certain confusion for us. Lastly, however, we remove from him even 'being' itself, as that is found in creatures; and then he remains in a kind of shadow of ignorance, by which ignorance, insofar as it pertains to this life, we are best conjoined to God . . . and this is the cloud in which God is said to dwell.

[Unde quodo in Deum procedimus per viam remotionis, primo negamus ab eo corporalia; et secundo etiam intellectualia, secundum quod inveniuntur in creaturis, ut bonitas et sapientia; et tunc remanet tantum in intellectu nostro, quia est, et nihil amplius: unde est sicut in quaddam confusione. Ad ultimum autem etiam hoc ipsum esse, secundum quod est in creaturis, ab ipso removemus; et tunc remanet in quadam tenebra ignorantiae, secundum quam ignorantiam, quantum ad statum viae pertinet, optime Deo coniungimur . . . et haec est quaedam caligo, in qua Deus habitare dicitur.][4]

[4] *Comm. in Sent.*, I, VII, 1, 1.

SELECTED BIBLIOGRAPHY

I. PRIMARY SOURCES. (Where not otherwise noted, I consulted the Parma Edition.)

Commentum in Quatuor Libros Sententiarum.
De Anima.
De Ente et Essentia. Edited by M.-D. Roland-Gosselin, O.P., Paris; J. Vrin, 1948.
De Sensu et Sensato.
De Potentia.
De Veritate.
De Veritate Catholicae Fidei Contra Gentiles.
Expositio in Epistola ad Hebraeos.
Expositio in Epistola ad Romanos.
In De Trinitate Boethii Commentarium.
In Librum Beati Dionysii de Divinis Nominibus Commentaria.
In Librum De Causis Expositio. Taurini: Marietti, 1955.
In Peri Hermeneias et Posteriorum Analyticorum Expositio. Taurini: Marietti, 1955.
In VIII Libros Physicorum Aristotelis.
In XII Libros Metaphysicorum Commentarium.
Opuscula Philosophica. Taurini: Marietti, 1954.
Opuscula Theologica. Taurini: Marietti, 1954.
Summa Theologiae. Taurini: Marietti, 1948.

II. SECONDARY SOURCES: Books

Adler, Mortimer J. *Problems for Thomists: the Problem of Species.* New York: Sheed and Ward, 1940.
Anscombe, G. E. M. *Intentions.* Ithaca: Cornell University Press, 1961.
Anscombe, G. E. M. and Geach, P. T. *Three Philosophers.* Oxford: Blackwell, 1961.
Balthasar, N. *L'abstraction métaphysique et l'analogie des etres dans l'etre.* Louvain, 1935.
Bennet, Owen. *The Nature of the Demonstrative Proof According to the Principle of Aristotle and St. Thomas Aquinas.* Washington: Catholic University, 1943.

Brennan, Robert E. *Thomistic Psychology; a Philosophic Analysis of the Nature of Man.* New York: Macmillan Co., 1941.

Brennan, Sister Rose Emmanuella. *The Intellectual Virtues according to the Philosophy of St. Thomas.* Washington: Catholic University, 1941.

Breton, Stanislas. *Etudes phénomenologiques. Conscience et intentionnalité sélon Saint Thomas et Brentano.* Vol. 19. Paris: Archives de Philosophie, 1956.

Bryar, William. *St. Thomas and the Existence of God.* Chicago: H. Regnery, 1951.

Chenu, Marie Dominique. *Introduction à l'étude de Saint Thomas d'Aquin.* Montreal: Institut d'études médiévales, 1950.

Chisholm, Roderick. *Perceiving: A Philosophical Study.* Ithaca: Cornell University, 1957.

Coady, Sister Mary Anastasia. *The Phantasm According to the Teaching of St. Thomas.* Washington: Catholic University, 1932.

Copleston, Frederick C. *Aquinas.* London: Penguin Books, 1957.

Dedek, John F. *Experimental Knowledge of the Indwelling Trinity.* Nundelein: St. Mary of the Lake, 1958.

Deferrari, Roy J. *A Lexicon of St. Thomas Aquinas.* Washington: Catholic University, 1948-49.

Donovan, Sister M. Annice. *The Henological Argument for the Existence of God in the Works of St. Thomas Aquinas.* Notre Dame, 1946.

Finance, Joseph. *De Cogito Cartesian et relexion Thomiste.* Vol. 16. Archives de Philosophie, 1946.

Gardeil, Henri D. *Initiation à la Philosophie de Saint Thomas D'Aquin.* Paris: Editions du Cerf, 1952.

Garin, Pierre. *Thèses Cartésiennes et Thèses Thomistes.* Paris: Desclée, 1932.

Garrigou-Lagrange, Reginald. *God, His Existence and His Nature.* St. Louis: B. Herder, 1934.

———. *The One God.* St. Louis: B. Herder, 1943.

Geiger, Louis B. *La Participation dans la Philosophie de S. Thomàs d'Aquin.* Paris: J. Vrin, 1942.

Gilson, Etienne. *The Philosopher and Theology.* New York: Random House, 1956.

————. *Realisme Thomiste et critique de la Connaissance.* Paris: J. Vrin, 1934.

————. *Le Thomisme.* Paris: J. Vrin, 1927.

————. *The Christian Philosophy of St. Thomas Aquinas.* New York: Random House, 1956.

Grabmann, Martin. *Thomas Aquinas, His Personality and Thought.* New York: Longmans, Green and Co., 1928.

Hawkins, D. *Causality and Implication.* New York: Sheed and Ward, 1937.

Hayen, Andre. *La communication de l'acte de l'être d'après Saint Thomas d'Aquin.* Paris: De Brouwer, 1957.

Henle, Robert J. *Saint Thomas and Platonism.* The Hague: M. Nijhoff, 1956.

Hoenen, Petrus. *Reality and Judgement According to St. Thomas.* Chicago: H. Regnery, 1952.

Isaye, Gaston. *La Théorie de la Mésure et l'existence d'un maximum sélon Saint Thomas.* Paris: Beauchesne, 1940.

Jolivet, R. *La Notion de Substance.* Paris: Beauchesne, 1929.

Klubertanz, George P. *The Discursive Power.* St. Louis: Modern Schoolman, 1952.

————. *St. Thomas on Analogy.* Chicago: Loyola University, 1960.

Knowles, David. *The Historical Context of the Philosophical Works of St. Thomas Aquinas.* London: Blackfriars, 1958.

Krempel, A. *La doctrine de la relation chez Saint Thomas.* Paris: J. Vrin, 1952.

Kuhn, Helmut. *Begegnung mit dem Sein.* Tübingen: J. C. B. Mohr, 1954.

Lyttkens, Hampus. *The Analogy Between God and the World.* Uppsala: Almquist, 1952.

Marechal, J. *Le Point de départ de la métaphysique.* 4 vols. Louvain, 1923-26.

Maritain, Jacques. *Existence and the Existent.* New York: Pantheon, 1948.

————. *A Preface to Metaphysics.* New York: Sheed and Ward. 1948.

————. *Les degrées de l'être.* Paris: Desclée, 1932.

————. *The Range of Reason.* New York: Charles Scribner's Sons, 1953.

McInerny, Ralph. *The Logic of Analogy.* The Hague: Martinus Nijhoff, 1961.

Mondin, Battista. *The Principle of Analogy in Protestant and Catholic Theology.* The Hague: Martinus Nijhoff, 1963.

Montagnes, Bernard. *La doctrine de l'analogie de l'être d'après St. Thomas d'Aquin.* Louvain, 1963.

Nagel, Ernest. *The Structure of Science.* New York: Harcourt, Brace & World, 1961.

Peghaire, Julien. *Intellectus et Ratio selon S. Thomas d'Aquin.* Paris: J. Vrin, 1936.

Peiffer, J. F. *The Concept in Thomism.* New York: Bookman Associates, 1952.

Penido, M. T. L. *Le rôle de l'analogie en Theologie dogmatique.* Paris: J. Vrin, 1931.

Pieper, Josef. *Guide to Thomas Aquinas.* New York: Pantheon, 1962.

———. *The Silence of St. Thomas.* New York: Pantheon, 1957.

Raeymaeker, L. D. *Introduction à la Philosophie.* Louvain; 1938.

———. *Philosophie de l'être.* Louvain; 1946.

Rahner, Karl. *Geist in Welt.* München: Kösel, 1957.

———. *Hörer des Wortes.* München: Kösel, 1963.

Roland-Gosselin, M. D. *Essai d'une étude critique de la connaissance.* Paris: J. Vrin, 1932.

Rousselot, P. *L'intellectualisme de S. Thomas.* Paris: Beauchesne, 1924.

Ryle, Gilbert. *The Concept of Mind.* New York: Barnes and Noble, 1949.

Sellars, W. F. *Science, Perception and Reality.* London: International Library of Philosophy and Scientific Method, 1963.

Sertillanges, Antonin G. *Foundations of Thomistic Philosophy.* St. Louis: B. Herder, 1931.

———. *S. Thomas d'Aquin.* Paris: Felix Alcan, 1925.

Sillem, Edward. *Ways of Thinking about God.* London: Darton, 1961.

Strawson, Peter. *Individuals, An Essay in Descriptive Metaphysics.* London: Methuen and Co., 1961.

Vanier, Paul. *Théologie trinitaire chez Thomas d'Aquin.* Montreal: Institut d'études médiévales, 1953.

SELECTED BIBLIOGRAPHY

Warnock, G. J. *Berkeley*. London: Penguin Books, 1953.

Wittgenstein, Ludwig. *Philosophical Investigations*. New York: Macmillan Co., 1953.

III. SECONDARY SOURCES: Articles

Balthasar, N. "A propos d'un passage controversé du 'De unitate intellectus' de S. Thomas d'Aquin," *Revue Néoscholastique de Philosophie*, XXIV (1922).

Boulanger, A. B. "Le 'Semi-agnosticisme' du P. Sertillanges et le Thomisme du R. P. Romeyer," *Revue Thomiste*, L (1950).

Chesterton, G. K. "St. Thomas the Agnostic," *Commonweal*, XIX (1933).

Corvez, M. "Existence et essence," *Revue Thomiste*, LI (1957).

Descoqs, P. "Sur la division de l'etre en acte et puissance d'après S. Thomas," *Revue de Philosophie*, XXXVIII (1938).

Dondaine, H-F. "Cognoscere de deo 'Quid est,'" *Récherches de Théologie Ancienne et Médiéval*, XXII (1955).

Dondeyne, A. "De prima via S. Thomae," *Collationes Brugensis*, XXX (1930).

————. "De tertia via S. Thomae," *Collationes Brugensis*, XXX (1930).

Fabro, Cornelius. "Knowledge and Perception in Aristotelic-Thomistic Psychology," *New Scholasticism*, XII (1938).

————. "Actualité et originalité de l'Esse' thomiste," *Revue Thomiste*, LVI (1956).

Gardeil, A. "A propos d'un cahier du R. P. Romeyer," *Revue Thomiste*, XIII (1929).

Henri-Rousseau, J.-M. "L'etre, valeur intelligible," *Revue Thomiste*, LI (1951).

————. "L'être et l'agir," *Revue Thomiste*, LIII-LV (1953-55).

Hepburn, Ronald. "Poetry and Religious Belief," *Metaphysical Beliefs*, London: SCM Press, 1957.

Jolivet, Regis. "La methode thomiste et la phénoménologie existentielle," *Sapientia Aquinatis*. Roma: Officium Libri Catholici, 1955.

Labourdette, M. "La théologie et ses sources," *Revue Thomiste*, XLVI (1946).

Landry, B. "L'analogie de proportionalité chez S. Thomas," *Revue Néoscholasitque de Philosophie*, XXIV (1923).

SELECTED BIBLIOGRAPHY

Maréchal, J. "De la forme du jugement d'après S. Thomas," *Revista di Filosofia Neoscolastica*, xv (1923).

———. "Le Dynamisme intellectuel dans la connaissance objective," *Revue Néoscholastique de Philosophie*, xxviii (1927).

McInerny, Ralph. "A Note on 'Thomistic Existentialism,'" *Sapientia Aquinatis*. Roma: Officium Libri Catholici, 1955.

Noël, L. "La critique de l'intelligible et de sa valeur réelle," *Revue Néoscholastique de Philosophie*, xxxvi (1935).

———. "La présence immédiate des choses," *Revue Néoscholastique de Philosophie*, xxviii (1925).

Roland-Gosselin, M. D. "De la connaissance affective," *Revue des Sciences Philosophiques et Théologiques*, xxvii (1928).

———. "Peut-on parler d'intuition intellectuelle dans la philosophie thomiste?" *Philosophia Perennis*, Vol. ii. Regensburg: J. Habbel, 1930.

Romeyer, B. "La doctrine de S. Thomas sur la vérité," *Etudes sur S. Thomas*. Paris: Beauchesnes, 1930.

Sertillanges, A. D. "L'etre et la connaissance dans la philosophie de S. Thomas d'Aquin," *Mélanges Thomistes*. Paris: J. Vrin, 1934.

Talbot, E. F. "Nihil est in Intellectu," *Revue de l'Université d'Ottawa*, iv (1934).

Van de Wiele, J. "Le Problème de la vérité ontologique dans la philosophie de Saint Thomas," *Revue Philosophique de Louvain*, lii (1954).

Vaissiere, J. de la. "Le sens du mot 'verbe mental' dans les écrits se S. Thomas," *Etudes sur S. Thomas*. Paris: Beauchesnes, 1925.

Van Leeuwen, A. "L'analogie de l'etre. Génèse et contenu du concept analogique," *Revue Néoscholastique de Philosophie*, xxxviii (1936).

Walsh, F. A. "Phantasm and Phantasy," *The New Scholasticism*, ix (1935).

INDEX

abstraction, 40-41, 53-54
absurdity, 158
agent intellect, 42, 53, 70, 76
analogy, 167-170; and act of
  knowing, 52, 63-64; of
  attribution, 66, 69, 168n;
  of "being," 64, 151, 167, 170;
  of proper proportionality, 19-21,
  67-68, 167
Anscombe, E., 6n
apologetics, 195-198
Aristotle, 22, 116, 126
Augustine, 28, 194
authority, 23-24
Ayer, A. J., 37n

Barth, K., 215
beatitude, 237, 242
behaviorism, 6
'being': as first concept, 65;
  modes of, 68
belief, 185
belief in God, 228-229
Blake, W., 224
body-soul polarity, 62-63, 73
Braithwaite, R. B., 216n, 217

Cajetan, 170
causal arguments for God, 89-90
causal models, 110
causal statements, 83-85
causality, 88; accidentally and
  essentially subordinated, 110;
  efficient, 114, 124, 133; final,
  122; secondary, 113-114; as
  transcendental, 152-154
charity, 264-265
Chisholm, R., 5n, 6n, 68, 83n,
  199n, 202n
Christ: his divinity, 250-251;
  his humanity, 232-233, 249
cognitio and *scire*, 32
cognitions of faith, 180-181,
  226-227, 240-241
common sense, 49
concepts: formation of, 40-42;
  significance of, 98-100
contingency, 126
conversio, 38, 183

Copleston, F. C., 126
cosmological proofs, 108-110
creation: doctrine of, 123, 126;
  ex nihilo, 20
credere deum, deo, and *in deum*,
  228-229
definition: explicit, 66, 87, 104;
  implicit, 67, 87, 105; by
  negation, 147-150; real and
  nominal, 136; relational, 140
deus absconditus and *deus
  revelatus*, 230
Dondeyne, A., 129

eschatology and intelligibility, 27.
  See also intelligibility
esse and *essentia*, 159
esse: as problem, 158-160
existence, 11-19, 64, 150;
  contingent, 102; and the
  judgment, 75-76, 159-160;
  necessary, 127, 173
"existence," as predicate, 17-18

faith, Chapter IV passim; common
  and proper, 235; dead and
  living, 246, 262; *ex auditu* and
  infusa, 235; imperfection of,
  230; and mystery, 249; objects
  of, 231; and reason, 226; and
  sacra scriptura, 232; and
  scientific language, 188-191,
  207-214, 218-219; species of,
  259; structure of, 228
Farrer, A., 211n
Findlay, J. N., 101n
First principles, 43, 157-158
five ways, 23, 107; first of,
  109-124, 155; second of,
  124-126, 155; third of, 126-131,
  155; fourth of, 131-134, 155;
  fifth of, 155
fundamental theology, 195

Garrigou-Lagrange, R., 26,
  110-112, 211n
Geatch, P., 18n
Gilson, E., 26, 75
God: attributes of, 33, 165-167,

176-177; and "existence," 11;
experience of, 192-193; and the
genera, 91, 125, 133, 153;
knowledge of, 3, 32, 164, 178;
and *per se nota existence*, 90-91
"God": and poetic language,
220-226; and theoretical
language, 188-191, 206-214
Gregory, Saint, 243

Hampshire, S., 76n, 231n
Hayen, A., 242
Henle, R. J., 24n
Hepburn, R., 108
Hick, J., 198-206
Hoenen, P., 81, 161n
hope, 234
Hopkins, G. M., 222-224
Hume, D., 37n, 83-84

"I-Thou" language, 219-220
id a quo and *id ad quod*, 138
ideal language, 13, 74, 79
imago dei, 255-259
imagination, power of, 49
intelligible species, 40-42, 53
intelligibility: of being, 54,
75-76, 157, 164; of God, 27,
80, 155-156; and necessity,
80, 86, 88, 161; and syntax,
49, 73, 78, 88
intentions, 5-7; religious, 8;
of God, 14
intentional beings, 93, 100
intentional entities, 17n
intentional images, *see* phantasm
intentional inexistence, 98-99
intentionality, 66

Kant, I., 75
Kaufmann, W., 27, 30
Kierkegaard, S., 192n, 251
Kuhn, H., 78

locomotion, 123
Lonergan, B., 42
lumen gloriae, 156, 233
Lyttkens, H., 171n

McDermott, T., 136n
McInerny, R., 171n

Maimonides, M., 131
Malcolm, N., 103-106
Maréchal, P., 42
Maritain, J., 26
mental images, *see* phantasm
mental state and physical state
language frames, 59, 63, 69, 71,
73, 219
models and religious language,
209-214
modus significandi, 137, 173
Mondin, B., 170n
morning and evening knowledge,
71, 78-80
mystical experience, 193

Nagel, E., 37n, 203n, 208
natura, 123, 140
natural theology, 3, 33, 156-160,
179-180, 227
necessary and synthetic
propositions, 81
necessary existence, 101-106,
126-127, 173
necessity: argument from,
126-131; formal, 81; natural, 84
Nicholas of Cusa, 28
noema of faith, 238

odds, 129-130
ontological argument, 91-106
opacity: notional, 141; referential,
140-143

paradox, hard and soft, 174
participation, 132
perception, 52-55
per se causal statements, 83
per se truths, 67, 81
per se nota truths, 83
phantasm, 38, 40-41, 55-62
phenomenalism, 60
phenomenology, 60
philosophical theology, *see*
natural theology
philosophy and theology, 22-34
Plato, 131
Proclus, 131
propter quid demonstration, 88
providence, 33, 134, 176-177
pseudo-Dionysius, 28, 173

quia demonstration, 89
Quine, W., 140n, 141

Rahner, K., 30n, 56n, 180n,
  196n, 260
Ramsey, I. T., 206
rapture, 193
'reality,' 65
reference, 4, 9, 51, 64-65; to
  God, 4; and incarnation,
  214-215; and meaning, 6;
  meta-empirical, 165; and
  predication, 4
remotion, 173-175
resurrection of Christ, 247-248
Ryle, G., 6n

sacra scriptura, 234
sanctification, 250
scientia, 233
scientia dei, 3, 32, 233-235. See
  also faith
scientia divina, 3, 32. See *also*
  natural theology
Sellars, W., vii, 5n, 6n, 7, 13n,
  36, 41n, 43, 44n, 51, 54n, 68,
  72, 80, 86, 101, 137n
semantical meaning, 50
sensation: act of, 39; and
  existential claims, 19; and
  perception, 56

Sertillanges, P., 30n, 42n
solipsism, 200-204
soteriological causality, 247
Stebbing, S., 208
Strawson, P., 9n
substantial unity and conceptual
  unity, 63-64
sufficient reason, 154
syntactical meaning, 44
synthetic a priori truths, 86-87

theology, philosophical and
  revealed, 227-228. See *also*
  natural theology; faith
transcendentals, 63, 131; as
  meta-linguistic terms, 153
Trinity, 254; similitude of, 260

Understanding, the Gift of,
  261-262

Van Buren, P., 216-217
verification, eschatological, 198
veritas prima, 237
visio dei, 233, 238

Warnock, G. J., 16
White, V., 30n, 31
Wittgenstein, L., 9
Word (intentional being) of
  God, 71, 80